Social Movements

Southern Illinois University Press : Carbondale and Edwardsville

Feffer & Simons, Inc. : London and Amsterdam

and Social Change ⌐

EDITED BY ROBERT H. LAUER

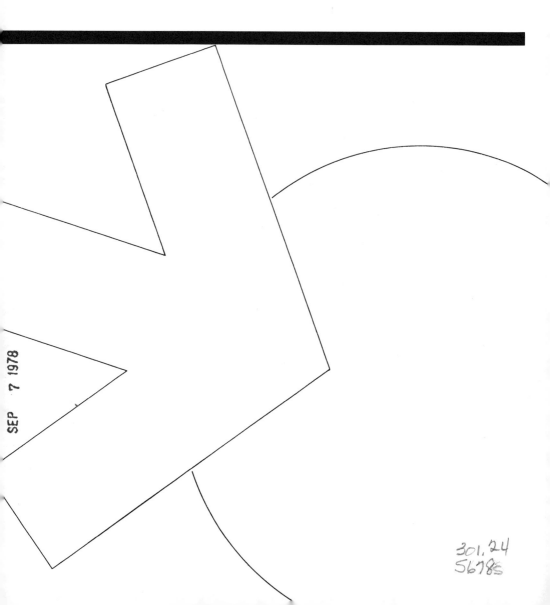

Library of Congress Cataloging in Publication Data
Main entry under title:

Social movements and social change.

   Bibliography: p.
   Includes index.
   1. Social movements—Addresses, essays, lectures.
2. Social change—Addresses, essays, lectures.
I. Lauer, Robert H., editor.
HN17.S59   301.24′2   76-18747
ISBN 0-8093-0771-5

Contents

v

Preface

Sociology is an exciting discipline, and nowhere is that more true than in the study of what Comte called social dynamics. Indeed, if this is the age of "future shock," if the world is changing so rapidly that multitudes of people are left in a state of psychic disruption, then the sociological study of dynamics is not only exciting but crucial to the well-being of man.

In spite of both the fascination and the urgency of the topic, the study of social change has only been seriously pursued in recent decades. The first sociologists concerned themselves with the subject of change, but subsequent generations of scholars left the area of change and relegated its study to the periphery of the discipline.

Furthermore, there has been a strange hiatus in sociology in that the study of change has been commonly separated from the study of social movements. As the introductory chapter indicates in some detail, the two topics are inextricably interrelated. Yet they have tended to remain separate fields within the discipline, and the study of each has normally been pursued with little reference to the other. One illustration of this hiatus is the source of the readings in this book—most do not come from mainstream sociological journals.

The purpose of this book, then, is to link together two fields that should not be divorced in the first place. I have tried to make this linkage as meaningful as possible by exploring the varied, logical interrelationships of movements and change. In addition, I have tried to maximize the interest of the readings by including a broad range of movements and a number of different social contexts. The reader will discover readings that relate to all of the different types of movements which have been identified in the literature: reform movements, expressive movements, and revolutionary movements. Some of these movements involve a particular social group—women, students, or minority groups. Others involve a cross section of the population. Some of the movements were located in other societies; most are or were American, though not all are contemporary.

Hopefully, then, the arrangement of the book and the readings which are included will not only enable the reader to gain insight into the manner in which differing kinds of movements relate to change, but will also stimulate research into this neglected area. The ubiquity and importance of movements and of social change demand the serious attention of the sociologist, and the demand is that we see these as interrelated rather than disparate areas of study.

Customarily one expresses gratitude to teachers or others who have influenced one's thought. In the case of this book, I can only give thanks to an anonymous reader of a previous manuscript of mine. That reader first suggested to me the importance of tying together the fields of social change and social movements. I am grateful to my secretary, Nancy Stephens, for help in typing and in attending to numerous details which must concern the editor of a book. Finally, I am grateful to my family; their appreciation of my scholarly endeavors and their unfailing love continue to undergird my existence and give it richness.

Robert H. Lauer

Edwardsville, Illinois
August 1975

Introduction: Social Movements and Social Change: The Interrelationships

ROBERT H. LAUER

In 1915, an anguished Chinese intellectual pleaded with the young people of his nation to be progressive rather than conservative. For, he said, the world's progress "is like that of a fleet horse, galloping and galloping onward. Whatever cannot skillfully change itself and progress along with the world will find itself eliminated" (Teng and Fairbank, 1967:242). This intellectual was affirming the need for collective human action and the efficacy of that action for guiding social change.

The same thought has been echoed by numerous and diverse others—from bankers to radicals—and forms a central assumption of this collection of readings. That is, the present work assumes that men may act collectively (in the form of a social movement) and thereby affect the direction of social change. Moreover, whether any particular group of people act collectively will not affect the fact of change; it will only determine whether that particular group participates in and helps to shape the direction of change. This is not to say, of course, that the direction of change will be that which the collectivity planned to effect; nevertheless, the direction of change can be affected by collective action.

At first, it may seem trivial or self-evident to assert that social movements affect the direction of change. But two facts must be borne in mind: first, discussions about the course of history have often been phrased in terms of the "great man" or "hero" theory versus the deterministic theory (Hook, 1943); and, second, the study of social movements and the study of social change have tended to be independent pursuits.

With respect to the first, the contrary theories of history, debates about whether great men produce or are produced by history tend to obscure the importance of collectivities as history makers. A good deal of sociological thought has minimized the significance of individuals in effecting change while emphasizing the importance of economics, technology, conflict, or culture. Auguste Comte, the father of sociology, argued that the direction of change is preordained, and that man could only facilitate the process, not alter it. By educating people to think properly, therefore, we can increase the rate of change towards a Positive (utopian) society, but we cannot shift the direction of change (Lauer, 1973:47). Spencer went even further in minimizing human action by denying that any such action could affect the rate of change—except to retard it. Interference in the social process can only impede progress, not accelerate it: "The processes of growth and development may be, and very often are, hindered or deranged, though they cannot be artificially bettered" (Spencer, 1874:401).

In more recent times, a theory of immanent change that minimizes the significance of individuals is found in Sorokin's writings. In a popular work, Sorokin (1942:23) explicitly denied the history-making role of individuals: "It was not the Hitlers, Stalins, and Mussolinis who created the present crisis: the already existing crisis made them what they are—its instrumentalities and puppets." Similarly, evolutionary theorists stress factors that transcend human action. Leslie White (1949:140) described culture as "a symbolic, continuous, cumulative, and progressive process." Furthermore, that process is self-generating; it circumscribes the life of individuals and explains all of human behavior. As a final example, Donald T. Campbell (1965:27) offers a "variation and selective retention" theory of evolution, in which the variations are "heterogeneous, haphazard, 'blind,' 'chance,' 'random,' but in any event variable."

Thus, both in sociology and the other social sciences a considerable amount of writing rebukes the great man theory of history. There is, of course, other writing that argues for the importance of individuals (Hook, 1943; Zimbardo and Ebbesen, 1970:144–56). But the point is that such debates obscure another alternative—a collectivity within a larger social entity that acts to effect social change. If we deny the great man theory of history, we still have not come to terms with the role of social movements. Thus, of the three possibilities, individual action, collective action, and suprahuman factors, this book focuses on the role of the second, a role which has often been lost in the midst of the debates about the importance of individuals and individual action.

With respect to the second point made above—the independence of the study of social movements and of social change—the situation is a little perplexing. The very definition of the social movement involves change. Consider the following examples:

. . . a collective attempt to reach a visualized goal, especially a change in certain social institutions. [Heberle, 1951:6]

A social movement is a collectivity acting with some continuity to promote a change or resist a change in the society or group of which it is a part. [Turner and Killian, 1957:308]

. . . large-scale, widespread, and continuing, elementary collective action in pursuit of an objective that affects and shapes the social order in some fundamental aspect. [Lang and Lang, 1961:490]

. . . a large-scale, informal effort designed to correct, supplement, overthrow, or in some fashion influence the social order. [Toch, 1965:5]

. . . socially shared activities and beliefs directed toward the demand for change in some aspect of the social order. [Gusfield, 1970:2]

. . . a group of people who are organized for, ideologically motivated by, and committed to a purpose which implements some form of personal or social change; who are actively engaged in the recruitment of others; and whose influence is spreading in opposition to the established order within which it originated. [Gerlach and Hine, 1970:xvi]

A social movement is a set of attitudes and self-conscious action on the part of a group of people directed toward change in the social structure and/or ideology of a society and carried on outside of ideologically legitimated channels or which uses these channels in innovative ways. [Ash, 1972:1]

In spite of considerable consensus on the definition of a movement, studies tend to focus on such matters as the organization of the movement, leadership and following, the recruitment and motivation of members, ideology, and the internal changes or developments in movements over time. The actual effects of the movement upon the social order have less commonly been investigated. Thus, the essential purpose of social movements, as specified in all the definitions given above, has been neglected in sociological studies. And the problem is compounded by the fact that books on social change seldom deal to any extent with the movement as a significant factor in social change.

One of the reasons that the two areas of study have been carried on relatively independently of each other is that much of the work in movements has been social psychological in nature, while scholars in-

terested in change tend toward either a Marxist or a conflict perspective. Turner and Killian (1957:6) have pointed out that the entire
field of collective behavior was "relegated to a peripheral and somewhat inferior position" in the early history of sociology, and that it was
those sociologists with a social psychological orientation who maintained interest in the subject. That the social psychological orientation
has remained prominent is evident in the kinds of studies that deal
with movements—the emphases noted above such as motivation,
leadership, and others.[1]

The readings in this book, then, are exceptions to the general tendency. Each has, in one way or another, integrated the study of the
movement with the study of change. I say "in one way or another"
because the relationship between social movements and social change
is more complex than the unidirectional effect we have been discussing to this point. As the Langs (1961:507) succinctly put it: "The
social movement, while itself a collective enterprise to effect changes
in the social order, is also a response to changes in social conditions
that have occurred independently of its efforts." Social change both
generates social movements and also results from social movements.
Furthermore, change in the larger society affects the development of
movements. In other words, to study a social movement in the context
of the larger society is not to study motion within a stable framework;
rather, it is the study of motion within motion. When we deal with a
social movement, we are dealing with two processes that intersect and
interact with each other—the process of the movement itself and the
processes of the larger society within which the movement is operative. This is why we must study any movement in terms both of its impact upon change and of the impact of change upon the movement.

Thus, the readings in this book are designed to explore fully the interrelationships between social movements and social change. In addition, therefore, to the impact of change upon the movement and
the movement's effects upon change, we will examine the matter of
strategies of change adopted by movements and the interesting question of the consequences of the movement gaining some measure of
success.

THE IMPACT OF CHANGE ON SOCIAL MOVEMENTS

Movements do not generally arise out of a stable context. Rather,
they arise out of a changing social order. In turn, the movements represent collective efforts to control change or to alter the direction of
change. As some of the definitions given above indicate, a movement
might develop in order to resist a particular change. More commonly,

movements aim at the control of change or at effecting certain shifts in the social order.

The fact that social movements are collectivities of people who are generally seeking to implement some kind of change is evidence that, contrary to many social observers, social change is not inherently traumatic (Lauer, 1971:882–84). Rather, social movements are an affirmation of the desirability of change and a choice of certain kinds of change rather than other kinds. In some cases, a movement may represent a commitment to virtually total change; we will deal with this further below. First, let us ask the questions of what kind of changes give rise to movements and how does ongoing change affect the development of the movement?

The changes that give rise to social movements have been explained in both sociological and psychological terms. Often, both modes of explanation are incorporated, but one or the other tends to be dominant. For example, an explanation that is basically sociological is the Marxist, in which developments in the class struggle result in the formation and action of a revolutionary movement. An explanation that is basically psychological emphasizes the needs of individuals. Such needs may be frustrated by societal developments and a reform movement may crystallize around the frustration. For example, Eric Hoffer (1951) argues that mass movements attract individuals because the movement satisfies "the passion for self renunciation." The same individual may be attracted to and may successively join what appear to be contradictory movements, therefore, since recruits are driven by their own emptiness and frustration rather than drawn by the purpose of the movement. Although the emphasis may differ in the two modes of explanation, both utilize elements of the other in order to fully explicate the genesis of the movement.

One of the most common explanations of the rise of social movements is that they arise in a context in which social change of some kind is perceived to result in deprivation or disadvantage by a group or groups. For example, Norman Cohn (1957) has shown how millennial movements have tended to arise in Europe during times of rapid social change. Such change, Cohn argues, combined with certain other factors, generates an emotional reaction on the part of large numbers of people and leads those people to seek magical solutions for their problems. This type of explanation is pervasive in sociological writings. As Rush and Denisoff (1971:160) summarize the matter, sociological analyses of social movements commonly argue that the movements "are products of problem situations, discontent, deprivation, strain, frustration, anomie, isolation, hopelessness, or status reassertion." It is important to keep in mind that such situations and feelings are themselves the result of societal changes, changes that lead certain groups to possess advantages or gain dominance over other groups.

It is also important to keep in mind that the sense of deprivation or disadvantage is relative and not absolute. That is, there are very few slave revolts in history. Those people who engage in a movement are most often rising or falling in the stratification system; they are some-where in the middle and not at the top or bottom. This observation goes back at least as far as Tocqueville (1955:175–77) who pointed out that the French were experiencing real gains in economic prosperity prior to the Revolution:

In 1780, there could no longer be any talk of France's being on the down-grade; on the contrary, it seemed that no limit could be set to her advance. . . . Moreover, those parts of France in which the improvement in the stan-dard of living was most pronounced were the centers of the revolutionary movement.

Such relative rather than absolute deprivation has often been iden-tified as a factor in the rise of social movements, including various kinds of movements. The basic idea is that social change results in disparities between what are perceived as legitimate expectations and what is actually obtainable; the disparities reflect the fact that the con-ditions of the group have become worse or the group has been ex-posed to new standards (Aberle, 1970:210). Thus, a social movement arises when some group defines itself as deprived or disadvantaged in some way. Such definitions, in turn, are grounded in social change that leads to the group either falling or not rising as it ought in the stratification hierarchy.

This means that social movements are more than economic phe-nomena, for the stratification hierarchy includes factors of prestige, power, and psychic gratification as well as economic factors. Mauss and Petersen (1973) illustrate this in their analysis of the "Jesus peo-ple" movement. They point out that the Jesus people appear to have developed out of disillusionment with happenings in the hippie com-munity. Pentecostal evangelists seized upon that disillusionment and converted many young people, offering them Jesus as a substitute for drug addiction. Obviously, economic deprivation cannot account for the rise of the Jesus people. Mauss and Petersen note that Charles Glock proposed five different kinds of deprivation: economic, organ-ismic (bodily deprivation), ethical (value conflicts), psychic (value am-biguity or a state of anomie), and social (need for belonging and for status). The converts to the Jesus people exhibited all of the latter four kinds of deprivation. Furthermore, there existed certain other factors necessary for the rise of a movement: the deprivations were shared by a number of people; they saw no other way to resolve their deprivation; and leaders appeared with an innovative way of dealing with the deprivation.

As the latter suggests, movements do not emerge merely because people sense deprivation. Movements require such things as an ideology, group norms, a "consciousness of kind" among members of the movement, and some kind of organization (Rush and Denisoff, 1971:185; Killian, 1964:430). What conditions are necessary in order for all of the above to emerge and a movement to appear rather than for people to pursue some other alternative? People could, in other words, retreat into the churches or develop psychosomatic symptoms or try to work within the political system when they sense deprivation. Why a social movement rather than some other route? Morrison (1971) has suggested five structural conditions which are necessary for the emergence of a movement in a situation of relative deprivation. First, a large number of people must experience the deprivation. Second, there must be a certain "density" of the deprivation—the people must be interacting and communicating with each other. (Recall Marx's argument that the peasants did not form a social class because of their lack of proximity and the necessary interaction.) Third, there must be similar roles and statuses among those experiencing the relative deprivation. (If the deprived are very heterogeneous, it is easier to attribute the deprivation to individual shortcomings.) Fourth, there must be a stratification system with well-defined boundaries and obvious power differences between the strata. And, finally, the existence of voluntary associations in the society facilitates the rise of the movement because they suggest that change can come about through voluntary, collective efforts.

All of the above is tentative. We need many more empirical studies in order to make a judgment about the validity of the relative deprivation thesis. Some scholars, of course, have already rejected that thesis and have posited other explanations for the rise of a movement. For example, it has been argued that changes in the structure of a society lead to changes in the resources available to groups and also generate new groups (industrialization creates the working class). As a result of these changes, protest movements emerge in the context of struggle between the various groups for power (Useem, 1975:22–23). In other words, movements here are viewed as manifestations of the power struggle among differing groups in a society, and the movement emerges whenever the structural conditions allow the mobilization of protest to occur. In any case, it is still social change which is viewed as necessary for generating the movement.

One other question which needs to be raised in terms of the bearing of change on the genesis of movements is whether we can link specific kinds of change with specific kinds of movements. Presumably, if we have sufficient information, we can predict the kind of movement that will emerge. If, that is, we know such things as various character-istics of the population (age, sex, religious orientation, education, and so forth), the structure of the society (the policy, economy, stratifi-cation system, and so forth), the kind or kinds of deprivation resulting from change, and the way in which the situation is defined by people, we can predict the kind of movement to emerge.

One effort to link specific movements to specific change is that of Roberts and Kloss (1974). They argue that there are three master social trends which have an "oppressive nature"—bureaucratization, cultural imperialization (including racism, colonialism, and economic exploitation), and industrialization. These trends give rise to, respec-tively, antibureaucratic, nativistic and nationalistic, and egalitarian movements. The movements, in other words, oppose the oppressive tendencies of the large-scale social trends. While appealing, this scheme falls short of an explanation of all movements. It does not, for example, account for the rise of such movements as the anti-por-nography or the Jesus people. The latter is defined by Roberts and Kloss (1974:41–42) as a "collective nonmovement," an alternative to a social movement. Their definition of social movements, in other words, is more narrow than that which is common in the literature. If we accept the general view of movements as efforts to implement or impede some kind of social change, Roberts and Kloss offer some good insights but not a comprehensive explanation. As noted above, we need to know more than the kind of change which has occurred. The latter must be combined with a knowledge of population charac-teristics, the structure of the society, the kind or kinds of deprivation involved, and the way in which the situation is defined before we can link specific changes with specific kinds of movements.

If social change is intimately involved in the genesis of movements, it is no less important in the development of movements. As pointed out above, the social movement and its social context are two interact-ing processes, each affecting the course of development of the other. At this point, however, we are concerned with the effects of social change on the movement. How is the movement affected by changes in its social context? As an example of the importance of the question, we may note the comment of the Langs (1961:510) about the Civil War: "Besides bringing a halt to several movements, the Civil War changed the character of many others—for instance, Abolition." The Abolition movement was not abolished by the war. Rather, it redirected its efforts toward retribution against the South. In addition, other movements were changed in character. For example, the war helped to effect the transformation of the temperance movement into a prohibition movement.

The course of development of a movement, then, cannot be adequately understood apart from the social context and, in particular, apart from changes which are occurring in that context. Events may effect changes in the climate of public opinion and strip a movement of its appeal and even of its legitimacy; the violence in Haymarket Square in Chicago in 1886 brought the mass movement for an eight-hour day for labor to a sudden halt. Legislative change may leave a movement bereft of a viable cause; various changes after the Depression made the Townsend movement (an effort to secure a national pension in order to prevent economic dislocation) basically irrelevant (Messinger, 1955). A slow rate of change may cause a movement to shift its emphasis on the kind of strategy needed to effect change; the black movement has become increasingly militant in the face of continuing frustration over the pace of change.

In sum, there is hardly any aspect of the social movement that is unaffected by change in the larger society. Whether we are dealing with the genesis, growth, ideology, program, recruitment of members, selection of strategies, or decline—all are a function of changes that occur in the social context. It is the purpose of the first section of readings to explore these relationships in greater detail and by concrete examples.

MOVEMENT STRATEGIES FOR CHANGE

In the second section, we turn to the question of strategy. How can the movement seize control of the direction of change in a society? Movements vary, of course, in the extent to which such control is defined as desirable. Revolutionary movements seek to gain absolute control. Expressive movements may acknowledge the very opposite—absolute lack of control—and strive to provide members with compensatory gratification. Reform movements typically fall in between the other two, striving to control the direction of specific changes rather than change in general.

But all movements must have a strategy for change. For even the expressive movement is seeking to effect change in its members. What kinds of strategies are available? What kind are viable? It is interesting that although such questions are crucial to the success of any movement, they have received scant attention from students of movements. Leaders of movements must answer such questions as who or what is to be the target of change and how that target is to be attacked. The following observation is applicable to any movement if we simply omit the word *revolutionary:*

Without a common approach to strategy it is impossible to build a common Movement. A common approach to strategy is needed to help pull together the present disparate, amorphous, confused and divided Movement into a serious, on-going and growing force for revolutionary change. [Green, 1971:142]

Strategic considerations are important for a variety of reasons. Most obvious, strategy relates to the achievement or failure of achievement of movement goals. A movement's strategy should be congruent with its ideology of change. For example, a movement with a revolutionary ideology should logically advocate a revolutionary strategy. As Mao (1967:343–44) pointed out, in order to resolve the antagonistic contradictions in a class society, "revolutions and revolutionary wars are inevitable." On the other hand, he has insisted, nonantagonistic contradictions (the kind to be found in socialist societies) must be dealt with in nonviolent ways such as "methods of discussion, of criticism, or persuasion, and education" (Mao, 1962:269).

I am not arguing that revolutionary change can be achieved only through armed insurrection, but am insisting that some congruence must exist between the goals of a movement, as expressed in its ideology, and the strategy employed by the movement. Mao achieved this in brilliant fashion by following Lenin's distinction between antagonistic and nonantagonistic contradictions, thus legitimating violent strategies to seize control of China and nonviolent strategies to continue the process of change. Some movements, such as the Libertarian and Women's Liberation in contemporary America, are essentially advocating revolutionary change while generally employing strategies appropriate for reform movements (education, pressure for legislation, and so forth). It would appear that one of three outcomes must occur where there is a contradiction between the ideology of change and the strategy or strategies employed: the goals of such movements will be modified; their strategies will be altered; or they will be considered failures.

The above discussion is based upon the premise that an appropriate strategy is one which is consistent with the stated goals of the movement. However, we must be cautious at this point for a number of reasons. First, most movements are heterogeneous in composition, providing not only differences about what is a viable strategy for achieving a particular goal, but also differences about which goals to pursue. And second, the stated goals may contain a certain amount of rhetoric; such rhetoric may be aimed at attracting members, at motivating members, or at influencing outsiders. In any case, the strategy may be consistent with goals somewhat different from those appearing in the rhetoric. Finally, every movement has multiple goals that relate to its survival and growth as well as to the purpose for which it was founded. We must therefore be cautious in drawing conclusions about the appropriateness of strategies. Nevertheless, it is important to recognize the possibility of a strategy that is inconsistent and inappropriate for the movement's real goals.

In addition to the importance of strategy in achievement of goals, there is the impact of strategy on recruitment and commitment of members. A movement's strategy may be its most intimate link with the public from which it must recruit members or, at least, recruit a base of sympathetic support. As Wilson (1973:226) puts it:

Social movements are often remembered more for the methods of persuasion adopted by them than for their objectives. This is because social movements relate to the general public through their tactical behavior, it is the "face" which the public sees and responds to. In comparison with this, the specific objectives of the movement, its constitution, and its sources of support may be relatively obscure.

Because of this importance of strategy to the movement's public image, leaders in the movement often face a dilemma—how can the necessary public image be retained while still employing an effective strategy? The dilemma is particularly acute in the case of militant movements. To be consistent and successful, for example, a revolutionary movement must adopt revolutionary strategies. But it thereby runs the risk of alienating potential members and of losing a mass base of support. On the other hand, if the movement leadership attempts to soften its tactics or moderate its strategy too much, it may antagonize its own members. The dilemma is well illustrated by the case of the civil-rights workers in the South during the 1960s (Wilson, 1973:236n). The workers insisted on walking down the main streets of Southern towns in interracial pairs, even though their leaders had warned against such a practice. The workers acted "on principle," while the leaders were concerned that the movement survive in a precarious situation. Movement members may define such concerns of leaders as compromise of principles or lack of courage. In some cases a movement may lose members if the latter feel that leaders are failing to put sufficient clout into the strategies; participation may be defined as nothing more than an exercise in futility.

Thus, a movement can recruit members only as it convinces people that it possesses a viable and legitimate strategy as well as a desirable goal. But the strategy is problematic for the leadership. Potential members may be lost through one that is defined as impotent. Leaders in social movements face a serious problem as they attempt to develop a viable strategy, maintain a desirable public image, and hold together a group of committed members. The difficulties of the task are illustrated by a New York City rent strike (Lipsky, 1968). The leader, Jesse Gray, organized groups and spent a good deal of time speaking in various parts of the city. But he neglected administrative details and antagonized lawyers (who were sometimes not paid). Furthermore, in order to satisfy the mass media's request for news and create a favorable public image, he exaggerated both the size and the success of the protest movement. Ultimately, the members received symbolic rewards but little in the way of significant change in their situation. In the short run, the members were satisfied. But the strategy was not a viable one in terms of achieving the initial goals.

In sum, the question of strategy is a crucial one for the movement. Unfortunately, there has been very little study of the matter.[2] The readings in the second section provide some materials relating movement strategy and social change. But much remains to be done, and the problem of strategy is one that demands serious and detailed consideration in the future. Certainly, leaders of movements have been acutely aware of the importance of strategy; students of movements would profit greatly by becoming similarly aware, and by seriously exploring the various problems of change strategies.

THE EFFECTS OF MOVEMENTS ON CHANGE

In the third section, we move on to the question of the effects of movements upon change. As noted above, movements are by definition collective efforts to implement or resist certain kinds of change. In the third, and longest, section, therefore, we will focus on this essential question of the movement's consequences for social change.

A first question is what do we mean by social change. Thus far in the discussion, as indeed in many discussions in the literature, it has been taken for granted that the meaning of change is self-evident. But what precisely is change? For suburban residents, the construction of a large shopping center may be viewed as a significant change. But can we designate that as social change? In other words, is any alteration of anything to be considered as change? In that case, virtually every movement could claim some measure of success. But such a broad usage of the concept cannot be allowed.

Generally, social change is defined in structural terms. Kingsley Davis (1949:622), for example, says that social change refers to "only such alterations as occur in social organization—that is, the structure and functions of society." Furthermore, he makes social change a part of the more inclusive cultural change, the latter including not only change in social organization but also changes in such facets of culture as art, science, technology, and philosophy.

Other authors follow Davis in distinguishing between social and cultural change, but some modify this. Lundberg and his associates differentiate between societal change and cultural change, and incorporate both into a definition of social change. Societal change "involves alterations in interaction patterns"; cultural change, on the other hand, refers to "modifications of social norms, belief systems, symbolic systems, values, or technology" (Lundberg, Shrag, Larsen, and Catton, 1963:583). These two aspects are incorporated into the definition of social change, which refers to "any modification in established patterns of interhuman relationships and standards of conduct."

While still rather broad, we will accept this as a working definition for this book. For however analytically separable, it seems to me that social and cultural changes cannot be empirically separable. As Washburne (1945:3) points out, the useful distinction between society and culture becomes problematic in the consideration of change because change in both areas "involves changes in man's approach to meeting his needs; and change in one is dependent upon change in the other."

As the readings in the third section will show, then, a movement may effect various kinds of social change—in the legal sphere, in various institutions, in patterns of interaction, and so forth. The changes may occur primarily in individuals. Movement members, for example, may develop an enhanced self-concept and a stronger capacity for coping with various frustrations as a result of participating in an expressive movement. Or the changes may occur primarily in the social structure. Widespread alterations occurred in the stratification system, the family, the economy, and other areas in China following the Communist revolution. The former, changes in individuals, would not be social change under the definition presented above. Some movements, in other words, effect psychological rather than social changes. Indeed, it is the purpose of some movements to effect only changes in those individuals who participate in the movement. The clearest examples of the latter are various religious movements that focus on spiritual elevation in the present and eternal bliss in the future.

Given the fact that movements may result in various kinds of change, we may ask two questions. First, what kind of change does a movement strive to implement? And, second, what kind of change does a movement actually implement? The latter means that the relationship between desired change and actual change is problematic.

With respect to the kind of change a movement strives to implement, we encounter considerable diversity. The revolutionary movement aims at total transformation while a reform movement may only seek to effect alterations in group status or changes in mobility opportunities or legislative change in behalf of a moral principle or minor adjustments in the distribution of power. A good example of the diverse aims of movements is provided by Wallace (1956b) in his delineation of "revitalization" movements. Such movements are deliberate and conscious efforts to construct a more satisfying culture through rapid change. But the specific change which is advocated may vary considerably. One movement may emphasize purification, the extirpation of foreign elements from the culture. Another movement may focus on the return to an idealized past state of the culture. Another may advocate the importation of foreign elements. And another may portray an idealized future which has never before been—but now will be—realized.

Thus, movements have various aims, and any assessment of the impact of a movement should take account of those aims. Such assessment must also take account of the actual effects of the movement: what kinds of changes can be identified specifically as resulting from the social movement? The question is a very difficult one. Social analysis generally is a complex affair because a multitude of factors are ordinarily at work. Even when we can identify certain changes that followed upon the activities of a movement, there is the bothersome question of whether those changes might not have taken place anyway. There is no final answer to such problems. We can only work carefully, try to account for all possibilities, and acknowledge the tentative nature of any conclusions.

With such caveats in mind, a number of things can be said about the impact of movements on change. First, the impact is quite different as we examine various movements. For some expressive movements the actual change seems to be in accord with desired changes—there is personal, psychological change, but social change is absent (and may be considered irrelevant). For reform movements, the relationship between desired and actual change varies. In some, the movement may attain success only to be thwarted later and seemingly doomed to endless frustration; the Prohibition movement fits this description. In others, perhaps in most, some changes are effected which are congruent with movement goals but the ideal goal or goals are never quite attained; the Women's movement in America has historically followed this pattern.

The latter description also applies to revolutionary movements. That is, revolutionary movements never effect the total changes which are defined as necessary and desirable. A good example of this is China, where ideological statements continually affirm the equality of the sexes. The liberation of women is said to be "a component part of the cause of liberation of the proletariat." [3] Moreover, it is claimed that in contemporary China the sexes are equal: "Women and men are equal by law. This was one of the first things the Party and People's Government proclaimed immediately after liberation." [4] In order to apprehend fully their liberation, of course, women must participate in production and in the political struggle, and that, it is said, is what the young women of China today are doing. In spite of the ideology and the assertions, the Chinese woman is not yet equal to the Chinese man (see chapter 9). Significant gains have been made in terms of role expectations, status in the family, and opportunities in education, the economy, and the polity. But the gains have not brought women to equality. For example, in the polity, as a recent study concludes,[5] the number of women is small by comparison with men. Furthermore, those women who hold top positions in the government concentrate on those problems which are traditionally of greatest concern to females. Finally, within ranks in the government, women tend to cluster in the lower levels of each rank. The revolution has brought equality in theory, but not—at least not yet—in practice.

Until this point, we have been assuming that the changes brought about by a social movement are in some way related to the changes desired by movement members. But it often happens that unanticipated and even undesirable changes may result from movement activities. The movement may even impede the very kinds of change it supposedly advocates. Feuer (1969) has argued this latter point with respect to student movements. He says that student movements have typically tried to attach themselves to some kind of "carrier" movement such as that of peasants, labor, or a racial group. But when this happens, "the evidence is overwhelming that the chances for a rational evolution and achievement of social goals have been adversely affected" (Feuer, 1969:8). Feuer provides a number of historical examples from a variety of societies to support his point.

It is not true, of course, that student movements always produce such undesired consequences. Youth in general, and youth movements in particular, have effected numbers of changes that were congruent with their goals (Lauer, 1973:176–86). But Feuer's point is an important one; we need to look for the "boomerang" effect in social movements, and for changes which were not anticipated. The notion of unintended and unanticipated consequences of social action has a long history in sociology,[6] and is applicable to social movements as well as to social action in general.

An example of analysis in terms of unintended and unanticipated consequences is provided by Ash's (1972:230–31) comparison of radical and reform movements in America. After noting that reform movements have been far more successful, she inquires into the actual consequences of radical movements, and argues that the latter have primarily been of help to the former. This happened because elites are impressed with the mild nature of reformist demands when they are confronted with the radical movement. By taking the edge off reformist demands and strategies, radical movements have both helped the reformers to succeed and have also insured their own failure in the process.

In sum, much work remains to be done with respect to the impact of movements upon change. We need to inquire into the change envisioned by the movement, the actual changes effected, and any unintended or unanticipated changes that resulted. I say "much work" because none of the readings in the third section deals with the issue in precisely the above terms. Nevertheless, each is valuable in touching upon one or more of the three aspects, and each shows in a concrete way how a movement can lead to some kind of change.

THE CONSEQUENCES OF EFFECTING CHANGE

We come, then, to the final problem, and the final set of readings. What are the consequences of effecting change *for the movement itself*? Any change that results from a movement will react in some way back upon the movement. This is in accord with the basic idea of the movement and the larger society being two interacting processes.

Before discussing the consequences of change, we should note a different problem: what are the consequences of *not* effecting change, and particularly of that change the movement strives to effect? Toch (1965:246) has argued that social movements are essentially efforts to cope with human suffering of various kinds; consequently, "if the aim of movements is the amelioration of discomfort, their success must be gauged in terms of their *felt* benefits rather than in terms of the *objective* changes they bring about." Presumably, the movement would continue to grow or at least hold its members as long as it provided sufficient psychic gratification, and this would be independent of any changes effected or stopped by the larger society. Undoubtedly, this would hold true for at least some movements. But the decline of the Communist party in the United States and the failure and breakup of radical student movements in the late 1960s and early 1970s suggests that failure to achieve change can be disastrous for a movement.

Oddly enough, success can also be disastrous for a movement—disastrous, at least, in terms of its initial goals. This is suggested by the famed "Iron Law of Oligarchy" which was described by Michels (1959). The law represents the tendency of social organizations to move away from democracy and towards oligarchy. Michels based his law upon a study of Socialist parties and labor unions in Europe. He found that the movement to implement democracy was thwarted by changes in the Socialist organizations. As the organizations grew more powerful in numbers and more complex in structure, many of the early, militant activities were abandoned and an increasing amount of time and energy flowed into maintaining a smoothly functioning organization. In a sense, then, the "success" of developing the organizational machinery necessary to implement Socialist goals subverted the movement.

Success—of whatever kind—does not then necessarily mark a point of triumph for a movement. The Women's Movement of the nineteenth and early twentieth centuries in America scored a number of "successes" including the right to vote. But, as William O'Neill (1968: 274–300) has convincingly shown, women in 1920 found themselves about where women had been in 1830. The movement had been content all along to win minor battles, but had sacrificed confrontation with more fundamental questions in order to win those battles. For example, the right to vote was won by appealing to reasons that would undermine the movement—middle-class women supported the effort because they were persuaded that they needed to vote in order to more fully fulfill their domestic functions. But it was precisely because of the oppressive and restrictive nature of those "domestic functions" that the movement had developed in the first place. Such ideological compromises, therefore, insured the failure of the egalitarian goals of at least part of the movement. Women could not be marshalled to fight for a new definition of sex roles while at the same time they were being asked to support programs because the latter would make their traditional domestic role more effectual.

In sum, we have confronted yet another area of the intricate relationships between social movements and social change that merits more detailed study. What are all of the consequences for the movement of either the failure to effect change or of some measure of success in effecting change? The readings in the last section provide interesting examples of movements that gain a measure of success and are altered in some way by that success. Hopefully, this and the other sections of this book will stimulate more serious empirical and theoretical studies. For the exploration of the relationships between social movements and social change has barely begun, but it offers the possibility of discovering rich insights into the nature of the social process.

NOTES

1. An effort to analyze movements in a Marxist framework while giving adequate scope to social psychological factors is provided by Ash (1972).
2. For a general discussion of strategies of change: see Lauer (1973:237–57). For a more elaborate treatment see: Hornstein et al. (1971).
3. *Peking Review,* March 16, 1973, p. 5.
4. *Peking Review,* March 9, 1973, p. 14.
5. Huey-ching Yeh, "Women in Communist China" (Master's thesis, Department of Sociology, Southern Illinois University at Edwardsville, 1972).
6. See, for example, Schneider (1971:669–70).

part 1

The Impact of Change Upon Movements

Introduction

As suggested in the introduction, social change in the larger society bears upon the entire career of the movement—from its genesis to its terminus. Social movements arise out of conditions of change, or specific movements flourish or falter because of various changes in the larger society. The elections in this first part serve to highlight various ways in which social change has an impact upon social movements.

In the first selection, John Israel delineates the manner in which a movement can arise out of change and, in turn, affect the direction of change. The activities of Chinese students were closely linked with the changes occurring—the Western humiliation of China, the Japanese defeat of China, the breakdown of Confucianism, World War I, the betrayal of China by her allies, World War II, and intensifying internal economic problems. These changes gave impetus to the growth of the Chinese student movement, and the movement, in turn, facilitated a specific direction of change in the social order, namely, the Communist assumption of power. We get here, then, a clear picture of the interaction of social change and social movements in a society. The movement was both a response to change and a factor influencing the direction of change.

I have earlier characterized the study of social movements as "motion within motion" to stress the processual nature of both the movement and the larger society. This motion within motion is clearly delineated in the historical sketch of the American student movement by Altbach and Peterson. Both the issues taken up by students and the fortunes of the student movement itself have been linked closely with

3

events in the larger society. In particular, political trends and international events such as war are strongly associated with both the issues
and the strength of the student movement at any particular point in
time. In the face of the two world wars, the movement virtually collapsed. At other times, the movement focused on diverse issues ranging from the right of free speech to the quest for peace.

With the student movement, of course, the shifting nature of the
issues pursued has been facilitated by the continually shifting membership of the movement itself. But even where the membership is
not so fluid, interaction with the larger society and changes in the
larger society will effect significant changes in the movement. In my
chapter, I show how the ideology, the program, and the recruitment
of members in Leary's LSD movement were affected as the movement
interacted with a changing society. In part, that change was rooted in
an unanticipated event—the birth of deformed children from
mothers who had used thalidomide during their pregnancy. This
resulted in new restrictions on drug use and heightened awareness of
the potential dangers of drugs. The restrictions, in turn, evoked a
response from the movement which intensified the conflict with the
larger society. Throughout the process of conflict, we may trace the
evolution of the movement's ideology and program.

Although the LSD movement changed, the direction of change was
such as to intensify rather than moderate its conflict with the larger
society. That is, the ideology and program changed in such a way as to
make the movement and the larger society wholly antagonistic toward
each other. It is possible, of course, for the ideology and program to
shift so as to become more socially acceptable; this has been the case
with a number of radical movements, as a later chapter will show.

When the movement diverges from the socially acceptable, however, its future becomes problematic. The LSD movement has apparently diverged into oblivion. A different outcome is depicted by
Gusfield in the fourth selection in this part. The Woman's Christian
Temperance Union has clung to its stand on total abstinence, has
thereby diverged from the larger society, and has consequently
changed both in certain aspects of its ideology and in its composition.

Changes have occurred in America with respect to both norms and
behavior about drinking. The WCTU found itself in a more hostile
social environment after Prohibition than before. Moreover, the
upper-middle-class women who had been the strength of the WCTU
had largely abandoned the temperance movement. The composition
therefore changed, with the leaders in 1950 being of a lower socioeconomic status than those of 1885.

The ideology changed early in the movement's history. At one point, there was great concern with various kinds of reforms. But as the conflict over Prohibition intensified, members' energies were consumed by an all-out assault on alcohol as the primary enemy of the underprivileged. In addition, the upper-middle-class became targets of scorn and attack after they abandoned the cause following the repeal of Prohibition.

In this first part, in sum, we see how every facet of the movement is affected by social change. Ideologies, for example, are not created ex nihilo and propounded without change to the larger society; they are carved out of social existence and are modified over the course of time as a result of social change. Whether we are investigating ideology, membership, program, career, or anything else about the movement, we cannot ignore change in the larger society, for the change is crucial to our understanding of the dynamics of the movement.

1

Reflections on the Modern Chinese Student Movement

JOHN ISRAEL

The students of the Sung dynasty (960–1279) would scarcely recognize their modern descendants. The former were seasoned scholars whose erudition secured their place in society. Through mastery of the prescribed classics, they aspired to the highest rungs of official-dom. Even degree-holders who failed to gain governmental positions became members of the "gentry" elite, entitled to special privileges and charged with numerous social responsibilities. Intellectals were also expected to criticize officials—even emperors—who failed to live up to the standards of the Confucian ethos. For two thousand years, the scholar-official elite served the Chinese state well.

By the time of the Opium War (1839–42), however, the traditional scholar had become an anachronism. The classics failed to prepare China for the multifaceted challenge of the modern West. Beginning in the 1860s, the Manchu (Ch'ing) dynasty sought reinvigoration through a series of reforms, but none were equal to the need. By the end of the nineteenth century, the combination of external pressure and internal decay had proved too much for the rulers of the sprawling empire. In 1911 the dynasty collapsed, and a republic was established. Republican aspirations were quickly crushed, however,

Reprinted by permission of *Daedalus,* Journal of the American Academy of Arts and Sciences, Boston, Massachusetts. Winter 1968, *Students and Politics.*

under the despotism of Yüan Shih-k'ai. From 1916 to 1949, national reunification eluded warlord rulers, the Kuomintang (KMT) government, and the Japanese. Throughout these years, reformers in various parts of the Chinese subcontinent followed in the footsteps of their Ch'ing forebears. In retrospect, even their boldest efforts were but preludes to the measures of Mao Tse-tung.

YOUTH AND REVOLUTION: 1895–1949

The Chinese student movement was both conditioned by and a condition of this historical transformation. Bridging traditional and modern movements was the Memorial of the Examination Candidates at the close of the First Sino-Japanese War (1894–95). More than twelve hundred scholars, who assembled in Peking for the triennial examinations, demanded a protracted war against Japan. In so doing, they played the historic role of heirs to their twelfth-century predecessors and forerunners of their twentieth-century successors. A truly modern student movement could, however, develop only with modern educational institutions. The first Western-style missionary college (St. John's) was founded in Shanghai in 1879, and the first modern public university (later to be called National Peking University, or "Peita") was officially established in Peking in 1898. But a certain ambivalence clouded educational reform: How could modern colleges prepare candidates for the traditional examinations? The contradiction was resolved in 1905, when the desperate dynasty abolished the thirteen-hundred-year-old examination system.

Thereafter no careerist incentive remained for memorizing the classics, nor was there assurance that alternative courses of study would bring success. The modern student thus felt an unprecedented degree of insecurity. His personal dilemmas were compounded by a pervasive sense of national shame stemming from China's backwardness and helplessness vis-á-vis the imperialist powers. Many resolved these problems by going abroad for study, hoping to return with the prestige of a foreign degree and a technological or philosophical understanding of the modern world. The Manchu dynasty, in its declining years, encouraged students to follow this path, assuming they would come home both skillful and grateful. By September, 1906, fifteen thousand Chinese were studying in Japan. From the government's point of view, the reform was a disaster; uprooted youths, free of Chinese controls and exposed to inflammatory ideas, provided an educated following for such radical reformers as Liang Ch'i-ch'ao and rebels like Sun Yat-sen. Students from all over China came together in Tokyo and returned to foment revolution. Recipients of government scholarships helped bring down the Manchus in 1911.

Deriving its energy from the unstable combination of China's historic grandeur and modern humiliation, the student movement developed an explosive potential. Its targets were oppression from abroad as well as inept government at home. It seemed increasingly obvious to young patriots that both would have to be eradicated if China were to become a strong modern state. The new education reinforced these sentiments. Reformers prescribed a stridently nationalistic course of study, conveyed to the younger generation through chauvinistic textbooks taught by patriotic teachers. Hence, the anti-imperialist theme of 1895 resounded with growing intensity in the twentieth century. In 1905 students joined merchants in an anti-U.S. boycott protesting discriminatory American immigration policies. When Japan presented Yüan Shih-k'ai with the infamous 21 Demands in 1915, Chinese students in Japan returned home by the thousands to join demonstrations against this threat to their nation's sovereignty.

The 1915 movement was a prologue to the Peking demonstration of May 4, 1919, which marked the emergence of students as a major force in national politics. The impetus for this historic demonstration was another manifestation of foreign imperialism, but its full significance can be understood only in the context of China's accelerating social and intellectual revolution. In the cities of China's eastern seaboard, where foreign-style institutions flourished under the protection of the unequal treaties, new social classes were emerging: bilingual merchants, financiers, and industrialists; an urban proletariat; a foreign-educated intelligentsia; and modern students. In the homes of the latter, a "family revolution" ensued as the experience, teachings, and institutions of the older generation became increasingly irrelevant to the needs and aspirations of the young. Revolutionary ideas were nationally disseminated through a multitude of popular magazines, newspapers, and political societies. The effects of these changes were felt both in cosmopolitan Shanghai, hub of economic modernization and refuge for China's political and intellectual rebels, and in Peking, which remained the nation's cultural capital.[1]

On December 26, 1916, National Peking University acquired a new chancellor, Ts'ai Yüan-p'ei. This remarkable man, who has been called "the moral leader of the new intelligentsia and one of the greatest educators and liberals in modern China" (Chow, 1960*b*:47*n*) promoted the startling idea that a university should be a forum for the free development of diverse views. To the horror of traditionalists, he brought to the Peita faculty such men as Hu Shih, who advocated replacing the time-honored literary language with the vernacular, and Li Ta-chao, who shortly later eulogized the Bolshevik Revolution and helped found the Chinese Communist party (CCP). Ts'ai's dean of the School of Letters was Ch'en Tu-hsiu, later the CCP's first secretary-general, but even in 1917 a cultural radical who supported the slogan "Down with Confucius and sons!" and recommended science and democracy as panaceas for China's ills.

The iconoclastic doctrines of these teachers found a receptive audience. Peita's students had ample reason to feel rebellious: their personal futures were uncertain; the republican revolution had ended in chaos; the country was at the mercy of corrupt militarists and foreign aggressors; and their own parents persisted in preaching obsolete notions of virtue and filial piety. The halls of Peita resounded with a cacophony of names and isms: Dostoevski and Kropotkin, Russell and Dewey, Shaw and Ibsen, Wilson and Lenin; democracy, equality, science, socialism, individualism, self-determination, nationalism, internationalism, and Bolshevism.

China's young rebels contrasted China's dreary present with a hopeful future. As war ended in 1918, they heard Woodrow Wilson promise equality to nations and dignity for mankind. They felt certain that the Versailles Conference would recognize the claims of their country, which had sent two hundred thousand coolies to aid the allies on the Western front. Principles of justice demanded that China regain her sovereign rights to the province of Shantung (birthplace of Confucius), seized by Japan in 1915. But youthful hopes proved illusory. By the end of January 1919, reports reached Peking that Great Britain, France, and Italy had signed secret treaties agreeing to support Japan's claims to Shantung. On the heels of these tidings came even more foreboding news: the Japanese had used the $74 Nishihara "loans" to bribe China's warlord government into acquiescence. Outraged by these events, representatives of various student groups gathered at Peita and planned an orderly protest demonstration for May 4. The demonstration began peacefully, but ended in violence when a group stormed the home of a pro-Japanese official, beat alleged traitors discovered within, ransacked the house and set it afire. News of May 4 reached China's new social classes via her modern communications. Students demonstrated in Tientsin, Shanghai, Nanking, Wuhan, and other cities. Workers staged sympathy strikes. Merchants joined an anti-Japanese boycott. Professors demanded the release of arrested agitators. Local student groups proliferated, and on June 16, 1919, delegates gathered in Shanghai and formed the National Student Association.

The organization of a national body was a formidable accomplishment, for the unifying influences of a common written language and shared nationalistic sentiments were counterbalanced by powerful centrifugal forces: mutually incomprehensible dialects, regional loyalties, and the country's size. Considering these obstacles and in view of China's lack of experience with representative democracy, it is not surprising that the national body came to function in a highly elitist manner. City and provincial congresses were composed of delegates popularly elected at constituent schools, and these groups in turn sent delegates to meetings of the national union. The structure operated, however, in a Leninist fashion, more centralist than democratic. Even at the local level, professional and amateur agitators skilled in propaganda, oratory, and controlling mass meetings were generally able to dominate the majority of less interested and less adept schoolmates. The absence of democracy notwithstanding, the National Student Association had become by the mid-twenties one of the most influential voices of public opinion in China. It was less effective, however, as an organ of control, and even during nationwide movements, the nature and intensity of student political activity continued to vary according to local educational, political, geographical, and cultural conditions.

The May 4 Movement was the turning point in China's cultural upheaval. Just as the revolution of 1911 had constituted a definitive break with efforts at monarchial reform, the New Thought of the late teens marked a radical departure from attempts at halfway modernization in the world of ideas. For the first time, eminent teachers and men of letters advocated wholesale Westernization and total abandonment of China's Confucian heritage. The reaction of educated youth was highly favorable; henceforth, the more novel and shocking an idea, the more likely it was to win a receptive audience. The demonstration of May 4 also ushered in a decade of radical anti-imperialism. Vehement protests against the unequal treaties alarmed China's foreign community, and an anti-Christian movement jolted missionary schools. Disenchanted with the fruitless promises of Wilsonian liberalism and wooed by Soviet envoys, alienated intellectuals and students formed the Chinese Communist party. Among them was Mao Tse-tung, a twenty-seven-year-old former Peita library assistant who had received his political baptism as a high-school student leader.

Sun Yat-sen, too, was carried along by the radical post-May 4 tide. Frustrated by twenty years of political failure, he welcomed the counsel of Comintern agents; he agreed to accept Russian aid, revamp the KMT along Leninist lines, form a united front with the Chinese Communists, and establish the apparatus for mass mobilization, including a Youth Bureau. During the mid-twenties, students under both KMT and CCP leadership organized workers and peasants for political action. In Canton, the KMT's newly founded Whampoa Military Academy set out to mold an indoctrinated military elite under Comman-

dant Chiang Kai-shek. Students from all over China flocked to this
mecca on the Pearl River.

As Chiang consolidated his forces, a series of atrocities by warlords
and foreigners stimulated student nationalism and boosted the fortunes of the KMT-CCP alliance. An incident on May 30, 1925, was the
most famous of these. Like the May 4 demonstration, the immediate
cause was an imperialist outrage: A Japanese foreman in a Japanese-
owned Shanghai factory had shot and killed a Chinese worker. Protesting students in the foreign-controlled International Settlement
had been jailed. When a crowd gathered in front of a police station to
demand their release, a British officer impulsively ordered his men to
fire. The slaughter of unarmed students by foreign police on Chinese
soil evoked a nationwide storm of protest. Twenty-four days later, indignation reached a new peak when British and French machine-
gunners mowed down Whampoa cadets and other youthful paraders
in Canton. On March 16, 1926, more anti-imperialist student demonstrators were massacred by troops of the Peking warlord, Chang Tso-
lin. When Chiang Kai-shek launched the Northern Expedition on
July 9, 1926, China's educated elite responded with enthusiasm to the
slogan, "Down with the Warlords and the Imperialists!"

Beneath the façade of unity, both KMT and CCP maneuvered for
the inevitable showdown. Chiang struck first. On April 12, 1927, he
began the Party Purification Movement. This anti-Communist campaign began in Shanghai and spread throughout the country. It resulted in the summary execution of many student radicals. The
purge, rupturing as it did the bond between KMT and a significant element of the younger generation, neutralized much of the enthusiasm that had been created by the success of the Northern Expedition
and the establishment of a national government in Nanking. A further blow to student activists was the ruling party's decision to discontinue mass movements. Student unions were to be replaced by apolitical self-governing associations, and youngsters were to stick to their
books.

Youth lost fervor for a government that wasted precious resources
in fighting warlords and Communist remnants at the expense of social reforms, but they also recognized the Nanking regime as China's
only hope. Indeed, they might well have set their sights on bureaucratic, technocratic careers had not Japan invaded Manchuria in September 1931. The Chinese government's failure to resist prompted
young war hawks to flock to Nanking. For three months in the fall of
1931, thousands of student zealots descended upon the capital, often
lying on railway tracks to halt traffic until free transportation was
provided. Foreign Minister Wang Cheng-t'ing (a former YMCA stu-

dent leader) was nearly beaten to death by a student mob on September 28. But the protest was relatively peaceful until December, when a radical minority from Peiping steered the movement in a revolutionary direction. Violent demonstrators manhandled KMT officials and wrecked the offices of the party newspaper, thereby forcing the government to adopt suppressive measures.

Once leftists had been jailed or driven underground, youthful nationalism was dampened by increasing political, social, and economic stability and by a hiatus in Japanese aggression. Official exhortations to "save the nation by study" apparently were making an impression. New moves by the invader, however, brought students once more to the streets in December 1935. The Japanese were demanding an "autonomous region" in North China, and Peiping students were alarmed by Chiang's ambivalent response: "We shall not forsake peace until there is no hope for peace; we shall not talk lightly of sacrifice until the last extremity." They feared they would become subjects of a North China Manchukuo.

Organized protest began at American-influenced Yenching and Tsinghua universities rather than at National Peking University, the traditional center of student politics. Yenching was a liberal missionary institution, and Tsinghua had originally been established with American Boxer indemnity funds as a preparatory school for Chinese students planning to study in the United States. Yenching was partly protected by extraterritoriality, and both schools were located five miles outside the city walls, which gave them some freedom from Peiping police controls. Large demonstrations on December 9 and 16 provoked a nationwide response among students and intellectuals reminiscent of May 4 and spawned a National Salvation Movement, which pushed Chiang toward a united front with the Communists and resistance to Japan. In May 1936 the proCommunist National Student Association was founded. The contrast between this and the troublesome but still loyal NSA dissolved seven years earlier by the Ministry of Training symbolizes the leftward trend among student activists during a decade of KMT rule.

The majority of the student generation of the 1930s committed themselves to no political party. They offered their allegiance to whoever would lead the country against Japan. Because they realized that only Nanking had the power to fill this role, they applauded Mao Tsetung's call for a national united front, but reserved their most enthusiastic support for Chiang Kai-shek when he indicated willingness to lead the nation into war. Though thousands of idealistic youth joined the Communists in the hills of Shensi between 1936 and 1939, tens of thousands retreated to the Nationalists' refuge in the southwest.

To the casual observer, the eight-year period of war witnessed an unprecedented unity of Chinese youth under the leadership of Chiang. Between the summer of 1938 and December 1945, there was practically no discernible student movement—not even a solitary protest against their wretched diet and rat-infested dormitories. Indeed, during the early war years, as the government fought, student rallied to China's defense and risked their lives to aid her hard-pressed armies. But by November 1938, a military stalemate had developed, and after December 8, 1941, it became apparent that the war would be won elsewhere than in China. Morale deteriorated behind the lines as the government diverted men and supplies to blockade the Communists, while inflation and black marketeering sapped China's economic and psychological reserves. In the colleges of Chungking, Chengtu, and Kunming, students pawned books and clothes to supplement meager government subsidies, prepared their lessons by kerosene lamps, suffered from malnutrition, and frequently contracted tuberculosis. Official policy dictated that these youths remain at their desks. Hoarded like the precious national resources they unquestionably were, the educated elite found no adequate outlet for their patriotic idealism. By late 1943, when students were finally encouraged to enlist in the army, cynicism had already begun to erode the foundations of academia.

The contrast with the Communist zones was striking. There students were trained and indoctrinated in special schools and sent to the countryside to mobilize the population for guerrilla warfare. The Communists emerged from the war with sufficient numbers of trained, dedicated young cadres to govern an area of a hundred million people. The nationalists had increased the number of students in institutions of higher learning from 41,609 in 1936, to 78,909 in 1945, and 155,036 in 1947. Aside from a loyal following in the Three People's Principles Youth Corps, however, these students were apathetic, if not hostile, toward the ruling party.

In the cities of East China that had been liberated from Japanese rule, the war's end reunited two groups—refugees returning from exile in the interior and residents who had collaborated, actively or passively, with the Japanese and their Chinese puppets. For both of these groups, the psychological effect of eight years of war had been disruptive.[2] The refugees nursed sentiments of self-pity and resentment. They viewed themselves as unsung heroes who had endured nearly a decade of unrequited suffering for the nation. Further sacrifice seemed unjust, especially since those who had remained behind seemed to have prospered by cooperating with the invader. Many of the latter, on the other hand, felt a need to atone for the compromises they had made.

Sensitive youth from these two groups crowded onto postwar campuses and provided the material for a series of student rebellions that reached a crescendo in the antihunger, anti-civil-war movement of May 1947. In the emporium atmosphere of Shanghai and other cities, wartime restraints had given way to an *enrichissezvous* atmosphere. An inflationary economy hungry for consumer goods favored importers, speculators, and influential officials. But in the schools, shortages and inflation meant further sacrifices for teachers and students. To returning refugees, the ramshackle housing, substandard diets, shortages of books and laboratory equipment, and restraints on freedom that had been endured as necessary during the struggle against Japan now seemed not merely unnecessary but intolerable. Students who had spent the war years in occupied China were inclined to sympathize with the Communists on practical and psychological grounds. Many felt that they had no future under the Kuomintang, which discriminated in favor of youngsters who had shared the bitterness of wartime "exile." The CCP, in contrast, presented itself as a forward-looking organization dedicated to universal ideals of youth. By enlisting in this noble cause, they might expiate feelings of guilt over the past and open up new possibilities for the future. In a contest that seemed to pit young idealists opposed to war and oppression against the old cynics responsible for these plagues, such students unhesitatingly cast their lots with the former.

Caught in a downward spiral typical of governments in the final stage of revolutionary overthrow, Chiang's regime vascillated between reform and force. Eleventh-hour moves to establish institutions of representative government failed to placate American and domestic critics and did nothing to halt political polarization, stem the devastating inflation, or prevent civil war. In this milieu, the Communists channeled youthful frustrations into demonstrations against civil war, malnutrition, American military misconduct, and Chinese police brutality. The government's response was "counterproductive"; bully boys beat demonstrators, and gunmen assassinated opponents, while official propagandists asserted that the highest priority of postwar reconstruction was the extermination of Communist rebels. Increasingly, the government became convinced that force was the answer in the cities as well as the rural areas. Police arrested thousands of students and intellectuals suspected of Communist sympathies and muzzled the left-wing press. Such action lent credence to Communist charges of fascism and won additional recruits for the widening ranks of Mao's supporters. As the People's Liberation Army swept southward, student reaction ranged from stoic acceptance to jubilation.

This historical survey must conclude on a cautionary note. While

Chinese students, individually and collectively, were important in their country's modern transformation and an essential ingredient in the victory of Chinese communism, the student movement was not a sufficient cause for this victory. Mao's contribution to Communist practice was not his utilization of students (a universal phenomenon among Communist parties), but his use of peasants in a political-military context. Students contributed heavily to the CCP's leadership and were a source of harassment to the KMT, but mass movements of urban intellectuals remained ancillary to the struggle in the villages and on the battlefield.

STUDENTS IN CHINESE SOCIETY

To understand the Chinese student movement, one must take a closer look at its participants. Who were the Chinese students? From what social strata did they come? Which of them played an active role in the events we have described? Unfortunately statistics are limited, and it is impossible to conduct thorough field studies. The answers to these questions must, therefore, be more in the nature of gross generalizations than of scientific findings.

China's students have always been members of an elite. The traditional scholar-gentry was, however, not primarily an economic class. The key to advancement was neither wealth nor social position, but education. Commoners often achieved gentry status, and gentry families lost their social standing over the course of several generations. Everything depended upon success in examinations that were open to poor and rich alike. Of course, the wealthy enjoyed obvious advantages: they could afford to give their sons years of leisure for education and to send them to school or to hire tutors. They could rear them in a world of scholars, a universe remote from the life of the poor peasant. Furthermore, the wealthy landowner or merchant might buy his son a degree, a procedure that supplemented the regular examination system. Hence, in pre-modern China, social mobility existed both in theory and in practice, though never to the extent suggested by the Chinese Horatio Alger tradition.

During the twentieth century, when college and even high-school attendance has involved living away from home, educational expenses have increased. Moreover, the prestige of a foreign degree made costly study abroad desirable for those aspiring to high government office. Hence, China's students were a highly urbanized, upper-middle- and upper-class group during the first half of the twentieth century. Available data do not answer the question: "Which elements of this elite were political activists?" As I have observed elsewhere, "disproportionate numbers of student radicals came from the lowest groups that could afford a post-grammar-school education—landlords and 'wealthy' peasants" (Israel, 1966). But how many of these radical thinkers expressed themselves in terms of political action is unclear. Communist recruitment in the schools was not necessarily from the most impoverished groups, nor were needy students averse to advancement via the KMT.

Regardless of which student sector may have been most active in politics, *all* students were members of a privileged elite. The cream of this elite were those who studied abroad, and it is noteworthy that these youths played a major role in the Chinese student movement from approximately 1905 to 1925. Personal confrontations with the modern world had a jarring effect on these students, as it so often does on young people from underdeveloped areas. Radical ideas and organizations in Japan, France, and (after 1917) the Soviet Union helped to turn these students toward revolutionary movements.[3]

By the mid-twenties, the importance of overseas student leadership had declined due to the increasing self-sufficiency and radicalization of the indigenous student movement, and the emergence of a KMT government supported by and largely staffed by returned students. Moreover, more and more students were going abroad for personal rather than patriotic reasons (Wang, 1966:149–50). The gap between returned and native students widened during the Japanese invasion of the 1930s, when many Anglo-American-educated academicians (as well as those trained in Japan) supported the government, sought help from the League of Nations, opposed the radical nationalism of the younger generation, and rejected student arguments that the national emergency made it imperative to interrupt normal education. In the middle- and late-forties, when war had fused the academic community, foreign-trained professors became increasingly impoverished, disillusioned and inclined to sympathize with student protests. A striking example of this metamorphosis was the American-educated poet, Wen I-to, whose criticism of the government and support of student radicalism led to his assassination in July 1946 (Hsü, 1958).

Both the economic position and the social outlook of China's students changed during the war. Previously, the average student was insulated from the stark reality of daily life among the four hundred million Chinese, even though groups of activists spread propaganda in factories and villages. Arduous journeys from occupied areas to Free China, however, made a lasting impression on these young people. Others gained still more unvarnished views of society after joining the regular army, guerrilla groups, or auxiliary military service organizations. After 1937, even the sons and daughters of the wealthy, cut off from their families, often found themselves living on the margin of starvation. To provide for these youths, the government introduced a system of scholarships, which soon supported tens of thousands of students. But wartime and postwar inflation virtually wiped out the Chinese middle class and lowered to a proletarian level the standard of living for scholarship holders, as well as teachers and other salaried officials. Though school food strikes had been common during the twenties and thirties, the "antihunger, anti-civil-war" movement of 1947 was the first nationwide student movement directed against substandard diets.

SOURCES OF YOUTHFUL REBELLION

The postwar student movement marked a victory for Communist propagandists who, after three decades of experience, had reached a high level of sophistication in wielding weapons of mass persuasion. But to assert that Chinese youth were duped by astute propagandists explains nothing. The question is *why* Communist slogans had such a wide appeal, *why* Leninism made so much sense to an educated elite, *why* Chiang Kai-shek was so easily cast in the villain's role, and *why* students helped to overthrow a lesser tyranny only to accept a greater one.

In the eyes of many observers, Chinese college students seem to have been driven to communism by their relentless hostility to legitimate authority. The diversity of targets of school strikes and nationwide movements—England, Japan, and the United States, Manchus, warlords, and KMT, capitalists and landlords, principals and teachers, family and state—certainly suggests that there was an underlying impatience with established power. This, too, requires an explanation. Richard Walker (1963:100) has written that China's students and intellectuals were victims of "the mystique of 'the Revolution' [which] assumed an almost mystical and sacred quality in the language of the new literati." As Walker observed, Kuomintang as well as Communist propagandists encouraged this semantic confusion. The students' profound commitment to the mystique was, however, based upon much more than confused semantics, as Robert A. Scalapino (1967:199) indicated in his trenchant analysis of Chinese students in Japan during the first decade of this century:

Many of the students, no doubt, became revolutionaries after a process of soul-searching and reflection that involved a consideration of alternatives, and used their intellectual facilities in reaching their decision. It cannot be denied, however, that the espousal of revolution was the most logical method of achieving an emotional release, a method with which reformism could not easily compete. To students discouraged and impatient, the commitment to revolution represented a concrete, dramatic personal act by which they could dedicate themselves to the cause wholeheartedly, unselfishly, and with finality. It did not involve them in any of the intricate compromises and potential corruption that reform efforts would inevitably evoke. It was a heroic, simplistic act so in tune with the psychological needs of the time.

This statement is remarkably applicable to students of subsequent periods—especially 1923–27 and 1946–49. There was evidently nothing mysterious about the popularity of the revolutionary mystique, nor was the mystique ubiquitous. During the most dramatic periods of the movement, student activists chose the most radical of mentors, but this by no means implies that all students at all times were willing to sacrifice short-range goals of national unity, social order, and educational development to take the path of revolution.[4]

The history of the modern Chinese student movement also demonstrates that rebellion against established authority did not necessarily imply rejection of all discipline. Anarchism did enjoy a vogue among Chinese students during the first two decades of the twentieth century, but its influence waned under the competition of communism and nationalism in the early twenties. A similar fate befell romantic and liberal individualism. Students' submission to Leninist leadership in the CCP and KMT suggests that they welcomed discipline in the name of nationalistic and revolutionary causes. Furthermore, every generation of students has upheld forces of unity and order when these appeared to be viable possibilities. Even in 1949 few students accepted the Communist revolution without reservations. Given a unified nation, unthreatened by enemies, many of them would have preferred the ideas of Hu Shih to those of either Chiang or Mao. Indeed, Hu's advocacy of literary reform, intellectual tolerance, political experimentalism, and the application of the scientific method to academic and social problems won a sympathetic hearing from students of the May 4 era and continued thereafter to find a sizable audience among nonactivists. Under conditions of imperialistic aggression and civil war, however, Hu's cosmopolitanism was unable to compete with strident nationalism. The rapid disintegration of the old social order called for something stronger than his prescription of "bit-by-bit, drop-by-drop" change.

The difficulties of the liberals were compounded by the social and mental chasm that separated Anglo-American-trained intellectuals from the realities of rural China. These men, who filled the majority of college positions, failed to win the support of socially conscious students. Their analyses seemed shallow, their solutions inadequate, their frames of reference irrelevant. More enduring was the alliance between student radicals and liberal and leftist writers whose years abroad had been spent in Japan, rather than England or the United States. From the 1920s on, the writings of Lu Hsün, Kuo Mo-jo, and others profoundly influenced the younger generation, but these men were victims of political polarization and became identified with the Communist camp.

China failed to develop a social democratic tradition, in part because her introduction to foreign ideologies was telescoped—the ideas of Marx and Lenin following close on the heels of liberal constitutionalism. Moreover, her cliques of progressive, democratic intellectuals were poorly organized and unarmed. The National Salvation Association, formed in 1936 as an offshoot of the December 9 Movement, provided some organizational cohesiveness for student patriots and their nonpartisan allies, and the Democratic League had its student following in the forties. Flanked by the armed, highly organized KMT on the right and CCP on the left however, the third forces were doomed. By 1949, the only choices left to the splinter parties and their student followers were to seek exile in Hong Kong or abroad, or to serve as window dressing on the mainland or in Taiwan. For most students, the cause of China seemed best served by remaining on the mainland and working with the new rulers.

STUDENTS AND THE RULING PARTIES: KMT AND CCP

Perennial student dissatisfaction with the *status quo* has created problems for both KMT and CCP rulers. By evaluating their divergent responses under varying conditions, one may consider whether the modernization process in China has made student rebellion inevitable.

The Kuomintang suffered from internal weaknesses as it entered the political-ideological arena. In retrospect, it seems clear that this ruling party, badly divided as it was, had slim hopes of satisfying China's college students. Filled with the high expectations common among youth in modernizing societies, these radicals were inevitably disappointed when mortal men failed to solve unsolvable problems. In industrialized countries, such as the United States and postwar Japan, young idealists may be expected to mature into integrated units of the "establishment." Yet this is impossible unless the established order offers well-defined rewards—social, economic, and psychological. Considering the series of convulsions that have shaken Chinese society since the mid-nineteenth century, it is not surprising that many of the young intelligentsia eventually were drawn into the Communist camp. Nor is it surprising that the temporary loosening of authoritarian controls in 1957 produced a student rebellion and that the staging of a massive revolutionary movement under official auspices was necessary to forestall another outburst a decade later.

But the CCP, for all its blunders, has controlled the student movement far more skillfully than its rival had. The Kuomintang's short-lived success with the younger generation ended when the Party came to power, and the abolition of extramural student organizations betrayed the KMT's lack of confidence in its own ability to compete with the Communists and other dissidents. Moreover, this negative policy failed to gain support from two key factions—the Ch'en Brothers' "Organization Clique" or "CC Clique" and the Whampoa Clique in the military. During the early and mid-thirties, these groups competed, more or less clandestinely, with Communist organizers in the schools. After the outbreak of the Second Sino-Japanese War, the party reversed its negative policy by establishing the Three People's Principles Youth Corps under Whampoa leadership. The corps's achievements, facilitated by wartime patriotism, were nullified after V-J Day. Under attack from jealous Party regulars, the corps was amalgamated with the Party in 1947.

In recent years, the Communists have been plagued by competition between civilian and military factions in their party for control of the youth movement. Since the failure of the Great Leap Forward, militant Maoists have criticized the CCP and its adjunct, the Youth League, for their policies of retrenchment. These ideological purists, led by Lin Piao and his adherents in the People's Liberation Army, circumvented the league and organized the Red Guards in the summer of 1966. The guards' countrywide crusade was made possible by the army's organizational and logistic support.

The generation gap, which perplexes Communist leaders today, is accentuated by a cult of youth that has provided opportunities and problems for adult politicians ever since the May 4 Movement.[5] Students led both KMT and CCP through their formative years, but both the KMT (which had been in existence for more than two decades before 1927) and the CCP (which had operated for nearly three decades prior to 1949) inevitably lost touch with the younger generation. The KMT, as we have seen, responded negatively to the challenge. During the early fifties, the CCP promoted student political action in a series of mass movements controlled by the party and the Youth League. But from the mid-fifties to the mid-sixties, functions of mass organizations were appropriated by the party-league apparatus, league leadership became the preserve of middle-aged men, and its membership grew older. The generational crisis is not likely to be resolved by the Red Guards' attempt to reaffirm the values of the youth cult by glorifying a seventy-three-year-old patriarch.

The Red Guard imbroglio reminds us that the CCP's relationship with the students has not been free of contradictions. Since the twenties, the party has realized the value of students in organizing workers, peasants, and intellectuals. By defining the class nature of students as wholly or partly *petit-bourgeois,* the party has been able to use them both as allies in united fronts and as scapegoats for the party's failures. Communist ideologists have, however, found reliance upon such a privileged elite embarrassing to the party of the proletariat. Thus, students have been expected to lose their sense of separate identity and to become one with the masses. Party ideologues repeatedly quote Mao Tse-tung's dictum:

The ultimate line of demarcation between the revolutionary intellectuals, on the one hand, and nonrevolutionary and counter-revolutionary intellectuals, on the other, lies in whether they are willing to, and actually do, become one with the masses of workers and peasants. [Mao, 1954:10–11]

Practical as well as ideological problems have compounded the party's dilemma. By the Yenan period, the CCP was no longer a clique of intellectuals, but a rural-based political-military movement. This made it difficult for the CCP to absorb the urban-intellectual youths who streamed in from Peiping, Tientsin, and other cities. From the viewpoint of the veterans of the Kiangsi Soviet and the Long March, these recruits were bookish and undisciplined. Thought reform was the Maoist cure for such ailments. The wartime movement labeled *cheng-feng* ("to correct unorthodox tendencies") was the first in a continuing series of attempts to remold students and intellectuals.[6]

Tensions underlying student-party relations since the mid-1920s still exist. Students remain largely bourgeois in family origin, hence untrustworthy, though their skills are needed as much as ever. CCP leaders fear that nearly half a century of revolution may be negated by residual habits of traditional careerism and modern professionalism among the young. The very structure of Chinese education contains built-in contradictions. The Communists inherited a university system modeled on the West's, manned by a Western-trained faculty, and designed to produce graduates dedicated to the disinterested pursuit of truth via "scientific" disciplines. With their newly acquired skills, these youths have sought to enter careers that would both further their own interests and modernize their fatherland. The Communists regard such attitudes as unfortunate hangovers from China's feudal and semicolonial eras. The pursuit of individual self-interest is thought to be incompatible with the development of the state, and the disinterested quest for scientific truth is considered secondary to the development of a "correct" Maoist *Weltanschauung*. The attempt to reconcile the contradictory purposes of education is formulated in the slogan, "Both Red and Expert." Changes in emphasis between these two desiderata have produced a series of crises, the most recent of which is the Great Proletarian Cultural Revolution with its offshoot, the Red Guards.

Red Guard membership initially was granted only to politically active students of proletarian origin. Youngsters with these qualifications had been accepted in institutions of middle and higher education during the Great Leap Forward, when it was more important to be Red than expert. It was they who suffered when the pendulum swung back, and academic performance became more important than ideological orthodoxy. Hence, in the spring and summer of 1966 they became enthusiastic recruits in campaigns to expel "bourgeois" chancellors, to revamp the system of entrance examinations, and to close the schools so that students could devote all their time to politics. These youth have but one hope for advancement in the highly competitive educational and economic systems—that political activism will replace academic achievement as the principal criterion of success. If the Communist leadership fails to satisfy their expectations, its quest for a generation of revolutionary successors will be doomed to failure. On the other hand, if it ceases to reward academic and technological achievement, its vision of a modern industrialized China will be shattered, and the country will be forced to fall back on its overcrowded rural hinterland.

Thus the CCP, like the KMT, has been trapped by its own ideology, by its failure to satisfy the expectations of youth who have taken the party's teachings too literally. The Nationalists lost their student following by not acting sufficiently nationalistic; the Communists are now threatened by rebellious youth who demand that they practice communism. The challenge posed by the Red Guards is likely to plague the party long after the current leadership struggle is concluded.

SOCIAL CHANGE AND THE STUDENT MOVEMENT

The course of the Chinese student movement follows logically from China's history. The nation entered the twentieth century stumbling in the shadow of her past brilliance. Unlike Russia, where centralized despotism made anarchism attractive, China was weak, divided, and exploited. Hence, the goals of the student movement were state-oriented, those of internal unity, solidarity against foreign foes, national power through modernization, and national identity through social revolution. Nationalism was equally important in helping students retain their personal identity as Chinese even while they were discarding their traditional heritage in favor of foreign innovations.

The nationalism of the 1905–11 movement was both racial and modern. Its assumption was that China would grow strong if the alien Manchus were dethroned and traditional governmental forms were replaced with republican institutions. Nationalism in the garb of anti-imperialism and anti-Christianity developed rapidly after the 21 Demands and reached its peak after the May 30 incident. Like anti-Manchu nationalism, it blamed foreigners for China's woes, and this enhanced its appeal. Students supported the goal of the Northern Expedition—national unification via military conquest—but failed to appreciate Chiang's continued obsession with this program during the Japanese invasion of the thirties. Civil war had less nationalistic appeal than anti-imperialistic war. Between 1937 and 1945, KMT and CCP vied for popular support, each arguing that it embodied the principle of national solidarity against the Japanese.

After the war, the KMT contended that its struggle against Communist rebels carried on the task of national unification begun in the fight against the Manchus and continued in the Northern Expedition and the anti-Japanese crusade. But instead of a decadent dynasty, venal warlords, or imperialistic Japanese, the KMT faced a resurgent Communist movement. Mao, who had also established his patriotic credentials during eight years of resistance, offered a "new democratic" China as an alternative to the discredited government of the postwar Kuomintang. Convinced that the KMT was the main obstacle to internal harmony and that continued attempts to extirpate the Communists could lead only to interminable civil war, the students became Chiang's harshest critics during the crucial period.

Even though successive generations of Chinese students may be characterized as nationalistic, this does not imply an absence of change. Political circumstances altered the quality of that nationalism from decade to decade. The most influential force for change was the intrusion of partisan politics into every sphere of student activity: hence, the enormous difference between the nonpartisan May 4 Movement of 1919 and the highly politicized May 30 Movement six years later, to say nothing of events in 1935 and 1947. This intrusion reached its logical conclusion after 1949, when the student movement became a tool of Party control. Partisan politics have similarly engulfed other areas of Chinese life—most notably in literature where the social consciousness of the twenties evolved into the revolutionary polemics of the thirties, the patriotic homilies of the war years, and then state indoctrination after 1949.

Student politics have also varied greatly in intensity. Movements have flourished in modern China when governments appeared weak and inept. Only those able to control the nation's territory, manage its educational system effectively, and carry out energetic programs in domestic and foreign policy have generally succeeded in avoiding massive student protest: hence, the frequency of student disorder during the late Ch'ing and warlord periods. The promise of unity and reform gave the Nanking government relative immunity from 1928 to September 1931, and from 1932 to December 1935. The December 9 Movement erupted in the least-controlled university (Yenching) of an insecure area (North China), endangered by vacillation in foreign policy. National resistance to Japan and tight KMT control of Southwest China's campuses dampened student protest during the war, but governmental weaknesses encouraged its reemergence in 1945.

There has been a tension in Chinese student thought between the desire for personal liberty and the quest for a strong state, but by and large liberty has been a secondary issue (Chow, 1960a:309). When the government has been strong, students have grumbled about suppression of civil liberties, but they have not rebelled. Only weak governments have had to answer for repressive policies. No rulers allowed greater academic freedom than the warlords who were more concerned with fighting battles than with running schools, but none elicited more bitter student opposition. KMT thought control failed because it was conceptually and operationally deficient, not because students valued freedom of thought above all else. CCP means of coercion have been more oppressive and more effective. The Communists mastered techniques of internal social control; the Kuomintang always seemed to approach students from the outside. Internal discipline, whether in a Peiping school or a Yenan thought-reform center, was more acceptable than external control by school administrators or military police. Pro-Kuomintang students were easily detected, labeled "running dogs," and isolated. Pro-CCP students were admired as self-sacrificing idealists.

Aside from its technical proficiency, the CCP was fortunate to arrive on the scene just in time to collect the fruits of revolutionary harvest. A century of national humiliation and a succession of thwarted reforms had imparted an irresistible allure to radical solutions. In the politics and literature of the students, as of the nation at large, unsuccessful fathers bequeathed a profounder radicalism to their sons. The generation of monarchial reform symbolized by K'ang Yu-wei (born

1858) was followed by one of republicanism epitomized by Sun Yat-sen (born 1866) and finally by the communism of Mao Tse-tung (born 1893). In this context, the neo-Confucianism of Chiang Kai-shek (born 1888), modeled as it was upon the conservative reformer Tseng Kuo-fan (born 1811), seemed strangely out of place.

The intellectual, psychological, and moral vacuum left by the breakdown of the universal Confucian order was too vast to be filled by the relativistic pragmatism of John Dewey and Hu Shih. A new and totalistic world view was necessary—one that would explain China's failures without undermining national pride. Hence, the appeal evoked by a theory that blamed imperialists and reactionaries, but exculpated the Chinese people. Leninism did this. It analyzed a perplexing and oppressive environment in simple terms and plotted a corrective course of action. In its united-front version (incorporated into Mao's New Democracy), Leninist doctrine reserved an important role for the *petit-bourgeois* intellectuals. This was essential to an intellectual elite whose consciousness of its own political preeminence had survived the demise of Confucianism.

Mao offered China's students an attractive blend of the modern and the traditional, a combination by no means unique to Chinese communism. Superficially, Chinese communism appeared to be anything but modern. Under Mao's hegemony, life in the regions was technologically primitive compared with the urbanized sector under Chiang. In terms of social mobilization, however, Mao's efforts to bring the masses into politics were most modern even though they drew upon an indigenous tradition of peasant rebellions. Mao adopted a radically modern ideology, but he *adapted* it to Chinese conditions by finding the source of absolute virtue in the downtrodden rural masses. In the Communist countryside, students found assurance that they could be both pure and progressive, radical reformers and 100 percent Chinese. On the other hand, Chiang's attempt to foster Confucian values in a foreignized urban environment seemed to combine the least appealing features of past and present.

Similarities between the recent Red Guard phenomenon and student movements of the past can be found only at a high level of historical abstraction. For example, frustrated careerism and betrayed idealism continue to unsettle China's youths. Students still view themselves as incorruptible social critics, and the purity of their protests is, as before, compromised by adult intrigue. One can isolate features of the Red Guards reminiscent of the traditional censorate, the Boxer uprising, and the post-May 4 student movements, to say nothing of the Hitler Youth (see Israel, 1967:26–30).

The historian, however, is more impressed by the discontinuities. The most striking of these is the change in scale. In December 1931, the capital city of Nanking was deluged with an unprecedented 16,600 demonstrators. In the late months of 1966, Peking received eleven million. This is indicative of a second fundamental change: the present government is the first in modern Chinese history capable of disciplining and mobilizing students on all levels throughout the country. Even the Red Guards, a product of internal struggle, testify most eloquently to this development. Unlike pre-Communist student movements, they represent an induced rebellion of part of the system against the whole, not a more or less spontaneous attack by an extra-legal revolutionary force. Finally, the nationalistic component of the Red Guards is relatively weaker than it was in pre-1949 student movements. To some extent, this is a tribute to the Communists' success in removing the two principal targets of student protest: internal disunity and foreign exploitation. But chaos, for which the Red Guards are partially responsible, has shattered national unity and invited outside interference. Thus, there is no reason to suppose that adulation of the Maoist cult has permanently superseded the tradition of nationalistic student protest.

NOTES

1. Joseph Tao Chen draws a vivid comparison between Peking and Shanghai in "The May Fourth Movement in Shanghai" (Ph.D. diss. University of California, Berkeley, 1964), pp. 2–3. These two cities, containing the majority of China's college students until 1937, have been the major vortexes of twentieth-century student politics. In contrast with other countries, the political capital has not necessarily played a major role. It is difficult to generalize about the geographical and institutional determinants of Chinese student movements, but nationwide political activity has usually concentrated in the liberal-arts colleges of the larger universities in major cities that contained several centers of learning. National institutions have generally been more active than provincial ones in the public sector, secular institutions more so than Christian ones in the private. Colleges relatively inactive in countrywide movements are not always spared turmoil based upon local issues.
2. For some of the observations in this paragraph and the following one, I am indebted to the insights of Professor Lucian W. Pye, who served in Peking and Tientsin from September 1945 to April 1946 as an intelligence and Chinese-language officer in the United States Marines. Letter to the author, September 12, 1967.
3. England and the United States produced fewer revolutionaries due both to the nature of society and education in those countries and to a natural selectivity of students going abroad: Those of radical proclivities went elsewhere by choice, and those of limited resources by necessity. Japan offered easy accessibility and inexpensive living, the USSR provided political subsidies, and France had a "work-study" program.
4. We may assume that no more than 10 percent of China's college students

were perennial activists and that less than 1 percent held positions of authority in local, provincial, and national organizations. Though an estimated three
thousand marched in Peking on May 4, 1919, and nearly eight thousand on
December 16, 1935, the inert majority could be mobilized only in times of
crisis. The diversity of student political credos is emphasized in Olga Lang's
study of college students in 1937. In interpreting her conclusions, summarized in Table 1 below, one should bear in mind that 1) students are categorized on the basis of their answers to open-ended questions; 2) 85 percent
of China's college students were in non-Christian institutions; and 3), as Miss
Lang notes, "whatever their political opinions may be, almost all students are
nationalists."

1. Political sympathies of college students in 1937

Political Tendencies	(Percentages) Male		Female
	382 Students of Christian Colleges	305 Students of Non-Christian Colleges	477 Students
Conservative	14	7	9
Fascist	19	14	11
Democratic	10	7	16
Christian	10	2	16
Radical	12	34	16
Nationalist	21	14	13
Not clear	14	22	19

Source: Olga Lang, *Chinese Family and Society* (New Haven: Yale University Press, 1946),
p. 316.

5. The writings of Pa Chin, portraying the breakdown of the traditional family, have been a mirror and a model for several generations of adolescent
rebels. See Pa (1958) and Lang (1967).
6. For the *cheng-feng* movement, see Compton (1952). For a study of "re-
molding" from a psychoanalytic point of view, see Lifton (1961), especially
Part 3, "Thought Reform of Chinese Intellectuals."

Before Berkeley: Historical Perspectives on American Student Activism

PHILIP G. ALTBACH AND PATTI PETERSON

American student activism has a long history, although it was only in the sixties that it received national attention and serious analysis. In 1823, half the Harvard senior class was expelled shortly before graduation for participating in disruptive activity, and students were involved in anticonscription campaigns during the Civil War.[1] Student activism before 1960, however, had no major impact on national policy, and prior to 1900, no organized student activist groups emerged. Yet there is a tradition of student involvement in politics in the United States, and many of the concerns of the activists of the sixties are reflected in the past.

This essay provides a broad historical picture of American student activism from 1900 to 1960. We have concentrated on organizations and movements, and have omitted a more detailed sociological analysis. Although religious student movements, pacifist groups, and conservative organizations are important during this period, it was liberal and radical student activity which exerted greater impact on the campus—hence our emphasis.

The American student movement prior to 1960 closely followed political trends in society. Members of the Intercollegiate Socialist So-

Reprinted by permission of the authors and publisher from volume no. 395 of *The Annals* of The American Academy of Political and Social Science. Copyright 1971, by the American Academy of Political and Social Science.

ciety (ISS), founded in 1905, were a "vanguard" among university students. But until major political crises mobilized large numbers of students, such groups remained small. The student movements which flourished prior to 1960 were generally linked closely with adult movements and no "generation gap" is readily discernible among activists. In fact, the independence of the current student movement might well be one of its strengths, since it is not necessarily bound by the organizational or ideological limitations of adult movements.

The student activism which developed in the early twentieth century took place in a context different from that of the modern American university. The colleges were much less in the mainstream of American life and academic community was much smaller than at present. In 1912, for example, there were approximately 400,000 students in American universities. Activism, even of the moderate type reported here, was confined to a very small proportion of the student community and to a relatively few institutions. Yet, the student "movement," if it can be called that, set the political tone of a basically apathetic campus community and influenced a small number of students who later played important roles in American public life. The foundations for student political activity on the campus were formed in the early years of this century.

EARLY ACTIVIST GROUPS

As the earliest major leftist student political organization, the ISS included among its early active members Upton Sinclair, Morris Hillquit, Jack London, Charlotte Perkins Gilman, Clarence Darrow, Walter Lippmann, and others later prominent in reformist and radical movements. Interestingly, most of the ISS founders were not students. From the beginning, the ISS was an educational organization, formed to "promote an intelligent interest in socialism among college men and women" (Lewack, 1953:4). While the major strength of the ISS was in the prestige colleges of the eastern seaboard, from 1910 until the outbreak of World War I it spread across the country, and by 1917 claimed sixty chapters with 2,200 members (Lewack, 1953:5).

The major thrust of ISS activity was educational. The organization's journal, the *Intercollegiate Socialist,* published regularly from 1913 until 1919 and featured articles on aspects of Socialist thought as well as on university-related issues and public affairs. ISS affiliates sponsored radical speakers on campus and often caused local crises over free speech. These speakers were the main educational thrust of ISS activity.

A number of themes emerged from ISS campus activities in the early 1900s, and also in its national conventions and summer conferences. The debate over American rearmament and entry into World War I caused substantial disagreement among members, and was a constant topic of discussion. Other popular topics were free speech on campus, immigration, a World Court, and various aspects of socialism.[2] In this period, there was relatively little attention paid to foreign affairs and, surprisingly, only slight emphasis given to internal university problems and academic reform. The ISS convention of 1916, however, voted to oppose the introduction of military training on campus.

The society did not take the complexities of ideological politics very seriously. In 1913, a questionnaire of 450 ISS members indicated that a third of the membership was non-Socialist, and a few members were even anti-Socialist.[3] If the *Intercollegiate Socialist* is any indication, the factional disputes over Socialist doctrine which characterized the 1930s and later periods were rare in the ISS.

As the Intercollegiate Socialist Society became more concerned with the creation of a broader movement, it began to shift its emphasis from the campus. In 1919, it changed its name to the League for Industrial Democracy, and its journal became the *Socialist Review*.[4] Although this was done to broaden the movement, the organization remained more intellectual than activist and most of its strength stayed on the campus.

Another organization which attempted to build a broad-based youth movement but which had some strength on campus was the Young People's Socialist League (YPSL). Organized in 1907 as the youth affiliate of the Socialist party, the YPSL claimed 4,200 members in 112 chapters by 1913.[5] Much of YPSLs membership was, however, off the campus. The YPSL tended to engage in more direct political campaigns, usually in support of Socialist candidates and other struggles, although it also carried on an active educational program.

Less obviously political than the ISS or the YPSL, the Student Christian Volunteer Movement (SCVM) played an active and important role on the campuses. Founded in 1886, the SCVM was a federation of various Protestant religious youth organizations, among which the YMCAs and YWCAs were perhaps the most active. The SCVM exhibited a strong sense of social concern, although prior to 1920 its main emphasis was on foreign missionary work. The SCVMs journal, the *North American Student,* was concerned with foreign missionary activity but also featured articles on problems at home. Some of the earliest articles supporting educational reform and women's liberation appeared in the *North American Student.* During both the pre-World War I period and the twenties, religious student organizations played a key role in bringing social concerns to the campuses and particularly to those colleges somewhat out of the mainstream of academic life, in which religious groups were the only source of social concern.

World War I and the postwar Red Scare of 1918–19 inhibited the student movement as it did the adult radical movement. Many liberal and radical intellectuals were perplexed by the war issue, and this question split the radical movement. The ISS did not support the war, but maintained a position which neither condoned nor condemned it and in the process lost much of its membership. The YPSL, which strongly opposed the war, was also decimated during the war.

THE MOVEMENT IN THE TWENTIES

The Issues

The twenties were a curious period in the history of the student movement, as they were for American society generally. The period was characterized by political apathy on and off campus, but at the same time exhibited some significant political and social currents. For example, the student movement strongly criticized the universities for the first time, and devoted itself to some extent to educational issues. A study conducted in 1926 showed that a majority of the 1,026 students responding opposed ROTC. In addition, college students were involved in a minor "cultural revolution." It can be argued that the "new" cultural patterns of the twenties which were stimulated largely by youth were in a sense similar to the hippie and other counter-cultural developments of the 1960s and 1970s. While the data are somewhat rudimentary, they seem to indicate that college students of the twenties were substantially freer in their sexual and religious attitudes and were in general more tolerant than their elders. Articles in student journals as well as commentary in intellectual magazines indicate that many socially conscious students felt that adult society was hypocritical, base, and anti-intellectual. Indeed, many of the charges sound very similar to those made at present by radical students.

The organized student movement of the previous decade was destroyed by the war and repression, and never regained its strength in the twenties. Much of the student activity which took place had no organizational roots and little continuity. The New Student, a journal founded in 1922, reported extensively on student events and tried to provide a communications link between disparate local groups. Despite the lack of organization, there was a good deal of ferment taking place during the twenties. The period was characterized by substantial repression; students with radical inclinations were often expelled from colleges, student newspapers were censored, and administrators often acted in a heavy-handed manner. Much of the thrust of student activism was aimed at establishing and protecting free speech on the campus. Campus newspaper editors protested censorship, and student groups attempted to bring radical speakers on campus.

Students cricicized "giganticism" in universities, and many of their criticisms have a very modern ring to them. Students complained that professors were boring and that there was too little contact with them, that academic bureaucracy was overwhelming the campus, and that they generally were alienated from their colleges. Articles reprinted in the *New Student* from college newspapers indicate that these kinds of criticisms were very strong. The twenties were a period of rapid expansion of higher education—the proportion of youth attending college rose from 4 percent in 1900 to 12 percent at the end of the twenties. This period was also one of rapid social change, and college curricula did not often keep up with currents in society.

The Groups

A number of student groups emerged in the 1920s which have been generally ignored because of the more dramatic events of the following decade. Strong student sentiment in favor of the League of Nations and for disarmament sparked the organization of the National Student Committee for the Limitation of Armaments. This group sent antiwar speakers to college campuses. In 1922, it merged with the Intercollegiate Liberal League to form the National Student Forum (NSF), and the new group claimed a thousand student members and several hundred graduate and faculty members. The NSF avoided general social reform issues, and its leadership tried to prevent it from getting a "radical" image. The *New Student* was the official organ of the NSF, and both the organization and the journal saw their image as stimulating thought and social concern among American college students.[6]

The National Student Forum was not the only group to emerge during the twenties. Organizations such as the National Student Federation of America (NSFA), the Student League for Industrial Democracy (SLID), and various Christian groups were attempting to unite students on social and, to some extent, political issues. The SCVM convention of 1923 considered a number of social action issues, and a number of radical speakers pressed for social change. Many Christian youth organizations passed strong antiwar statements at their meetings and, in 1924, a group of 700 Christian students at an SCVM convention took a strong pacifist stand under the leadership of the Fellowship of Youth for Peace, an affiliate of the Fellowship of Reconciliation, a prominent pacifist organization.

The SLID claimed seventy-five student chapters and about 2,000 student members in 1927. Its major activities included campaigns against ROTC on campus, organizing student committees to defend Sacco and Vanzetti, and campaigning against American intervention in Nicaragua and Mexico (Lewack, 1953:9–10). Among the SLIDs active members in the late 1920s were Walter Reuther, Sidney Hook, and Max Lerner. Indeed, one observer in the 1950s stated that one of the SLIDs main functions in the twenties was to train leaders for the labor, Socialist, and other reform movements.

A forerunner of the present-day National Student Association, the NSFA was founded in 1925. The NSFA was a loose federation of student governments, and was interested mainly in international cooperation and understanding among student groups. Other efforts at student involvement in the twenties were issue-oriented.

Single-issue conferences were common. For example, students gathered at Bear Mountain, New York, in 1924 to discuss "Youth's Standard of Living." Among the sponsors of this meeting—foreshadowing the coalitions of student groups in the 1930s—were the YPSL, YM and YWCAs, Young Workers' League (the youth group of the Communist Party), Rand Students League (Socialist), and the Ethical Culture Society. In 1927, the first conference of the American Federation of Youth, representing fifty youth organizations, met and went on record favoring a nationwide campaign against compulsory military training, militarism, imperialism, and child labor. Conventions of religious students were addressed by SLID speakers, and often took radical or reformist stands.

THE THIRTIES

The 1930s saw the growth of the first mass student movement in American history. The most important campus issue was the antiwar question; thousands of students were involved in many American colleges. For the first time, the student movement engaged in a political campaign which, although ultimately unsuccessful, aroused substantial public support on and off the campus. Despite its size—the American Student Union claimed 20,000 members in 1938, and several hundred thousand students participated in peace strikes during the decade—the impact of the student movement should not be overestimated. For the most part, the activities of radical students were a reflection of other, more significant, social movements and organizations.

The generation gap, so much a part of the political rhetoric of the sixties, was absent during the thirties. Politically active students were generally affiliated with adult political groups and usually took their cues from the adult movement. Even the antiwar movement was stimulated as much by conservative isolationists as by radical students. Finally, the activism of the thirties was mainly confined to metropolitan centers, most notably New York City, and to the more cosmopolitan campuses. The majority of colleges was unaffected by the political ferment taking place. Despite these limitations, the student movement of the thirties was one of the most significant in American history, and in terms of proportions of students involved in activism, perhaps more significant than the New Left of the 1960s.

The student movement of the thirties had a number of key foci. It was not generally interested in issues of academic reform. In fact, the continuing criticisms of the educational system which were made in the twenties generally stopped in the thirties. Students fought battles over ROTC and over free speech on campus, and occasionally defended academic freedom, but in general their concerns were more political. The antiwar issue was the most volatile campus question of the thirties despite the Depression and other domestic crises, perhaps reflecting the overwhelmingly middle-class student population. The more ideologically sophisticated students were also involved in labor organizing, and in the internal politics of the significant left-wing movements of the period.

The Radical Trend

The early thirties saw the radicalizing of existing student groups and the formation of new leftist organizations. The Student League for Industrial Democracy, perhaps the most important left-wing campus group with an historical tradition, moved substantially to the Left although it maintained its Social Democratic orientation. The Socialist and Communist parties, which had been unenthusiastic about campus organizing in the early thirties, became active in the universities by 1933. In 1931, the National Student League was organized with Communist support and eventual domination. While the NSL was more radical than SLID—its program included an effort to "promote student participation in the revolutionary movement against capitalism"—it tried to appeal to a range of student opinion. NSL received national publicity when its members went to Harlan County, Kentucky, in 1932 to support striking coal miners. SLID and NSL did work together, however, in organizing "united front" antiwar campaigns on campus in 1931 and 1932 and in the American Student Union.

The thirties also radicalized the Christian student movement. The

Council of Christian Associations, the organization uniting the YM
and YWCAs, published a pamphlet in 1931 entitled "Toward a New
Economic Society" in which collective ownership of natural resources
and public utilities was advocated.[7] Older national leaders of the Ys
became disturbed at the council's publication and disavowed its Socialist position. The SCVM placed less stress on overseas missionary
work and paid more attention to domestic problems. Resolutions
passed at the first National Assembly of Student Christian Groups in
1938 indicated religious students had become more radical. One resolution, passed by a substantial majority, stated that capitalism and fascism were unacceptable and that the goals of the Coöperative Movement and of Marxian socialism were preferred (Campbell, 1938:12).

The Peace Issue

The most dramatic campus issue of the period was peace and disarmament. A poll conducted by the Intercollegiate Disarmament Council in 1931 indicated that 39 percent of the 22,627 students polled at
seventy colleges would not participate in any war and 33 percent
stated that they would fight only if the United States were invaded.[8]
The Brown University *Daily Herald* polled approximately 22,000 students in sixty-five colleges; and of the 15,636 students who responded, around 50 percent stated they would bear arms only in case
of an invasion of the United States. Students also fought over civil
liberties and academic freedom, and with somewhat more success
than they had had in the twenties. The most dramatic case involved
the editor of the Columbia University *Spectator,* who was expelled
from the university in 1932 for publishing "misrepresentations." One
of the first successful campus student strikes took place over this issue.

Events in Europe and a continuing domestic crisis greatly increased
the constituency for radical student activism in the United States. By
1935, the most active student groups were the SLID (Social Democratic), the National Student League (Communist), religious pacifist
groups such as the Fellowship of Reconciliation, social-action-minded
religious groups like the Ys, and the National Student Federation of
America (Liberal). Attempts at unity among progressive students
were made during the early thirties, such as the National Conference
of Students in Politics in 1933, but the major united-front student
group was the American Student Union (ASU), which functioned
from 1935 to 1939.

Like many of the other campus trends of the period, the formation
of the ASU reflected broader events in society. The Communist International's stress on the formation of "united fronts" provided the

major impetus for the ASU and other similar groups among other constituencies. The ASU was basically a union of the Communist NSL, the Socialist SLID, and various unaffiliated liberals.[9] From 1935 until 1937, there was an effective sharing of power between Socialists and Communists, due in part to Liberal support of the Socialist position. By 1937, however, the Communists were able to take control of the ASU and from that time until the ASUs demise it slavishly followed the turns of Communist policy.

The Oxford Pledge was a center of controversy in the ASU, and a key issue in the student movement as a whole. In 1933, the Oxford Union adopted a resolution that stated that under no circumstances should one fight for "King and Country." The ASU adopted an American version of the pledge in 1936 and it became the center of campus organizing by both the ASU and various liberal and pacifist groups. National student peace strikes were organized from 1935 until 1939, and these attracted great public attention. Among the most successful strikes, one took place in April 1935 which involved more than 150,000 students and had the support of a number of liberal college presidents, and another in 1938 involved more than 500,000 students. On many campuses these "strikes" involved only a one-hour work stoppage, however. The campus peace movement lost support as groups like the ASU closely followed Communist policy in supporting collective security, and as war in Europe looked increasingly possible.

Despite the fact that in 1938 the ASU claimed 20,000 members in 150 colleges and 100 high schools, all was not well with the organization. ASUs reversal of its antiwar stand and its increasingly clear Communist domination disillusioned many students. Vocal Socialist and pacifist groups also took away some ASU supporters. The final blow to the organization came when collective security was abandoned by the ASU at the time Stalin signed the Nazi-Soviet nonaggression pact. ASU membership dropped to 2,000 in 1940, and the organization soon went out of existence.

The "Active Left"

At the same time that mass "united front" student groups were functioning, the political parties and sects of the Left were also active on the campuses. The Young Communist League, clearly the largest of the political groups, claimed 22,000 members in 1939, both student and non-student. The Young People's Socialist League continued to function during this period, and although it took more of an interest in students than it previously did, its effectiveness was limited by in-

ternecine factional disputes. Smaller political student groups affiliated with Trotskyist, pacifist, and other tendencies on the Left also existed, although it is unlikely that their combined membership was
more than 3,000 nationally, with a major segment concentrated in
New York City. One of the political trends of the thirties, on the
campus as well as more broadly, was a splintering of the radical movement. Student groups spent much of their time fighting each other.
The major thrust of the student movement was leftist during the
1930s, but there are indications that not all politically conscious students were radicals. The liberal National Student Federation of
America continued to function throughout this period. Furthermore,
students were involved in a number of antistrike activities in the thirties, indicating that conservative activism also existed. Right-wing
Berkeley students helped to break the San Francisco general strike,
and some radical students were thrown into the lake at the University
of Wisconsin in 1937. There are no indications of a major right-wing
organizational thrust on the campus at this period, but sentiment did
exist.

The student movement of the 1930s involved large numbers of
students in impressive demonstrations and in large organizations. But
in the last analysis it failed to build a viable movement. Its lack of interest in campus issues and its deep involvement in the factional politics of the Left cut it off from many students. The adult movement
allowed the students little autonomy, and when political difficulties
emerged on the adult level, the student movement immediately collapsed. Yet, the student movement of the thirties involved impressive
numbers of individuals, many of whom received their political education in the movement, and many are the parents of today's generation
of activists (see Flacks, 1967).

THE FORTIES

The contrast between the thirties and the following two decades is
dramatic. With the onset of World War II, the American student
movement simply collapsed. Radicals who opposed the war were disillusioned and confused by the splits in the adult radical movement
concerning the war and related foreign policy issues. Other radicals
and liberals threw themselves behind moves for collective security and
supported the Allied cause. And with American involvement in 1941,
many students volunteered or were drafted into the armed forces and
campus activism came to an end. The most active groups on campus
were such organizations as the Student Defenders of Democracy.

The immediate postwar period saw a number of efforts to revive the student movement, but none of these was very successful. The first postwar convention of SLID, held in 1946, was attended by only forty delegates from twelve schools. Communist activists organized the American Youth for Democracy (AYD) in 1943, which sought to combine campus-oriented issues with opposition to the beginning of the Cold War. While AYD had a respectable membership, it did not inspire major student support, nor was it a force on the campus. Perhaps the most successful postwar student groups were those related directly to the desire for a durable peace; among these students, many were returning veterans anxious to complete their studies and settle down to a job. The United World Federalists had a short period of support on the campus, and engaged in various kinds of educational programs aimed at convincing Americans to give up their national sovereignty and join in a world government.

The liberal movement also was reflected in a number of student groups which were formed around 1948. These organizations reflected in part a growing anti-communism, both on and off the campus, and a desire to counter groups like the AYD, as well as large numbers of students who supported Henry Wallace's presidential campaign in 1948. The Students for Democratic Action (SDA), founded in 1947, was an affiliate of the liberal, anti-Communist Americans for Democratic Action. It attracted substantial support on the campus but did not engage in major campus-oriented campaigns. There was a brief upsurge of student political activism during the 1948 presidential election campaign. The Young Progressives of America, formed largely with AYD initiative, provided strong campus support for Wallace's election campaign, and involved thousands of students under Communist direction. When the Wallace forces were roundly defeated, many of those who were active became disillusioned and left the political scene altogether.

Efforts at reviving the student movement in the late 1940s faced substantial odds. The mood of the campus, as of the country at large, was decidedly apolitical. As previously mentioned, many veterans returned to their studies and were anxious to finish their academic work quickly. The student movement itself was unable to shift its attention to campus issues, such as overcrowding in universities, poor housing conditions, and other problems created by the returning veterans. The adult Left was in substantial disarray and could provide no guidance, and no independent student groups existed which could strike out on their own. But perhaps the major reason was the general political climate in the country, which was confused in the immediate postwar period, and increasingly anti-Communist and conservative during the 1950s. The Korean War, the development of the Cold

War, the Communist coup in Czechoslovakia, and the increasingly anti-Communist foreign and domestic stance of the American government, combined to make radical or even liberal student organizing difficult.

THE FIFTIES

The one major national student organization founded in the late 1940s reflected many of the trends which have been noted. The United States National Student Association was founded in 1948 in the flush of international student unity and cooperation. It was not long before the NSA became involved in the Cold War, and its stand became strongly anti-Communist.[10] The NSAs early support was impressive—some 1,000 student leaders representing 1,100,000 students and more than twenty national student organizations attended the founding convention of the NSA—but the organization never achieved major active support on the campus. It was from the outset a federation of student governments without grass-roots support. Although there was a small minority of Communists in NSA, and a rather substantial minority of conservative Catholics, the NSAs policies were from the outset "mainline Liberal." Recent disclosures of the CIAs involvement in NSAs financial affairs are not so surprising, considering the political climate in the early 1950s and the strong anti-Communist position of NSAs liberal leadership during this period.[11] Although clearly the largest and probably externally the most influential student organization of the 1950s, the National Student Association made very little impact on its more than one million student "members."

The 1950s were also a period of direct political repression and general apathy. Investigations by Senator Joseph McCarthy and various congressional committees instilled fear in many liberals and radicals. Faculty members were forced from their jobs in some cases because of their political views, and loyalty oaths became common. Journals like the *Nation* and the *New Republic* chronicled the silent generation, and the liberal press decried the apathy of the young. Right-wing student groups gained some prominence on the campuses for the first time in years. The pro-McCarthy Students for America, founded in 1951, had a short period of strength in the early 1950s; and other conservative groups were founded, often with substantial outside financial support, later in the decade. The Students for America was a blatant arm of McCarthyism with a national security division that maintained direct liaison with antisubversive government agencies. The Intercollegiate Society for Individualists, founded in 1957, reflected an intellectual concern for right-wing libertarianism, while the Young Americans for Freedom (YAF), founded in 1960, is a more activist-oriented, conservative student organization.

It is a curious paradox that although antiwar feelings among students in the 1930s and the 1960s helped to sustain active radical student movements, similar tendencies among students in the 1950s had no organizational effect. The Korean War was never very popular on the campuses. A poll taken in 1953 indicated that 26 percent of those responding were strongly opposed to the war while 36 percent had strong reservations (Suchman, Goldsen and Williams, 1953:173, 182). No groups emerged to mobilize this feeling, and as a result the campus was virtually silent on the subject of the Korean conflict.

Despite pervading apathy and repression, left-wing student groups did survive the 1950s, providing some organizational continuity which kept radical thought alive in the United States during a rather difficult period. The Communists changed the name of their student group from American Youth for Democracy to Labor Youth League, to reflect shifts in party policy. The LYL maintained a small number of chapters during the fifties, mainly in New York and a few major campus centers, and it was subjected to substantial repression by campus authorities and others. The pacifist Fellowship of Reconciliation maintained a presence on the campus and was especially active among seminarians. The Young People's Socialist League and the SLID both continued to function, although with memberships varying around two hundred each. As in the twenties, religious student organizations kept the spark of social reform and political concern alive on many of the less politically active campuses. Groups like the YM-YWCA were especially active in this area, and they provided a forum of radical speakers, and engaged in some mild social action campaigns.

THE SIXTIES AND THE "NEW LEFT"

The end of this narrative brings us to the beginnings of the New Left. The late 1950s saw a rebirth of student activism in the United States and the emergence of some of these organizations and political concerns which contributed to the student movement of the 1960s. A number of crucial developments was taking place outside the campus which had a major impact on the student movement. The end of the Korean War and a period of somewhat greater tolerance in the United States made political activism a bit easier. The "beatniks" indicated the first stirrings of a major counter-culture. The 1954 Supreme Court decision on segregation and the beginning of an active

and militant civil rights movement focused the attention of students
on a key issue in American society for perhaps the first time. The
growing consciousness of the dangers of nuclear war stimulated the
resurgence of a peace movement. It is significant that the student
movements of the postwar period placed little emphasis on university-
related issues. This lack of concern with the environment of the student continued until the early 1960s, when questions of educational
reform and of the university generally became important issues.

The student movement of the late 1950s had strong intellectual
concerns. It was interested in moving beyond the stale ideologies of
the "old Left" sects and in breaking new ground. Substantial disillusionment with the Communist party was evident after Khrushchev's
speech denouncing Stalin, and especially after the Soviet invasion of
Hungary in 1956. Several new journals were founded which reflected
a searching for fresh ideological currents. *Studies on the Left,* founded
by graduate students at the University of Wisconsin in 1959, *New University Thought,* from the University of Chicago, and several other
journals began to establish the ideological and tactical basis for a new
radical movement.

The New Concerns

Several new student organizations and campaigns emerged at the
end of the 1950s which reflected new concerns of politically conscious
American students. The Students for a Democratic Society (SDS),
perhaps the most publicized organization of the New Left, emerged
from the Social-Democratic Student League for Industrial Democracy. While SLID changed its name to SDS in 1959, ties were maintained with the adult League for Industrial Democracy until 1963,
and SDS received a financial subsidy during this period. The ideological and tactical development of the SDS, while beyond the scope of
this essay, reflects some of the changing emphases of the student
movement. As the SDS became more radical it broke its ties with the
LID, indicating a trend away from student involvement in the adult
"old Left" political organizations.

The three main threads of student activism in the late 1950s were
civil liberties, peace, and civil rights, in chronological order. Ad hoc
civil liberties groups such as the Committee to Abolish the House
Committee on Un-American Activities aroused interest in issues of
academic freedom and civil liberties. These efforts culminated in violent demonstrations in San Francisco in 1960. The peace movement
emerged from two major trends—the traditional pacifist organizations such as the Fellowship of Reconciliation, and newer, liberal

groups such as the National Committee for a Sane Nuclear Policy (SANE). The student affiliate of SANE was founded in 1958 and, although it included many left-wing students, it generally followed SANEs liberal policies. Its major focus was on ending nuclear testing. The other major student peace organization, the Student Peace Union (SPU), was founded in 1959 by a combination of pacifists and moderate radicals. The SPU was for a period the largest radical student group in the United States, with a membership of about 5,000 in some 100 campus groups. The civil rights movement is perhaps the most important stimulus for the recent upsurge in student activism. While the major successes of the campus civil rights movement took place in the early 1960s, many of the roots were established in the fifties. Many students supported groups like CORE and the NAACP, and small civil rights demonstrations occasionally took place. In the days before black power, it was easier for white middle-class college students to involve themselves in campaigns for equality and integration, and the plight of the Negro caught the attention and sympathy of the campus.

While the 1950s saw a reestablishment of radical and social action organizations on campus, the major mood of the campus remained, in the words of the *Nation,* silent and apathetic. Only a tiny proportion of the student population was involved in any of the new organizations, and most campuses remained placid. Yet, groups like SDS, SPU, and the newly formed Student Nonviolent Coordinating Committee (SNCC) caught the attention of some students and indicated a trend away from reliance on adult guidance. New student journals helped to lay the ideological foundations for the new movement. The period can, in the words of one radical journal, be characterized as one of hope in the midst of apathy.

Easy generalizations concerning student activism in America are impossible. While there is a clear historical tradition of student activism, each period is marked by distinctive factors. The American student movement in the period under consideration was never a direct threat to the established order nor did it play a leading role in any of the social movements of the period. Nevertheless, American students in the 1920s were among the most socially conscious elements of the population. Students were influential in at least one political struggle, the antiwar movement of the thirties. Throughout the period under consideration, the majority of the American student community was never involved in a major way in politics. Even during the 1930s, most of the campuses were untouched by activism, and in the less active 1920s and 1950s only a tiny minority of the student population was involved in politics.

Perhaps more important than the number involved, however, was the fact that the student political movement—mostly of a radical nature—helped to shape the political and intellectual climate of the campus and particularly of the prestigious universities. The impact of the university on student activism has hardly been mentioned in this essay, although it is of importance. During this period, the numbers of students on American campuses increased from 355,000 in 1910 to 3,580,000 in 1960. The university was transformed from an important yet somewhat "ivory tower" institution into the "multiversity" at the center of economic and political life. Higher education was transformed from a preserve of the upper middle classes to a much broader phenomenon.

Despite substantial differences between periods and among organizations, there are a number of generalizations that can be made with regard to the period between 1900 and 1960.

1) There is little evidence of generational conflict in the organized student movement. There was discontent with adult cultural forms in the twenties and some conflicts between youth and adults in groups ranging from the YMCA to the YPSL, but few direct attacks on adult institutions. Throughout this period, student activists worked closely with and generally took direction from the adult political movement.

2) The student movement generally limited its tactics to educational campaigns and nonviolent and legal direct action. This generalization seems to hold regardless of political ideology throughout the period.

3) The thrust of the student movement was in general directed at broad social issues and not basically concerned with the university itself. Although there was some concern with academic issues in the twenties, most activists were more interested in political questions.

4) The organized student movement was not part of any kind of a "counter-culture" or other similar effort. The radical political groups felt that the basic necessity was a change in power relationships in society and social reform.

5) Student activism involved not only radical (or conservative) organizations, but religious and other groups. For several periods, groups like the YM-YWCA were in the forefront of student social action programs.

6) With the exception of the late 1950s, the student movement followed political trends in society and in the adult radical movement.

A comparative analysis of the student movement of the pre- and post-1960 period is beyond our present scope. It is clear that while there are some similarities, there are also important differences. Quick comparisons will probably result in errors, as student activism has been shaped by the different circumstances of varying historical periods. If there is any lesson from this consideration, it is perhaps that student activism is very much tied to events in society and on the campus. Although the movement on a number of occasions acted as a conscience for its generation, or at least kept radical traditions alive, it never exhibited the potential for revolution.

NOTES

1. Seymour Martin Lipset's recent essay, "The Historical Background of American Student Activism" (mimeographed, 1970), gives a detailed description of the early origins of American student activism.

2. Harry Laidler's editorial accounts in the *Intercollegiate Socialist* offer some idea of what ISS concerns were. A good example of convention discussion topics can be found in vol. 4 (October–November 1916).

3. *Intercollegiate Socialist* 1 (February–March 1913): 13.

4. Some members were concerned that the society's name might exclude noncollegian members and some expressed concern that it might give the impression that the ISS was affiliated with the Socialist party.

5. "Report of the Young People's Department of the Socialist Party of the U.S. to the International Young Socialist Congress," *Young Socialist Magazine*, June 1914, p. 12.

6. *New Student* 1 (May 3, 1922): 1.

7. "Student Radicalism," *World Tomorrow* 14 (June 1931): 181.

8. George Rawick, "The New Deal and Youth" (Ph.D. diss., University of Wisconsin, 1957), p. 282.

9. The best account of the American Student Union is Draper (1967:151–89). Draper's account reflects the Socialist faction of the radical student movement.

10. The most adequate account of the early period of the NSA can be found in Martin McLaughlin, "Political Processes in American National Student Organizations" (Ph.D. diss., Notre Dame University, 1948). The author writes from a strongly anti-Communist viewpoint and was himself involved in the founding of the NSA.

11. For an assessment of the NSA-CIA affair, see Stern (1967).

Social Movements: An Interactionist Analysis

ROBERT H. LAUER

A social movement is, by definition, a dynamic phenomenon. It cannot, therefore, be adequately analyzed within a structuralist conceptual framework.[1] As Blumer (1951:202) says, a "temporal and developmental perspective" is necessary. While certain structural concepts are valuable analytic tools, their usefulness is greatly enhanced through the addition of the temporal and developmental dimension.

In analyzing the significance of *structural strain,* for example, we must not only identify those strains that are factors in the initiation of the movement, but also those that develop during the movement's subsequent history, giving it shape and direction. Likewise, in the analysis of factors of *conduciveness,* we must not disregard the temporal variation in those factors that results from the interaction of the movement with the larger society.

There have been attempts, of course, to deal with the dynamics involved. Over four decades ago, Dawson and Gettys (1929) identified four stages which characterize successful movements: an initial stage of unrest, a popular stage of excitement, a formal stage, and institutionalization. More recently, Wallace (1956b) delineated the five ideal-typical stages through which "revitalization movements" go. These stages are the "processual structure" of the movement, and include a

Reprinted by permission of the author and publisher from *Sociological Quarterly* 13 (Summer 1972).

steady state, a time of intensified individual stress, a time of cultural distortion, a time of revitalization, and the resultant new steady state. Turner and Killian (1957:328–29) discuss how public reaction may impel movements into revolutionary, peculiar, or respectable stances vis-à-vis the larger society.

There have also been attempts to study facets of movements (as opposed to the movement in its totality) in terms of the dynamics. Although they did not go into detail, Gerlach and Hine (1970:170) note that ideologies may shift as a result of the interaction between the movement and the larger society. And Toch (1965:26 f.) points out a "four-step road" through which people become members of a movement.

Most of the above, however, tend to deal with fixed sequences rather than with interactive ones. Toch (1965:227) does note, on the other hand, that throughout its existence "the life cycle of a social movement shows the ever-present impact of the outside world." The present essay is an effort to draw out that impact by viewing the movement as an interactive phenomenon vis-àvis the larger society.

From an interactionist perspective, then, structural concepts are given a temporal dimension, and the variations that occur are a consequence of the interaction process. In the interactionist framework, social life "takes on the character of an ongoing process—a continuing matter of fitting developing lines of conduct to one another" (Blumer, 1966:538). The present essay applies this perspective to historical data to generate propositions about the dynamics of a social movement. The movement analyzed is the effort by Timothy Leary and others to legitimate the use of LSD. This effort is viewed as a concrete expression of a more diffuse movement (Blumer, 1957:145) involving the use of drugs which has characterized the last decade.

Furthermore, the movement was a combination of what Turner and Killian (1957:328–29) call a "peculiar" and a "revolutionary" movement. It was peculiar in that it was "inconsistent with the basic value structure of society." The type of opposition generated was more than the ridicule and ostracism accorded the peculiar movement, yet generally less than the violent suppression characteristic of the revolutionary movement. As Turner and Killian point out, however, a change from one of these two types to the other is rather frequent in the case of any concrete movement.

Since the LSD movement was an effort to promote and legitimate a form of behavior labeled as deviant, the analysis which follows has a problematic utility for other kinds of social movements. It is, moreover, difficult to judge the validity of the conclusions for other kinds of movements because existing studies have not sought to delineate interactive sequences. The propositions that are developed, therefore, must be tested by the analysis of other movements, and, hopefully, this will stimulate research in a neglected area. A historical résumé and a descriptive analysis of the characteristics that define Leary's effort as a social movement will provide a necessary background for the interactionist analysis.

LEARY AND THE LSD MOVEMENT

The natural history of the LSD movement begins with one of the numerous serendipities that have characterized the progress of science. In 1943, Dr. Albert Hofmann, a biochemist, had accidentally ingested a small amount of the drug in the laboratory. However, Leary's experience with the hallucinogens occurred in 1960 at a mushroom party in Mexico. There he tasted psilocybin, which produces effects similar to LSD but of shorter duration. Leary and Richard Alpert, both with Ph.D.'s in clinical psychology and both teaching at Harvard, began an intensive program of experimentation with the drug.

Initially, the two psychologists administered psilocybin to a group of thirty-eight people, primarily intellectuals and artists. The results of this first experiment convinced the researchers that they were dealing with a substance of revolutionary social import. They envisioned its use in psychotherapy, in the facilitation of creativity, and as a means of gaining insights in scholarly pursuits. In 1961, a second project was initiated—a rehabilitation program in the Massachusetts Correctional Institution involving the use of psilocybin. The experimenters also took the drug, sharing the experience rather than merely observing it: "The most obvious result of these experiences is the closeness that develops among men who have been enlightened together. Even afterwards, in the somnambulance of normal reality, the bond remains" (Leary and Clark, 1963:253).

Although some Harvard faculty members began to display some skepticism and opposition to the research, the administration did not react until two undergraduates were confined in mental hospitals after ingesting hallucinogenic drugs. But David C. McClelland, director of the Center for Research in Personality, defended the research, and the administration did nothing more than secure an agreement that undergraduates would not be used in the experiment. On October 8, 1961, however, McClelland issued a mimeographed memorandum at a staff meeting [2] which stated that those who took psilocybin exhibited certain questionable characteristics, including social withdrawal, interpersonal insensitivity, a feeling of omniscience combined with religious and philosophical naïveté, and impulsive behavior.

Misgivings and tacit disapproval exploded into open controversy in February 1962, when the *Harvard Crimson* published an article about the experiments. A state inquiry was conducted and a requirement was established that a licensed physician should be present whenever the drug was administered.

Pressure from hostile colleagues at Harvard continued, and Leary and Alpert took a group of people interested in the "mind-expanding" drugs to Zihuatanejo, Mexico, for the summer of 1962. On their return to Harvard in the fall, they began a determined campaign for "internal freedom," i.e., for freedom to use hallucinogenic drugs. In October 1962, Leary announced the formation of a private organization, the International Federation for Internal Freedom. IFIF applied for incorporation, and began an active program of expansion.

In April 1963, Leary disappeared from Cambridge without giving the university formal notice of his departure. President Pusey and the dean of the faculty conferred with the Harvard Corporation, which immediately relieved Leary of his position and stopped his salary. On Mary 27, 1963, Pusey announced that Alpert had been fired for breaking the agreement not to give psilocybin to undergraduates.

Alpert and Leary declared that they would give their full attention to IFIF. But because of the greater restrictions on the use of drugs that followed the thalidomide tragedies,[3] they decided to continue their research in Mexico. Thirty-five persons, primarily mature business and professional people, went to Zihuatanejo "for the purpose of studying the transpersonative effects of group interaction with the concurrent use of LSD-25" (Downing, 1964:144). From the point of view of IFIF, this was to be a center both to demonstrate the value of psychedelic drugs and to train people in their administration and use.

The experiment was short-lived; the participants were forced by the Mexican government to leave by mid-June, ostensibly for "engaging in activities not permitted to a tourist." [4] In August 1963, Leary and Alpert moved to Millbrook, New York. They were received genially, as reflected in the title of a local editorial: "No Witch Hunt Here."

On December 14, 1963, Leary announced that the IFIF had been dissolved because of restrictions on the use of psychedelic drugs. Roughly three years later he held a press conference and announced that he had founded a new religion, the League of Spiritual Discovery, based on the use of LSD, peyote, and marijuana. Goals of the league were expressed in "the metaphor of the present—turn-on, tune-in, and drop-out." [5]

The formal organization of the league was rooted in a twofold purpose: to give shape and meaning to the psychedelic experience and to bring about the legalization of the psychedelic drugs and of marijuana. But the movement experienced increasing societal hostility combined with new encounters with legal authorities during the latter part of 1966 and throughout 1967. By June 1967, the initial acceptance of the Millbrook residents had changed to opposition, ranging from tacit disapproval to open hostility toward the esoteric activities of Leary and his guests.

Throughout this period, Leary continued to write, lecture, and direct the activities of his guests at Millbrook, which he began to call the "Mother Church" of the league. An Associated Press release in February 1968 reported that Leary planned on vanishing from public view for some time. He would, he said, go underground in a campaign to win recognition as a modern messiah. His plans called for the continuation of the league and of the Millbrook estate. Leary himself was going underground to escape harassment.[6] Eventually, he asserted, he would be recognized as the wisest man of the twentieth century.

To what extent, then, does the above description sketch a social movement? Blumer (1951:202) has identified a number of distinguishing characteristics of social movements, including a well-defined objective or goal, an organization and structure, leadership, membership characterized by a "we-consciousness," a guiding set of values, and normative expectations.

The objective or goal of the LSD movement basically was to obtain the freedom to use drugs that expand consciousness. Leary formed two organized structures to implement this goal—the IFIF and the league. He himself was the acknowledged leader of the league, though an internal hierarchy also functioned. The "we-consciousness" of the members was evident from quotes in a number of sources, e.g.: "Taking the drug is such an overwhelming experience that we soon realized that those of us who had done so had something wonderful in common. We wanted to be together constantly, to share time and space." [7]

Although certain values and normative expectations had evolved, they did not crystallize into a unified system, for the movement quickly experienced a certain factionalism and splintering. The Neo-American Church was founded in 1964 by Arthur Kleps, a psychologist. His group was primarily concerned with withdrawal and "the appreciation of Transcendental Reality" (Braden, 1967:214). Blum (1964:130) has identified three major factions: the psychologists, who stress growth of personality; the psychiatrists, who stress personality growth in a medical context; and the religionists. The latter include the two subgroups of Christian and Eastern. One value was common to all, however—the positive value of the drug experience. And this value led to a shared conviction that the experience should be legalized.

GENESIS OF THE MOVEMENT

The LSD movement can be said to have begun with the appearance of an elemental ideology—the conviction regarding the potential value of hallucinogenic drugs. Those who shared the conviction and participated in the activities based on it comprised an interest group.[8] Certain factors were highly conducive to the pursuit of the interest of this group:

1) The federal laws relevant to the use of the drugs were loose and ambiguous. The United States Narcotics Bureau, for example, stated that it was unable to act in regard to hallucinogenic drugs for the drugs were not listed in federal narcotics statutes as addictive substances.

2) The drugs themselves were readily available. Distributors of investigational drugs were supposed to ascertain for themselves whether prospective buyers were qualified to use the drugs. A brief form asked for the purchaser's educational background, research facilities, and proposed research.

3) The Harvard setting, and the association of Leary and Alpert with the Center for Research in Personality, gave credibility, prestige, and freedom to the research.

4) Experimental subjects were readily available. Harvard students provided Leary and Alpert with an unlimited number of eager subjects. Because of the Harvard connection, prisoners at the Massachusetts Correctional Institution were also available. And the familiarity with and approval of the use of drugs by certain artists and intellectuals gave the experimenters yet a third source of subjects.

5) One other possible factor is the use of drugs as an accepted feature of American society.[9] This, then, is the first phase of the genesis of the social movement—the appearance of an elemental ideology, the initiation of certain activities that express that ideology, and the existence of factors of conduciveness that permit the activities.

In the second phase, stress appeared in the form of reaction from the social environment. This reaction involved an attempt to define and delimit the activities of the interest group. The stress first appeared as reservations and opposition on the part of certain faculty members at Harvard. After the hospitalization of the two undergraduate students, the experimenters were required to agree not to use undergraduates in their research. Thus, initial stresses elicited a reaction that began to close the avenues of conduciveness. The stress was intensified by reports and letters in the *Harvard Crimson* and by the state inquiry.

The third phase involved the response of the interest group to the initial stresses. The group continued working, but refused undergraduates the use of the drug (with the one exception that provided the grounds for Alpert's dismissal).

It should be noted that a number of alternatives were open in each of the three phases. For example, in phase one the researchers could have chosen to observe the effects on selected subjects, or shared in the effects by ingesting the drugs themselves, or tried some combination of the two. The decision to share in the effects rather than simply observe them narrowed the subsequent field of alternatives. McClelland later declared that the more Leary and Alpert took the drugs themselves, the "less they were interested in science." [10]

In phase four there was heightened interaction between the interest group and its social environment, leading to an intensification of efforts to control and of resistance to that control, and, finally, to the emergence of the social movement. When drugs were no longer readily available, the pair of researchers continued their work in Mexico, and, upon their return, they formed IFIF. With the establishment of a formal organization, the interest group crystallized into a social movement.

The foregoing analysis leads to a first proposition: the genesis of a social movement involves an interactional process between an interest group and its social environment, the course of which is marked by: a) an increasing intensification of stress; b) a constriction of the legitimate avenues of conduciveness for the expression of activities of the interest group; and c) a selective choice of alternatives that results in a sequential divergence of consensus between the interest group and its social environment regarding the legitimacy of the values, norms, and/or goals of the former.

DEVELOPMENT OF IDEOLOGY AND PROGRAM

Neither the ideology nor the program of the LSD movement appeared in a fully developed, integrated form during the first years. Both evolved in the interactional process as the movement and the larger society defined and redefined, adjusted and readjusted, to each other. As noted above, Gerlach and Hine found in their study of the Pentecostal and Black Power movements a development of ideology as a result of interaction with the establishment (religious and political). Laue (1964) identified "doctrinal modifications" in the Black Muslim movement over a period of time. The concern here, then, is with an identification of the social factors that helped to formulate the ideology and program of the LSD movement. With regard to the former, a process of formation can be identified clearly in at least three areas:

1) *Development of a symbol system to express the ideology.* The use of drugs seems to involve the individual inevitably in a non- or antirational, mystical kind of experience. William James, who experimented with the effects of nitrous oxide, noted that drugs produce mystical states, and that these states (1902:414): "break down the authority of the non-mystical or rationalistic consciousness, based upon the understanding and the senses alone. They show it to be only one kind of consciousness. They open out the possibility of other orders of truth."

In an address to the International Congress of Applied Psychology in August 1961, Leary was already echoing this pattern of thought. He claimed that all behavior consists of learned games, but only the individual whom we usually call a mystic has perceived the game structure of behavior. Our task, he argued, is to see the mind as the "game-playing fragment" of the "brain-body complex." As such, the mind is "a useful and entertaining tool but quite irrelevant to survival and indeed usually antagonistic to well being" (Leary, 1962:57).

Nevertheless, Leary was still expressing his ideas in scientific terms at this point. In the *Harvard Crimson,* he expressed a concern for the problems created by such drugs. He envisioned the use of drugs as a catalyst to thought, with students applying insights gained from the use of the drug to specific problems in their own fields. And he was publishing the results of his experiments in the professional literature (e.g., Leary, Litwin, and Metzner, 1963).

It is important to note at this point that the nature of the LSD experience can be described in diverse ways. Blum (1964:16) reports a young man who had used LSD describing the experience in approximately the following way: "Really, when I first took LSD, I didn't know how to describe what had happened. It was intense and important, very much so, but there were no words for it. But after talking with others who had taken it, I could see that they were talking about the same thing. They did have words for it . . . and so I started using these words myself." The young man reports that the same thing happened to his wife, who said little about her experience until she had "learned how to talk about it" from others. Blum (1964:64) also points out that people tend to relate the kinds of experiences which they expect to have or which another tells them they are having.[11]

While at Harvard, Leary was still making an effort to express his work within the scientific symbol system. But his Harvard colleagues defined his work as antirational and antiscientific. After the break with Harvard, the movement more fully embraced a mystical symbol system. Leary turned to the East, and, in particular, to Tibet. The *Tibetan Book of the Dead* was adopted as the sacred scripture of the movement. The work was revised in order to transform "Buddhist metaphors and the hallucinatory content appropriate to a pastoral people . . . to the visions ecstasies, and terrors of our times" (Leary, Alpert, and Metzner, 1964:185).[12] The revised work was published in 1964 as *The Psychedelic Experience: A Manual Based on the Tibetan Book of the Dead.*

To sum up, the LSD experience can be described by more than one symbol system. During his Harvard experiments, Leary tended toward a mystical symbol system, but still sought to express his research in scientific terminology. The definition of the work as antirational and antiscientific and the disaffiliation with the university gave impetus to this tendency, and led to the adoption of a mystical symbol system.

2) Development of the idea of the "messiah game." I have already briefly mentioned Leary's "game" theory of behavior. The use of "game" denotes that all behavior is "artificial and culturally determined" (Leary, 1962:51). A game is a learned cultural sequence that involves rules, goals, rituals, language, and values. A culture maintains its stability by blinding its members to the fact that these five characteristics are game structures. So, for example, we play the "nationality game," and it is treason not to play it. But once an individual becomes aware of the game nature of behavior, he can choose his own game, learn its rules, rituals, and concepts, and play it fairly and cleanly.

In February 1968, Leary embarked upon the "messiah game," and this led to his decision to go underground. He declared that history shows that once you commit yourself to the "messiah game," you are going to encounter trouble with the Establishment.

The ideal of the "messiah" game evolved both out of interaction with the larger society and out of certain internal factors. Among the internal factors, two are crucial: the feelings of superiority that inhere in the drug experience, and the homage accorded to Leary by his adherents. With regard to the former, Blum (1964:55, 86) reports that LSD users frequently describe nonusers in terms that convey a sense of their superiority over the latter. This is fertile ground for the development of the "messiah game."

The homage accorded Leary by his followers is also a function of a number of factors: Leary's own charisma; the gratitude of the followers toward the man willing to assume the risks of leading their movement; and the need to have a worthy leader. This homage was intensified by their perception of Leary as a persecuted man. In testimony before a Senate subcommittee in May, 1966, Arthur Kleps said: "We regard him with the same special love and respect as was reserved by the early Christians for Jesus. . . . On the day prison doors close behind Tim Leary, if these ill-considered laws of religious suppression are upheld by the courts, this country will face a religious war." [13] Leary's definition of himself as a modern messiah was greatly facilitated by continued conflict with officialdom. Continuing oppressive experiences are necessary for a messiah, since one of the functions of the messiah is to rescue his followers from an evil society. There are no messiahs in socially respectable organizations. The development of this aspect of the ideology depended upon continuing social efforts at suppression.

3) *Development of the idea of social withdrawal.* During the first psilocybin experiments, Leary and Alpert saw the drugs as tools for creating a social utopia. They were convinced of the drug's therapeutic and creative social value. But their research received social condemnation, and the rejection by society led to their rejection of society. Speaking to the National Student Association Congress in 1967, Leary advised the delegates to "drop out" and detach themselves from society, and to "drop in to life" through the use of drugs.[14] The original stance of Leary was that of a social therapist; the developed stance was that of a social isolate.

With regard to the development of the program of the movement and of the organization designed to implement the program, the following brief outline sketches the process of change:

1) Bieberman (1967:17) describes the original group as being as "idealistic as children, brave as Christian martyrs, and full of wisdom. They were an indissoluble family, destined to go forward, hand in hand, to win souls and bring in the Kingdom." This grand program, however, was resisted by the university, and these pressures led to the organization of IFIF.

2) With the formation of an organized effort, increasing thereby the possibility of realizing the aims of the movement, suppressive efforts were intensified. Adverse publicity, professional criticism, and governmental pressures were directly applied. The IFIF was formally dissolved.

3) Governmental regulations against LSD were made increasingly stringent. States passed restrictive legislation, and federal pressures were exerted in the universities.[15] The government obviously had no intention of allowing the promiscuous use of LSD. Without some kind of formal organization, the adherents of the ideology had no means to effect changes in this situation. In 1966, therefore, Leary announced the formation of the League for Spiritual Discovery, which

would give shape and meaning to the psychedelic experience and seek to legalize the use of both psychedelic drugs and marijuana. A month later, Leary asserted: "We have a blueprint and we're going to change society in the next ten years." [16] But there is no evidence that the league pursued such a program. Its primary thrust seems to have been in the direction of trying to persuade the larger society of the values of using hallucinogenic drugs.

4) Pressures were unrelenting following the founding of the league. A flurry of popular articles in 1967 warned of the extreme hazards of the drug. James Goddard said that the use of the drug is "like playing Russian roulette on a sugar cube." [17] Ultimately, Leary announced his plans to go underground.

Under conditions of continually increasing pressure, then, the movement went through two cycles of aggressiveness and withdrawal (formation and dissolution of IFIF, formation of the league and the decision to go underground). The program was characterized by a progressive narrowing and increasing specificity—from the grand scheme to create a utopia, to the more limited program of encouraging, supporting, and protecting research; to the narrower and more specific effort to give shape and meaning to the psychedelic experience itself; and to the specific attempt to legalize the use of the drugs.

We may now present a second proposition: the development of the ideology and program of the social movement occurs during the interaction between the movement and the larger society, and may be characterized as a selective process in which: a) the stance of the movement vis-à-vis the larger society is defined; b) the rationale for group behavior is more sharply delineated; c) the goals of the movement are clarified through a narrowing of their scope and an increasing specificity; and d) through trial and error effective means are sought for attaining goals in the face of social resistance.

By calling the process a selective one, I mean to emphasize that the development of ideology and program is a function of the interaction process itself, with the members of the movement selecting from a range of alternatives those that allow them to respond to the larger society in a way they deem appropriate and necessary.

MOTIVATIONAL FACTORS IN RECRUITMENT

Students of social movements have commonly dealt with members of the movements in terms of the kind of people that are likely to join. Heberle (1951:94–100) identified four types likely to find a movement attractive: those who believe in the righteousness of the cause; those who have an emotional attraction (to a leader, for example);

those who have a traditional impetus; and those who anticipate personal gain through membership.

A typical characterization of recruits is that they are deprived in some way. Hoffer (1951) argued that the "true believer" lacks self-confidence and has a strong need to feel a part of something that transcends himself. Geschwender (1968) has recently set forth three temporal phenomena (rising expectations, relative deprivation, and downward mobility) and one nontemporal phenomenon (status inconsistency) as factors in predisposition toward participating in movements. Clearly, all involve deprivation.

By contrast, Gerlach and Hine (1970:79 f.) found the deprivation thesis to be of little use. The critical factor was face-to-face contact with members of the movement. Therefore, members are not necessarily the most deprived segments of the population nor even those who experience relative deprivation. The LSD movement supports Gerlach and Hine's thesis; it appealed strongly to mature, educated, and successful people. Among the thirty-five participants in the Zihuatanejo project, for example, were six clinical psychologists, five businessman, three physicist-engineers, three teachers, three artists, a rabbi, a minister, a psychopharmacologist, an editor, and an architect. Problems of recruitment, therefore, must be dealt with by identifying the kind of people who do join the movement and the interactional process by which one or another kind of people found the movement attractive. The question to be answered here is what motivated successful, educated individuals to attach themselves to the LSD movement?

The meaning of a movement to its adherents is a function of three factors: the societal definition of the movement; the movement's self-definition; and the adherent's or potential adherent's own definition, which is derived from his perception of the first two.

The LSD movement's self-definition, in terms of its assumptions and what it offered, has been well summarized by Downing (1964:149–50). Essentially, the assumption was made that the process of socialization limits and distorts individual personalities. The effects of the drug are to make the individual aware of this, and to free him. He gains understanding of the totality of reality in a nonverbal way. "The result is greater serenity and lessened anxiety."

In 1966, Leary stated that he expected more than a million new members within the next few years. While this may be discounted either as facile optimism or delusion born of desperation, the fact remains that certain facets of American society indicated a potentially widespread receptiveness to the movement in terms of its self-definition. That is, among white, educated, prosperous Protestants, certain patterns would indicate a potential positive response to a movement of this kind: 1) the widespread use of drugs (sleeping pills, tranquilizers, and so forth); 2) the popularity of peace-of-mind literature, indicating a felt need for anxiety reduction; 3) the resurgence of glossolalia, or "speaking in tongues," and Pentecostalism in Protestant churches, indicating a renewed interest in and receptiveness to pure emotional experiences.[18]

Nevertheless, the movement made no significant gains in the number of its adherents, for the societal definition of the movement characterized it variously as hazardous, weird, and illegal. Professional critics of the use of LSD emphasized that the drug has no inherent benefits; rather, the drug is like a scalpel—helpful when used by the physician, but otherwise merely a dangerous implement (Kurland et al., 1967:33–34).

Consequently, while certain aspects of the movement's self-definition could strongly motivate potential adherents, these were more than counterbalanced by the societal definition. And those to whom the movement appealed most were precisely those who were least likely to be willing to risk association with an ostracized, illegal group.

In addition, other elements of the self-definition developed which had a negative effect on the educated and successful, namely, the ideology of "dropping out." This was not a part of the initial movement. On the contrary, as shown above, the initial thrust was toward utopian reconstruction as well as personal growth. The drop-out ideology developed through interaction with a hostile social environment, and had the effect of "turning off" potential adherents. The self-definition, then, had an ambivalent appeal; one way in which the ambivalence was resolved was by accepting the use of LSD without joining the movement.

We may now set forth a third proposition: The motivation to join a movement is a function of the intersection of the movement's self-definition and the societal definition with the individual's interests and felt needs. The movement, therefore, will only be able to recruit sufficient numbers to the extent that: a) its self-definition generates specific appeal for disaffected groups in the society; or, b) it secures a societal definition of at least partial legitimacy.[19]

The LSD movement foundered because it failed in both of the above. The self-definition generated an appeal that was ambivalent and of prime interest to those who, while sensing that certain needs might be met in the movement, had too much stake in the existing order. And the societal definition was one of total rejection; neither the movement's goal—legitimating drug use—nor its activities—continuing use of and experimentation with drugs—were defined as legitimate.

NOTES

1. The structuralist framework has been well articulated by Smelser (1962). Much of the analysis in this essay may be understood vis-à-vis Smelser's explication.

2. *Reporter,* August 15, 1963, pp. 36 f.

3. Federal regulations were tightened in February 1963.

4. *New York Times,* December 15, 1963, p. 64.

5. *New York Times,* September 20, 1966, p. 33.

6. A United States Appeals Court had upheld a thirty year jail sentence and $50,000 fine against Leary the previous September. This stemmed from a 1966 conviction in Texas for transporting and concealing marijuana.

7. Downing (1964:164) describes the members of the Zihuatanejo community as "having a group ego, the usual process of group identification having been carried to a point where the individual member extended the boundaries of his own self-concern to include the individual intrapersonal concerns of the other group members."

8. Simmel (1950:317) defined an interest group as an association based on a particular interest and involving "objective member contributions" rather than "everybody's psychological knowledge of everybody else."

9. In 1965, for example, 24 million prescriptions for amphetamines and 123 million for sedatives and tranquilizers were filled. And most Americans are probably aware of the value of drugs in psychotherapeutic practice. However, LSD is a drug of a quite different kind—a dangerous drug—and is used for quite different purposes—esoteric and exotic experiences rather than aiding in adaptation to conventional society. Making such distinctions would seem to predispose people against acceptance of the movement. On the other hand, part of the rhetoric of the movement involved pointing out the widespread usage of drugs, and Gerlach and Hine (1970:79 f.) have shown that a crucial factor in the spread of movements is face-to-face recruitment. In other words, members apparently found it useful in rationalizing their behavior and evangelizing others to note the amount of drug usage in the society. Consequently, this factor worked both to inhibit and to facilitate the work of the movement, and it is not clear whether the net effects were the former or the latter.

10. *Reporter,* August 15, 1963, pp. 36 f.

11. Becker (1953) early pointed out that the definition of marijuana-use as pleasurable is the result of a social process and not of the inherent pleasure of the physiological effects of the drug.

12. That the break with the scientific symbol system was complete is illustrated by Leary's comment about the evaluation by Downing, a psychiatrist, of the Zihuatanejo project: "The interpretations, appraisals, and observations of Joseph J. Downing . . . are his own and differ from those which we would make. It is natural and proper that Dr. Downing choose his own metaphors to describe the events of that time" (Blum, 1964:185).

13. Reported in *Christianity Today,* June 24, 1966, p. 46.

14. *New York Times,* August 18, 1967, p. 17.

15. Dr. James Goddard, Commissioner of the United States Food and Drug

Administration, cautioned more than 2,000 college and university administrators about the illegal use of LSD. The FDA was also reported to have
placed undercover agents at some of the larger universities in an effort to
locate distributors of LDS.

16. *New York Times,* October 2, 1966, p. 6.

17. *U.S. News and World Report,* April 10, 1967, p. 12.

18. Regarding the widespread use of drugs as a factor, see note 9 above. With
regard to the others, the point is that they are indicators of needs which could
find fulfillment in the kind of program offered by the LSD movemnt. The
peace-of-mind literature appealed to considerable numbers of people. It is
more difficult to assess the response to the Pentecostal movement, which, like
the LSD movement, is a radical departure from conventional society. For
some evidence that the response has not been negligible, see the materials in
the bibliography offered by Gerlach and Hine (1970:237–41) and the news
item in *Christianity Today* (November 24, 1967), p. 12.

19. By partial legitimacy I refer to the fact that a movement may be defined
as having legitimate goals which are sought through illegitimate or improper
means; or it may be defined as having illegitimate or questionable goals which
are, however, pursued through legitimate means. In both cases, the movement, while maintaining a certain tension with the larger society, may be formally tolerated.

Social Structure and Moral Reform: A Study of the Woman's Christian Temperance Union

JOSEPH R. GUSFIELD

Social changes affect the fortunes of organizations and movements no less than they do the fate of individuals. Movements which try to alter the manners, tastes, and daily habits of large numbers of people are peculiarly vulnerable to shifts in the culture of the population. Few social movements in American history have achieved as many successes and witnessed as many disappointments as the temperance movement. In the one hundred and fifty years during which the organized movement has been a significant part of American life, it has gone through a process of "boom and bust," from activity and success to quiescence and failure. The last seventy-five years have been particularly beset with steep rise and equally steep fall. The high point of the movement was reached in the passage of the Eighteenth Amendment and the nadir in Repeal and the period following.

This essay examines the Woman's Christian Temperance Union, one important segment of the temperance movement, during the last eighty years. We have tried to discover the way in which the movement has changed and some of the reasons which help explain that change.

Reprinted from *American Journal of Sociology* 61 (November 1955), by permission of the author and The University of Chicago Press, © 1955 by The University of Chicago Press.

THE PROBLEM

Previous studies of social movements have dealt largely with organizations that have increased in numbers and influence. Such studies have indicated a gradual modification in the structure and ideology of the movement. As the movement grows, it tends to adapt itself to its society and to substitute the values of organizational power and prestige for its original goals. This process has been described in the now familiar theory of the "institutionalization of social movements." [1]

Recently, Messinger has shown how the adaptive process has affected a declining social movement, the Townsend Movement (Messinger, 1955). Here the adaptation to loss of influence and adherents was in terms of the loss of the movement's actual mission and the emphasis on the preservation of the organization as such. New activities of the Townsend clubs are understandable only as devices to perpetuate the organization's membership, income, and power.

The WCTU cannot be called a "successful" movement. Its fundamental goal, the changing of American drinking habits, is less realizable today than in earlier periods. Neither is it analogous to the movement in decline. Membership figures indicate that the size of the organization, while less than before Repeal, is still above two hundred thousand and actually growing now in membership (Table 1).

1. WCTU membership by decades

Year	Membership
1881	22,800
1891	138,377
1901	158,477
1911	245,299
1921	344,892
1931	372,355
1941	216,843
1951	257,548

Source: Treasurer's reports in *Annual Report of the National Woman's Christian Temperance Union* (Evanston, Ill., 1881–1951).

While the WCTU is far from decline or death, temperance norms have lost a great deal of their power in American culture. Their political power, as pressure groups, is far less than before and during Prohibition.[2] The percentage of "dry" communities in the United States is far less than in the period before the passage of Prohibition, and fewer Americans are abstainers today.[3]

The change in American drinking habits and the increased permissiveness of drinking norms have presented the WCTU with an environment more hostile to the doctrine of total abstinence than was true in the years of the organization's formation and development. The reaction of the WCTU to this changed situation forms the subject of this essay. We want to know whether the change in environment has led to changes in the goals and doctrine of the movement. We further seek to explain changes, or lack of change, in the organization.

Several possible modes of reaction suggest themselves to us. Faced with a now more hostile environment, the WCTU might change to achieve greater acceptance within the new norms. This would entail giving up much of the earlier mission for the sake of organizational values, which is the adaptation suggested by the Townsend Movement cited above. Second, it is conceivable that we may find little changes which increase the gap between the public and the organization.

THE PRE-PROHIBITION PERIOD: TEMPERANCE AS
SOCIAL WELFARE

Moral reform and social welfare. The American temperance movement during the nineteenth century was a part of a general effort toward the improvement of the worth of the human being through improved morality as well as economic conditions. The mixture of the religious, the equalitarian, and the humanitarian was an outstanding facet of the moral reformism of many movements.[4] Temperance supporters formed a large segment of movements such as sabbatarianism, abolition, woman's rights, agrarianism, and humanitarian attempts to improve the lot of the poor.

In these efforts there is evident a satisfaction with the basic outlines of the economic and social system. What is attempted is the extension of the system to include the underprivileged. The reforms proposed attempt to alleviate suffering through humanitarian actions by those in advantageous positions or to reform the habits of the suffering as a way to the improvement of both their character *and* their material situation. There was clearly a relationship between the two.[5] Moral reformism of this type suggests the approach of a dominant class toward those less favorably situated in the economic and social structure. Barnes (1933) has pointed out that many of the social movements of the nineteenth century were composed of people bent on reforming others rather than themselves. Abolitionists were rarely former slaveowners. Except for one short episode in the 1840s,[6] the temperance movement has drawn to it people of little or no experience with drinking.

The goals and doctrine of the WCTU were part of this humanitarian moral reform movement in the period before Prohibition. This is most evident in the late nineteenth century but remained a strong aspect of WCTU activities well into the Prohibition period.

In its auxiliary interests the WCTU revealed a great concern for the improvement of the welfare of the lower classes. It was active in campaigns to secure penal reform, to shorten working hours and raise wages for workers, and to abolish child labor and in a number of other humanitarian and equalitarian activities. In the 1880s the WCTU worked to bring about legislation for the protection of working girls against exploitation by men. During the late nineteenth century several committees were active among lower-class groups, among them the Department of Work with Miners, the Department of Work with Lumberers, and the Department of Work among Railroadmen,[7] which directed their efforts toward converting the worker to Christianity, bringing him material comforts, and spreading the gospel of temperance.

The activities of the WCTU in the pre-Prohibition era appear to be the actions of a socially dominant group, essentially satisfied with the major outlines of the social structure. The social welfare efforts can be viewed as attempts to raise the lower classes to a level of behavior held out to them by the dominant middle-class citizen. This view is supported by the paternalistic character of much of WCTU social welfare activity during this period. For example, in 1882 the WCTU established a Kitchen Gardens Department to train "uneducated and untrained girls" in the arts of cooking and household management. The aim of this activity was explicitly stated as the preparation of housemaids, and it was hoped that occupational training would protect the girl from the temptations of city life.[8] The same training and the same rationale are found in the WCTU industrial schools established to aid "fallen women." [9]

The WCTU played an important role in the leadership of the woman's movement in the late nineteenth century, but this was not the only concern of the organization with questions of social justice. The labor movement had strong support from the WCTU. The Knights of Labor aided the temperance activities of the WCTU. The WCTU supported the struggle for the eight-hour day and the six-day week [10] and many of the strikes of the 1890s, though it balked at the use of violence. Its support of the labor cause is illustrated in the report of the Committee on the Relations between Temperance and Labor for 1894. Employers were urged to refrain from "kindling the spirit of animosity among those already struggling under the iron heel of oppression" and thus provoking violence.[11]

These are illustrations of the interest of the WCTU during the nineteenth century in economic and social reform. It is difficult to find activities in which moral reform is clearly distinct from economic or social reform. Prison reform, for example, was stressed as a way to rehabilitate character, to convert men to Christianity, and to prevent the suffering of prisoners.

After 1900 this humanitarian interest appears less frequently, although it is still an important aspect of WCTU activities. Two things become evident. First, the humanitarianism and the equalitarian concern for the poor have greatly decreased. The Committee on the Relation of Temperance and Labor, for example, has shifted its major concern from labor issues to the propagation of the temperance cause among workers. The reports of this committee after 1900 show an interest in the morals and character of the worker. Thus in 1909 the report of this committee stated: "Urge working men and women who work for wages to cultivate a sense of responsibility in the thoroughness of their work and to consider their employer's welfare as well as their own."

The second point is that humanitarian concerns are not ignored, although decreased in emphasis, prison reform and child welfare receiving considerable attention. Between 1900 and 1920 the WCTU allotted one of the largest segments of its budget for its center at Ellis Island devoted to aiding incoming immigrants. In 1919 a huge Americanization project was begun, reminiscent of the paternalistic pattern described above. It set aside $40,000 for the purpose, the second largest single appropriation in its history.

After 1900, however, the moral reformism of the WCTU is more frequently separated from a concern with the underprivileged. With the development of the Anti-Saloon League after 1900, temperance aims become important in the campaign for legal sanctions against the sale of alcoholic beverages. Yet the emphasis on the lower classes as the object of WCTU reform is still present.

Temperance as reform of the underprivileged. An effort to improve the lot of the poor and the underprivileged was not only displayed in the WCTUs auxiliary concerns. The very doctrine of temperance can be seen as directed toward changing the habits of the lower classes. The materials usually depict the drunkard as a worker. Temperance is frequently presented as the solution to economic problems, the route to success, whereas drinking is seen as the path to economic and social ruin. The WCTU did make some efforts to promote temperance sentiment among socially elite groups through a Department of Drawing Room Conversion. These proved unsuccessful and were abandoned.

A popular slogan of the temperance movement, in the nineteenth century, was that "drink is the curse of the working classes." Total abstinence was viewed as the solution to the problem of poverty. A story entitled "The Strike at Dennis Moriarity's" illustrates how the WCTU saw temperance as the answer to the worker's problems.[12] Dennis, son of a workman on strike, refuses to fetch beer for the strikers, insisting that they could pay their bills, even while on strike, if they didn't drink. The strikers are impressed by his reasoning. One says, "It's the saloon that hurts and keeps us poor. I've been wondering all this while why Debs and the rest of the leaders didn't see it."

In the above story the immigrant as well as the laborer is the central character. Irish and German immigrants were often depicted in the fiction of the WCTU as drunkards or shown in the process of reformation. Often it was the son or daughter of the immigrant who effected the reformation through his or her experiences with the WCTU.[13] This type of story again presents the idea that acceptance of temperance is a mode of assimilation into middle-class life.

That temperance is a key to class position is seen in the fates of the middle-class man who violates the temperance norms and the lower-class immigrant who accepts such norms. Lapses are punished by the loss of economic and social position. The WCTU was active, both before and after the turn of the century, in spreading the idea that "lips that have touched liquor shall never touch mine." Through its young girls' groups it tried to make sobriety in the male a prerequisite for marriage. The following story from a WCTU journal illustrates the awful consequences of drink for the middle-class male:

> Ned has applied for a job, but he is not chosen. He finds that the potential employer has judged him to be like his Uncle Jack. Jack is a kindly man but he spends his money on drink and cigarettes. Ned has also been seen drinking and smoking. The employer thinks that Ned lacks the necessary traits of industriousness which he associates with abstinence and self-control.[14]

The implications of the above story seem clear. The man who wants to succeed must have the requisite character. He must appear to possess the characteristics of sobriety which indicate the other virtues of thrift, industry, and self-control. Temperance is thus a way not only to conform to morality but to achieve social and economic welfare. The WCTU was acting as a vehicle of progress and improvement of the poor and underprivileged.

Analysis of committee reports. We have classified the various committee reports found in the annual reports of the WCTU. The treatment of issues in these reports demonstrates the existence of the humanitarian reformist orientation in earlier periods. As Prohibition struggles became fiercer, the WCTU decreased its humanitarian interest.

Moral conformity appeared apart from a concern with the welfare of the downtrodden. For example, the Department of Rescue Work had been interested in the improvement of the working girls' morality, wages, and living conditions as one consistent goal. By 1916 this department was chiefly concerned with efforts to limit fashion changes in the name of morality. The social welfare interest had disappeared. The interest in temperance more frequently appears unrelated to other welfare considerations. It is not until after Repeal, however, that the reports indicate unalloyed moral reform and temperance interests more frequently than humanitarian reform unalloyed or mixed with other interests (Table 2).

2. Classification of WCTU committee reports by period and by interests

	Interests (Percent of Total Reports) *				
Period	Humanitarian Reform	Moral Reform (Unalloyed)	Temperance (Unalloyed)	Other	N
1879–1903	78.6	23.5	26.5	15.3	98
1904–28	45.7	30.7	33.1	18.0	127
1929–49	25.8	37.0	48.2	1.2	81

Source: Sample of every fifth *Annual Report* of the WCTU.

* Percentages total more than 100 percent due to several interests in some committee reports.

Humanitarian reform and social dominance. The great concern of the WCTU with the lower classes was a dominant feature of its aims during the period from its formation in 1874 to the passage of Prohibition. It is not drinking per se that is emphasized but the drinking problems of the poor and the working classes. Even where drinking in upper classes is berated, a prime concern is the impact of upper-class drinking patterns on the lower classes.

In its temperance doctrine as well as in its alliances with social movements of a reformist nature, the WCTU attempted to cope with the problems posed for urban America by the advent of urbanism, immigration, and industry in the late nineteenth century. The large industrial working class with its alien culture clashed with the rural image of virtue. A social group whose own position was relatively secure could best react to this threat by ameliorative reforms. The doctrine of temperance appears to function in this fashion in the pre-Prohibition period. Implicit in the logic of the activities and the doctrine of the WCTU was a basic satisfaction with the social order.[15] The problems of the underprivileged can be solved in two ways. In one, greater kindness and humanitarianism can be extended to those who have not been fortunate. This is the motif in activities such as prison reform, work with "fallen women," better labor conditions, and other reform measures described. The demand for greater equality for women is an attack on the system of male superiority, but this is not generalized into an attack on other parts of the social and economic system.

Second, the doctrine of temperance itself suggests a solution consonant with the dominance of the group and the concern with injustice and suffering. If the lower classes and the immigrants will acquire the habits and social codes of the native middle classes, their problems will be solved. In short, assimilation into middle-class, Protestant culture is the reformist solution the WCTU offered in the pre-Prohibitionist period.

It is noteworthy that, prior to the 1920s, we find no condemnation of the American middle classes in WCTU literature. The good, churchgoing people of American Protestantism are seldom depicted as drinking. It is to this class that the WCTU looks for support of its aims. In defending the canons of sobriety, the WCTU could act as a representative of this class. An article in the *Union Signal* in 1889 put this as follows: "The class least touched by the evil thus far is that which here, as elsewhere in the land, forms its bone and sinew—the self-respecting and self-supporting class whose chief pleasures in life center in and about the home." [16]

THE "MORALIZER-IN-RETREAT"

The political strength of the temperance movement in America has been greatest in those states with large proportions of Protestant and rural populations.[17] With the decline in supremacy of the rural culture, both in city and in country, the norms of temperance have become less respectable. The advocates of temperance now face a more hostile environment in which they cannot enunciate a moral code and assume large segments of population in agreement with them. In the phrase of David Riesman (1950:195), they are "moralizers-in-retreat." [18]

With the repeal of the Eighteenth Amendment, the WCTU found itself in a radically new situation. It could no longer assume that the norms of abstinence were really supported by the dominant middle-class elements in American life. The total abstainer became a figure of disapproval and ridicule rather than a figure of power and respect.

WCTU leaders interviewed generally felt that the total abstainer no longer had a position of respect in the community.[19] They saw this as a change which has affected the churchgoing middle classes as well as the secularized groups. The same theme is evident in the journals and in the speeches and reports from convention proceedings. The following interview excerpts are fairly typical:

> There has been a breakdown in the middle classes. The upper classes have always used liquor. The lower classes have always used liquor. Now the middle class has taken it over. The thing is slopping over from both sides.

> You know that today church people drink. That's the reason for the poor showing of the WCTU. It's been that way since Prohibition. There are many that believe but won't sign the pledge. They are afraid that they might want to take a drink.

The WCTU was seen, by the leaders interviewed, as lower in prestige today than in an earlier period when temperance norms held a stronger position in the American society. Leaders contrasted the prestigeful social composition of earlier periods with the present composition. Examples such as the following appear frequently in the interviews:

> When this union was first organized, we had many of the most influential ladies of the city. But now they have got the idea that we ladies who are against taking a cocktail are a little queer. We have an undertaker's wife and a minister's wife, but the lawyer's wife and the doctor's wives shun us. They don't want to be thought queer.

> I remember when the X's lived in the house that is now the Hotel W. They were the finest people in the town, and they were temperance people.

> When I joined, women of prominence and social prestige were in it. They were the backbone of the churches and the schools.

The WCTU is recognized by its membership as having retreated from a past position of greater influence, power, and prestige. To be a member of the WCTU is therefore harmful to social acceptability in many groups. It opens her to ridicule from people whose opinion is important to her.

This is frankly realized by the WCTU. The literature of the organization does not hide the fact. For example, a membership drive pamphlet contained the following description of one type of WCTU member, Mrs. I-Would-if-I-Could: "She wouldn't think of asking for money or inviting anyone to join. She knows the organization is not especially popular in some groups. . . . There are times when she prefers not to mention her membership."

Local leaders also described the low esteem of the WCTU in their communities:

People don't like us. Some of the churches don't respect us.

Well, as you have probably learned, this isn't the organization it used to be. It isn't popular, you know. The public thinks of us—let's face it—as a bunch of old women, as frowzy fanatics. I've been viewed as queer, as an old fogy, for belonging to the WCTU. . . . This attitude was not true thirty years ago.

The WCTU is acutely aware of what it has been and of what it has become. The present position of unpopularity might lead to several different types of reaction. One possible position would be a reversal of past doctrine and the embracing of a doctrine of moderate drinking. This would be the acceptance of the new standard of the middle classes. Another possibility might be a de-emphasis of temperance aims and a substitution of other aims, such as those of a social welfare nature or an attack on "popular" enemies, such as drug addiction or juvenile delinquency.

The alternatives considered above all imply the importance of maintaining the popularity and acceptance of the organization in middle-class circles. If the organization should attempt to maintain its old doctrines, it could no longer be representative of prestigeful segments of American life. With the social base of dominance undetermined, can the WCTU continue a reformist attitude toward lower classes, or must it become a sectarian critic of the class it once represented?

MORAL INDIGNATION: CENSURE OF THE
NEW MIDDLE CLASS

The characteristic doctrine of the WCTU is no longer humanitarian reform of the underprivileged. Instead it is an indignation directed against the middle-class moderate drinker. Total abstinence is presented as behavior morally demanded, apart from social welfare considerations. The new standards of the middle class are seen as defections from the traditional morality of abstinence.

"Moral indignation" as used here is not equivalent to the use of the term by Ranulf (1938:13). We are not concerned with the "disinterested tendency to inflict punishment" but rather with the quality of anger generated by the failure of others to recognize standards of morality which the actor recognizes. The definition of "indignation" given by *Webster's New Collegiate Dictionary* accurately conveys our meaning. It is "righteous wrath" and "anger excited by that which is unworthy, base, or disgraceful." In understanding this emotion in the WCTU, we must keep in mind the fact that abstinence was once a respectable middle-class doctrine. The middle-class drinking habits are not only in conflict with WCTU norms; they are defections from past standards.

A fiction story in the *Union Signal* illustrates this sense of moral indignation toward the new doctrine of temperance.[20] The story is entitled "Today's Daughter." Ruth, sixteen, is taken to a party at the home of a new boy who has just moved into the neighborhood. The boy has told Ruth's family that he is glad the new house has a game room in the basement. Aunt Liz is suspicious. She knows that many of the houses in the neighborhood now have bars in the basement game rooms. Ruth's mother tries to still these suspicions: "We're not living in the Victorian period. . . . I'm sure the Barrets are alright [*sic*]. They joined the church last Sunday." Aunt Liz's reply greatly unnerves Ruth's mother: "As if that meant respectability *these days!* Many's the church member who drinks and smokes and thinks nothing of it."

This episode contains the significant parts of the current position of the WCTU. Here are people of moderate incomes, in the same neighborhood and members of the same church as the WCTU adherent, yet the indexes of social class, religion, and ethnicity are no longer good assurances of abstinence.

Conflict between the doctrine of the total abstainer and a new "middle-class psychology" is evident. The following story is an apt illustration in which the new middle class is criticized for defection from the Protestant norms which supported and sustained the temperance doctrine. The story is entitled "When Yesterday Returned." [21] Jane, the heroine, reveres her "old-fashioned, Christian grandmother" who taught her the temperance pledge. Jane's mother ridicules temperance as prudishness and says that it hinders her social position. The struggle between the two groups, the newer and more prestigeful moderate drinkers and the old-fashioned abstainers, is epitomized after Jane scolds a visitor who asked for whiskey before dinner.

> When the guest had gone her mother informed her in no uncertain tones that "such plebian mannerisms" were rude. And furthermore if there were to be any more such old-fashioned, prudish notions exploited before such persons as Mr. Forsythe, the family's opportunities for social prestige would be lost forever and Jane's visits to her grandmother curtailed.

The figures of the underprivileged poor and the laborer no longer appear as the center of WCTU interest. In their place is the middle-class, churchgoing moderate drinker. Toward him the WCTU displays resentment rather than reformist concern. Typical remarks of interviewees stress the moderate drinker:

We fear moderation more than anything. Drinking has become so much a part of everything—even in our church life and our colleges.

Since Repeal, people are drinking who wouldn't have before. They are held in great regard. The social drinker has a greater effect on children than the drunkards.

In past decades moderate drinking might have subjected the drinker to fear of loss of reputation or damaged career.[22] Some writers have lately maintained that career routes more and more demand the skills of fellowship, personal attachments, and the ability to be the "good fellow" (Riesman, 1950:130–44; Mills, 1951:91–100, 182–88). This means that the culture may place great value on tolerance of others, in drinking as well as in other behavior. This makes the moral reformer even more reprehensible in the life of the new middle-class culture.

In reaction to this, the WCTU has poured out wrath against the defector from standards of abstinence who talks of taking an "objective" stand toward the problem. One interviewee complained of the Yale School of Alcohol Studies:

You as a teacher must take a stand against smoking and drinking. Do you know of the Yale center? Well, I went down there one night. When they were through, you didn't know whether they were for it or against it. They didn't want to commit themselves. What can they expect students to do?

This attitude has made it difficult for the WCTU to cooperate with organizations which viewed drinking from a social welfare interest in curing or preventing alcoholism. Insistance on the vital importance of legal restriction of the sale of drink has continued. The president of the WCTU took an "unbending" position when she said: "Between right and wrong only one ground is possible and that is a battle ground." [23]

The fact that "good people" are drinking is a chronic complaint among interviewees and in the pages of WCTU literature. One membership pamphlet voices this lament as follows:

The greatest difficulty to be found today among youth, in anti-alcohol education, is the fact that "good people" are using liquor. Beautifully gowned women sipping their cocktails in lavish cocktail lounges give the impression that it is an extremely cultured thing to do. . . . Even within some of the best homes, the bar is set up. [Smith, 1953]

The social position of the moderate drinker in the concern of the WCTU is not that of the poverty-stricken, the socially elite, or the non-churchgoer. It is rather the class from which the WCTU formerly drew its power and which formed the base for a doctrine of social reformism. Interviewees stressed the change in the churchgoer as the cause for the new respectability of drinking.

> The churches aren't helping, some of them. We went to the home of a professor for a church meeting, and she [his wife] served sherry. The football coach's wife makes no bones about it. She serves liquor.

> It creeps into the official church boards. They keep it in their iceboxes. . . . The minister here thinks that the church has gone too far, that they are doing too much to help the temperance cause. He's afraid that he'll stub some influential toes.

> The churches aren't doing enough. . . . Many nominally take a stand, but many don't follow it locally. There was one churchman in L. who had beer at his daughter's wedding. Another churchman in H. had wine at a wedding that really flowed. And this was the Church of the Brethren!

The WCTU has not attempted to reformulate its previous temperance doctrine in the direction of popular acceptance, despite the changed milieu in which it must operate. Rather it has swung in the direction of a greater sectarianism which carries it strongly into conflict with previous sources of adherence. How can we explain this? Why has it not accommodated to the new situation? Some light may be shed on this question by the analysis of the social composition of the movement between the years 1885 and 1949.

Increasing class distance. We have studied the social composition of local leaders in the WCTU through the use of directories of officers published in annual state WCTU reports. These list the local officers and their addresses for each city, town, and village in which there is a unit. With these lists, we then utilized city business directories, which gave us the occupation of the husband of the officer.[24] We were limited in choice of cities by availability of state reports for each of the four years chosen—1885, 1910, 1925, 1950—and by the availability of city directories for each of the cities and years. However, we were able to compile comparative data for thirty-eight cities in five states (Table 3).

The results of this study indicate that the socioeconomic status of the local leadership has diminished during the period 1885–1950. There has been a relatively steady decrease in the percentage of professional people, proprietors, managers, and officials and a relatively steady increase in the skilled and unskilled groups. More and more, the social base of the WCTU appears to be lower middle class and lower class rather than the earlier picture of upper middle and lower middle classes.

This suggests an answer to the question posed above. The present social composition of the movement cannot duplicate the pretense to

3. WCTU local leaders classified by husband's occupation for state and year

State and Year	Professional and Semi-professional	Pro-prietors, Managers, and Officials	Cler-ical and Sales	Skilled Labor	Unskilled and Semi-Skilled	Farm	Total (%)	N
Connecticut:								
1885	25.7	20.0	22.9	22.9	5.8	2.9	100	68
1910	21.0	31.6	13.2	21.0	10.6	2.6	100	34
1925	3.8	15.4	21.2	36.6	21.1	1.9	100	51
1950	12.4	18.6	25.0	29.2	14.8	0.0	100	52
Michigan:								
1885	17.8	33.3	6.7	28.9	8.9	4.4	100	42
1910	15.3	19.4	19.4	26.4	15.3	4.1	100	72
1925	13.0	14.6	18.8	24.6	27.6	1.4	100	66
1950	13.2	7.1	16.6	26.2	36.9	0.0	100	77
Illinois:								
1885	20.0	35.6	11.2	24.4	8.8	0.0	100	50
1910	14.5	22.0	20.4	25.4	15.2	2.5	100	136
1925	11.8	19.3	23.5	19.3	24.4	1.7	100	124
1950	12.4	14.2	16.8	25.6	31.0	0.0	100	127
Minnesota:								
1885	25.6	33.3	15.4	17.9	5.2	2.6	100	38
1910	14.0	19.3	27.3	28.9	9.6	0.9	100	116
1925	12.7	22.8	20.1	28.9	15.5	0.0	100	151
1950	10.3	17.6	23.6	31.5	17.0	0.0	100	164
Maryland:								
1885	22.2	44.4	27.8	5.6	0.0	0.0	100	15
1910	13.6	36.4	40.9	9.1	0.0	0.0	100	22
1925	16.7	35.2	20.4	18.4	9.3	0.0	100	57
1950	21.4	33.3	21.4	16.8	7.1	0.0	100	41
Total:								
1885	22.6	30.4	26.1	22.1	6.5	2.3	100	193
1910	15.1	22.0	21.8	26.6	12.3	2.2	100	348
1925	12.0	21.2	21.0	25.3	19.6	0.9	100	392
1950	12.4	16.3	20.3	28.2	22.8	0.9	100	408

social dominance from which a reformist position is possible. Further, the very class structure of the movement accentuates the split between the upper and the lower middle classes which appears in the interviews and documentary materials. A uniform middle-class culture is less of a reality than it was in earlier periods.

One would anticipate that the groups most susceptible to norms en-

couraging drinking are precisely those upper-middle-class groups
making up the world of the professional, business executive, and
salesman—the new middle classes whose religion is less evangelical
and whose norms emphasize fellowship, toleration, and leisure.
These seem to be the groups who have left the WCTU. Their higher
socioeconomic status would have afforded them leadership had they
remained.

The data suggest that temperance norms have filtered down to
lower socioeconomic groups. The moral indignation of the movement
is explainable by the resentment engendered by the defection of the
upper middle class. These are no longer available as models with
which the religiously oriented in America can identify. The quality of
"moralizing" has ceased to be respectable. The adherents of rural
nineteenth-century values epitomized in the doctrine of total abstinence do not have available tangible models of success and prestige
in social levels above them. Nevertheless, they nourish expectation
that the values on which they have been raised will be the values of
groups above them in status. Their resentment is understandable as a
response to the realization that their expectations are no longer true.

This study has demonstrated a shift in the doctrine and social composition of a moral reform movement. The earlier stages of the
WCTU were shown to have been characterized by an attitude of
moral reform directed toward the lower classes. In this stage, social
composition data indicate that the WCTU represented a socially dominant class.

Today the WCTU is an organization in retreat. Contrary to the expectations of theories of institutionalization, the movement has not
acted to preserve organizational values at the expense of past doctrine. In adhering to less popular positions, it has played the role of
the sect and widened the gap between WCTU membership and
middle-class respectability. Analysis of social composition in this stage
indicates that the movement is today less upper middle class in composition than in earlier periods and more lower middle and lower
class in composition. In this respect, as well as in the changed drinking
norms of the upper middle classes, the split within American Protestant middle classes has been widened.

The moral indignation of the WCTU today is a very different approach to temperance and to the American scene from the reformism
and progressivism of the late nineteenth and early twentieth centuries. The plight of the "moralizer-in-retreat" is the plight of the
once powerful but now rejected suitor. The symbols at his command
no longer ring true in the halls where once they were heard with great
respect. He cannot identify easily with those above him in status,

because they now repudiate his morality. It is the sense of the historical shift, fully as much as the absolute clash in values, that has soured
his reformism and generated his resentment.

NOTES

1. The basic statements of this approach can be found in Troeltsch (1911:I,
331–43); Weber (1947:363–86); Park and Burgess (1921:865–74); Blumer
(1939:167–222). The general approach has been utilized in many studies. Examples of these are Niebuhr (1929); Pope (1943); Clark (1949); Michels
(1949); Lipset (1950); Muste (1928).
2. Odegard (1928) has analyzed the extensive power of the Anti-Saloon
League during the Prohibition and pre-Prohibition periods.
3. Jellinek (1947); "How Hard Do Americans Drink?" *Fortune* 47 (1953):
121–25, 146–48, 153–54. The trend toward greater permissiveness in American drinking norms is, as we shall show, clearly recognized by the WCTU as
well as by other temperance leaders. In this regard see Warner (1946) and
King (1951).
4. Cf. Schlesinger (1950:3–15); Barnes (1933); Bestor (1952).
5. Everett C. Hughes has pointed out the moralistic elements in the attitude
of George Pullman in the construction of Pullman, Illinois, in the late nineteenth century. The material conditions of the town would, Pullman felt, develop the moral qualities which made better human beings as well as better
workers. Such workers would have the traits of sobriety, industry, thrift, and
loyalty (cf. Everett C. Hughes, "A Calvinistic Utopia" [unpublished]).
6. The Washington movement was the response of former drunkards, who
made an organized attempt to reform drunkards. The rest of the temperance
movement would not unite with them (cf. Krout [1928:182–222]).
7. Historical material of this chapter is largely based on reading of the annual
reports of the National Woman's Christian Temperance Union and samples
of the WCTU journal, the *Union Signal*. The data cover the years 1874–1953.
For a complete statement of the material presented here cf. Joseph R. Gusfield, "Organizational Change: A Study of the Woman's Christian Temperance Union" (Ph.D. diss., University of Chicago, 1954).
8. *Annual Report of the WCTU* (1884), pp. 47–51.
9. *Annual Report of the WCTU* (1889), p. 62.
10. Not only were the speeches of Frances Willard, president of the WCTU
from 1879 to 1898, very favorable to labor but the committee reports reveal
similar prolabor sentiments (cf. *Annual Report of the WCTU* [1889], p. 144; *Annual Report of the WCTU* [1894], p. 147). The general attitude of the WCTU
toward the six-day week was a mixture of religious sabbatarianism and social
justice (cf. *Union Signal*, January 1, 1885). For a fuller treatment of the relations between the WCTU and the labor movement see Earhart
(1944:245–59).
11. *Annual Report of the WCTU* (1894), p. 447.
12. *Union Signal*, October 11, 1894, pp. 2–3.

13. During the agitation of the Woman's Crusades of 1873, out of which the WCTU emerged, the struggle against "demon rum" was often carried out as one between the churchwomen and German and Irish saloonkeepers. The accounts of the crusades contain many examples of the immigrant as the opponent of sobriety (cf. Wittenmyer [1878]; Stewart [1888]).

14. *Union Signal,* January 1, 1883, p. 6.

15. There were some efforts toward a more revolutionary position in the late nineteenth century. Frances Willard, the leader of the WCTU from 1879 to 1898, was an outspoken Socialist and tried to make the WCTU follow her position. Despite her great power and influence in the movement, she did not succeed.

16. May 16, 1889, p. 3.

17. Odegard (1928:24–35); cf. Gosnell (1942:101–2); Siegfried (1927:70–90).

18. Cf. Lee (1944).

19. Interviews were conducted with forty-six local and national WCTU leaders. The local leaders were active in upstate New York and in Chicago; the national leaders, members of the staff of the WCTU National Headquarters in Evanston, Illinois.

20. *Union Signal,* December 25, 1937, pp. 5–6.

21. *Union Signal,* June 3–July 29, 1939.

22. In some American industries this still remains true, as in the International Business Machines Corporation, under the leadership of Thomas Watson (cf. *Time,* March 28, 1955, p. 83). Watson may be taken as one of the last of the temperance reformers in positions of dominance. His attitude of strong disapproval toward employee drinking on or off the job is viewed as unusual enough to warrant comment both in *Time* and in the IBM communities.

23. *Annual Report of the WCTU* (1952), p. 87. Recently, with the retirement of the past president, there has been a "softer" attitude toward the Prohibition question and toward cooperation with non-Prohibitionist antialcohol groups. The general condemnation of the middle-class drinker still remains the focus of WCTU doctrine, however.

24. In the case of widows we used the last occupation of the husband. In classifying occupations, we utilized United States Employment Service, *Dictionary of Occupational Titles* (Washington, D.C.: Government Printing Office, 1944).

part 2

Movement Strategies for Change

Introduction

The strategies for change which movements adopt have received little attention in the literature. The question of strategy is of obvious crucial importance for movement members themselves, but it is also important to the sociologist striving to understand the phenomenon of social movements. Heberle (1951:362–65) notes three reasons why strategies are important for analysis: 1) the strategy and tactics selected may determine whether a movement is defined as legitimate; 2) the strategy and tactics may lead to cooperation or disjunction with other movements; and 3) controversies over strategy and tactics may lead to internal disruption and schism in a movement.[1] In addition, strategic decisions may determine whether or not a movement is successful in attaining its goals.

The importance of strategy to the movement itself is illustrated by the extensive work of Marxists. Lenin, for example, gave considerable attention to the question of strategy, and showed himself in both his writings and his actions to be a brilliant strategist. The pamphlet "What Is to Be Done?" laid out a strategy involving an elitist-led movement. The revolution would come (contrary to Marx's formulation) as a result of a unified, highly disciplined core of professional revolutionaries, who would educate and direct the masses. These professionals would, in turn, be guided by theory, for Lenin insisted that no movement was possible without theory. Indeed, all Marxists—from Lenin to Mao—have insisted upon the importance of theory in formulating strategy; those who depend upon the spontaneous rising up of the masses, argued Lenin, are amateurs rather than revolu-

81

tionaries.[2] Thus, Marxist leaders have attended with great seriousness to the question of strategy, and to the relationship of strategy to theory.

What kinds of strategies are available to movements? The Langs (1961:535) suggest that strategies may be categorized according to the means of action: "The distinction among strategies based predominantly on education, on mobilizing mass support through propaganda, and on force seems meaningful." In the first selection in this part, I try to develop a more elaborate typology of strategies, suggesting that three differentiating factors may be identified: who implements the change (the movement or the larger society); how much force is required for the change (nonviolent or coercive/violent); and the proximate target of the change (individuals or the social structure). I then suggest how movement ideology and interaction with the larger society bear upon the choice of one or more of six different strategies: the educative, small group, bargaining, separatist, disruptive, and revolutionary.

The other two selections in this part offer two approaches to strategy which have contrasting functions. The first, which I label an "analgesic strategy," generally serves to provide psychological support for movement members rather than to change the social order. Rosen offers us a portrait of the emotional climate of millennial movements and of the functions of an analgesic strategy. As Rosen points out, such movements arise out of the misery of oppression. Sometimes they may be a reaction to a thwarted revolutionary attempt; sometimes they simply emerge out of the wretchedness of a dominated people.

Although the millennial movement is always critical of the present situation, the strategy for change involves behavior that more often provides psychological support rather than a force for social change. It is what I have called the "small group" strategy, because it focuses on the individual as the proximate target of change, is nonviolent, and perceives the movement itself as the social group implementing the change. The small group strategy tends to be analgesic in function, and the millennial movements well illustrate this. For while magic, symbolic behavior, and religious ritual may enable movement members to survive in a dehumanizing environment, they are unlikely to effect any meaningful change in that environment.

The final selection offers what I label a "power strategy." The analgesic and power functions are not mutually exclusive. That is, a power strategy may also function to provide psychological support. Marx argued that revolution is necessary in order to cleanse psychologically and renew an oppressed people. Furthermore, a power strategy may not be any more successful in changing the social order than an analgesic strategy. Nevertheless, the analytical distinction is useful; one has the basic potential for giving psychological support while the other has the basic potential for effecting social change.

The black power ideology delineated by Benson yields two of the types of strategy which I have offered. For the ideology identifies the social structure as the target of change and insists on the need for coercive/violent methods. The more extreme advocates, however, would argue that the movement itself must effect the change, while the more moderate would allow for the larger society to effect the change. Thus, both the disruptive and the revolutionary strategies apply here. In either case, the ideology means the legitimation of a coercive/violent strategy, a strategy that stresses the need to exercise power in the face of a coercive social order.

Benson's chapter illustrates another point made in this book. He not only outlines the ideology that legitimates power strategies, but also shows how that ideology emerged out of interaction of the movement with a changing society. The decision in the larger society to pursue a war on poverty created an organizational context in which the black power ideology clashed with a more moderate ideology and emerged triumphant. Thus, the power tactics employed by members of the black civil rights movement are legitimated by an ideology that was fashioned in interaction with the changing society, a society that was changing in part because of previous actions of the movement. Again, we see clearly how the movement and the larger society are two intersecting and interacting processes, motion within motion.

NOTES

1. The distinction between strategy and tactics is that the former refers to a more general design or plan of action, while the latter refer to concrete and specific actions that are congruent with the nature of the strategy. Thus, a movement might have an educational strategy, and its tactics might include propaganda, classes, paid advertisements, and so forth.
2. For a brief discussion of Lenin's ideas on strategy, see Keep (1967:135–58). The pamphlet "What Is to Be Done?" may be found in Lenin (1950:V, 203–409).

5

Ideology and Strategies of Change: The Case of American Libertarians

ROBERT H. LAUER

Studies of social movements have probed into such matters as the genesis of the movement, recruitment of members, the natural history of the movement, factors involved in the success or failure of the movement, and others. But, as Turner (1970:146) points out, little has been done in the way of investigating strategies which may be pursued by a movement in the attainment of its goals. What kinds of strategies may be employed in order to effect change, and what factors enter into the choice of certain strategies over others? Little help is offered in the literature.

Generally, the matter of strategy has been handled in cursory fashion. Blumer (1951:111) simply argues that the tactics employed by a movement will depend upon the nature of the situations and the cultural background of the movement. Heberle (1951:362, 364) notes that the same objectives may be pursued by differing means, and that if the movement is radically opposed to the existing order it may resort to "tactics which are incompatible with the legal order." That a variety of strategies is perceived to be appropriate for attaining objectives is clear in those social movements, such as the black movement in America, in which radically different strategies are used either successively or simultaneously (Lewis, 1970:149–90). But the question still remains as to the reasons for the choice of particular strategies, and also the types of strategies from which the choice may be made.

Turner (1970:147) identified three very general types: persuasion, bargaining, and coercion. Other typologies of change strategies have been developed outside the context of the study of social movements. Chin and Benne (1969:32–59) categorize strategies into three groups: empirical-rational, normative-reeducative, and power-coercive. These three were developed on the basis of their underlying assumptions about human motivation. The empirical-rational assumes that rational men will act in accord with self-interest when this is shown to them. The normative-reeducative assumes that in addition to rationality and intelligence, men act in accord with normative patterns which demand certain attitudes, values, skills, and relationships. New commitments to new norms must therefore be generated. The power-coercive strategy assumes that men act in accord with compliance to superior power, whether that power be legitimate legal authority or some other kind.

One other effort to classify strategies is that of Walton (1965), who reduces all strategies to two groups—those involving power tactics and those utilizing attitude change activities. Walton made his classification on the basis of differing objectives. The power strategy aims at "concessions in substantive areas," while the attitude strategy aims at "improvements in relationships."

The purpose of this chapter is: to develop a typology of strategies with specific reference to social movements (as Turner sought to do); to show how the typology reflects the assumptions which are implicit in the choice of strategy (as Benne and Chin and Walton sought to do); and to suggest how the various strategies relate to ideology and to the interaction of the movement with the larger society. Such a typology will enable us to see the assumptions about man and society that are implied in the choice of strategies, and will provide a basis for further exploration into the factors that determine the choice. The typology will be developed in the context of an examination of the diverse strategies employed and advocated by a particular movement—the American Libertarian.

THE AMERICAN LIBERTARIANS

Although at least one author has tried to discount the relationship (Le Fevre, 1965), the Libertarians stand in the anarchist tradition. That tradition exhibits considerable diversity, but a shared conviction of all anarchists involves "a belief in individual freedom and a denial of authority, especially in the form of the State" (Krimerman and Perry, 1966:6). With specific reference to libertarian philosophy, Hospers (1971:5) summarizes it as follows: "it is a philosophy of personal liberty—the liberty of each person to live according to his own choices, provided that he does not attempt to coerce others and thus prevent them from living according to their choices . . . thus, libertarianism represents a total commitment to the concept of individual rights." As such, the libertarian philosophy will either opt for very limited government or no government at all. "Limited" government here means limited to such functions as protection against external enemies; in no case is the authority of the government to coerce the individual acknowledged as valid.

Obviously, there are many who sympathize with or hold to a philosophy very similar to the above without being a part of the Libertarian movement. How many Americans, then, both accept the philosophy and identify themselves with the movement? For a variety of reasons, it is difficult to even estimate the number, but there is a growing body of literature and a number of organizations which have emerged. Wingo (1970) declared that libertarian groups were among the fastest growing on campuses: "Two years ago their meetings were small and local; now they are held on major campuses, attracting students by the hundreds from all over the country." Nevertheless, as a movement the Libertarians remain quite amorphous. Specific groups may be identified, such as campus groups and clusters of nomads. But, perhaps in keeping with their basic anarchist perspective, there are no centralized loci of activities and no key figure or figures who may be identified as outstanding leaders. If highly influential leaders may be said to exist at all, they exist in those authors who espouse Libertarian ideas in books and magazines. It is in the literature rather than in specific groups or individuals that we get the clearest notions of who the Libertarians are.

Some of the dominant themes which appear in the literature include:

1) Inherent oppression in the exercise of political power. Sam Weiner, one of the founders of the Libertarian League, has said that "we have nothing to fear so long as no group in society is given political power to rule over others." [1]

2) Rejection of political means for attaining social objectives. Even the attainment of social order (which Libertarians, like anarchists generally, vigorously affirm) is conceived in nonpolitical terms. Any society must have order, but that order does not derive from the polity. Rather, Libertarians "must see that this order is imposed from below in response to the popular will, and not institutionalized along dictatorial lines." [2] When most Libertarians speak about revolution, therefore, they are not referring to a political phenomenon, but to a social transformation. And the strategies for attaining that transformation,

as I shall indicate below, are diverse, but rarely do they involve political action.

3) Denial of the rights of and sociological reality of the state. The state has no moral rights which individuals do not have. To sanction behavior on the part of the state which is not sanctioned for individuals is to sanction immorality. For example, theft is commonly regarded as immoral. But when the state taxes citizens, and employs force or the threat of force in order to secure the taxes, it is stealing from those who are taxed. Consequently, to legitimate the state's right to tax is to sanction theft (Friedman, 1970).

Furthermore, the state has no sociological reality. That is, Libertarians are methodological individualists. Society has "no existence independent of, different from or greater than the existence of the men who compose it"; society is merely a "group of men related by interdependence, involving communications, commerce and/or purposeful physical contact" (Wollstein, 1969:8). This theme forms a logical basis for the next one.

4) Celebration of freedom and individualism. Freedom and individualism are recurring themes, and they are inextricably tied together. Freedom is generally conceived in terms of the individual's ability to act without restraints. Social well-being will follow from the pursuit of individual well-being. To act in accord with self-interest, therefore, is to act morally, while to sacrifice oneself in behalf of God or society is both individually and socially destructive. These ideas find bountiful expression in the writing of Ayn Rand, who has been avidly read, says Wingo (1970), by virtually all students who identify themselves as Libertarians. Rand (1961:25) argues that individual freedom cannot be attained apart from laissez faire capitalism: *"Intellectual* freedom cannot exist without *political* freedom; political freedom cannot exist without *economic* freedom; *a free man and a free market are corollaries."* As a concomitant of the celebration of freedom and individualism, therefore, Libertarians often speak of the ideal social organization in terms of voluntary, free market associations.

LIBERTARIAN STRATEGIES OF CHANGE

The question is, however, how is this ideal social organization to be attained? What strategies can be employed to extirpate the existing political state and its power and establish a social order based on voluntary, free market associations? Since the basic elements of Libertarian ideology, as sketched above, do not logically define a particular strategy, it is not surprising that we find a number of strategies advocated. In both behavior and writings, Libertarians espouse at least four different strategies of change: educative, disruptive, separatist, and revolutionary.

My impression is that the educative strategy is the more common of the four. It is based upon the premise of man's rationality: "The rational animal alone of all of earth's species was confronted with alternatives of existence: to be man or not to be, to think or not to think, to create or loot" (Wollstein, 1970:2). Animals have no choice; they must operate by force within the environment as it is given to them. But man can create his world via his capacity for rationality.

Further, it is argued that society is only a group of men who act in harmony on the basis of shared beliefs. If, therefore, the individuals who compose a society share a belief in communism, the social order will be a communist one; if, on the other hand, those individuals share a belief in voluntarism, they will create a social order on the basis of a free market. The belief in voluntarism will not lead to disorder or chaos; contrary to the fears of those who cleave to the collectivist ideology, the free market system is a "symphony of order and movement" (Wollstein, 1969:9).

The educative strategy, then, assumes that men can be persuaded rationally to see this "symphony of order and movement" as well as the freedom that resides in such an order. Once having seen that, they will accept the philosophy and proceed to build the proper social order. This, it will be noted, is precisely the type of strategy that Chin and Benne called the "empirical-rational." Men act on the basis of self-interest, and where this can be demonstrated rationally to them, they will accept and follow it.

Furthermore, according to those who advocate it, only the educative strategy will prove efficacious. The state will never be eradicated by destroying the men who rule, because other men would simply replace them. The only hope for a free order lies in the replacement of statist ideologies with a philosophy of freedom. Men must be persuaded rationally to accept new beliefs, beliefs about true human freedom. And true human freedom demands that men make their own decisions, direct their own existence, and form their own voluntary associations. Government by men must be replaced by the "administration of things" (Le Fevre, 1965; Tannehill and Tannehill, 1970).

The disruptive strategy is advocated by those who feel that something more than rational persuasion is required if the state is to be destroyed. The state will only be eliminated, in this view, when it is crippled by action on the part of those who oppose it. The services of the state, therefore, must be replaced by the services of Libertarians. It has been proposed that Libertarians establish "alternative institutions" and "pre-emptive actions" that will replace the activities of the state (d'Aureous, 1969).

From pamphlets, articles, and interviews with Libertarians, a number of suggestions come for ways to disrupt the functioning of the state. The black market has been suggested as a way of exchanging goods that circumvents state control. Means of resisting tax and drug laws could be developed and sold, thoroughly clogging the courts when the state tried to take repressive action against resisters. Taxpayers might, for example, simply refuse to pay property taxes en masse (as happened in a Pennsylvania township). Or voters could be persuaded to reject any increase in taxes, closing schools in the process. Libertarians have helped form the National Taxpayers Union in order, in part, to lobby Congress for a radical cut in defense and welfare spending and organize local tax-resistance groups.

Although the specific tactics are innumerable, the basic thrust of the disruptive strategy is to deprive the state of revenue while at the same time clogging the courts and creating great expenses in prosecuting resisters. The idea of disruption as a coercive technique is not, of course, unique to Libertarians; others have recognized its potential (Pivan and Cloward, 1970).

There are those, however, who envision the necessity of even greater force, and advocate a revolutionary strategy. It is not true, as Reichert (1967:865) asserted, that all American anarchists agree that the "social revolution must be nonviolent and unpolitical in character." Most Libertarians do press for social revolution, but some— probably a very few—advocate revolution against the state. One of the more articulate advocates of political revolution is Karl Hess, whose checkered career has included editing of *Newsweek,* writing speeches for Barry Goldwater and helping write the 1960 and 1964 Republican party platforms, and serving as an associate editor of *Ramparts.*

Hess (1969:3) argues that the growth of state power is "a dynamic of the system itself and not merely a function of factions within the system." Consequently, the only way to stop the growth of the power is to oppose and destroy the system itself through revolutionary action. Hess, along with members of the Student Libertarian Action Movement, have called for alliance with various New Left groups in order to achieve the destruction of the state. A 1970 publication of the Student Libertarian Action Movement, *The Match!,* noted that some SDS. members, more anarchist than Marxist in their thought, have joined with SLAM. in common revolutionary action.

Libertarian revolutionaries have supported a number of New Left causes, including the effort to gain student power, the antiwar and antidraft movements, and the Black Panthers. The one ideological element that legitimates all such alliances is the conviction that the present state must be destroyed via revolutionary action.

The revolutionary strategy includes the notion of vanguardism. That is, the revolution would be waged by a vanguard of ideologically pure Libertarians, who would bring about the "consciousness" necessary for revolution to succeed. The vanguard would flood the masses with the propaganda necessary both for their support of the revolutionary action and for their acquiescence to the new order. In this view, then, the masses are seen not as rational beings who can be educated to pursue their own self-interests, but as short-sighted opportunities who must be manipulated. A SLAM. member, Stephen Halbrook, has argued that the masses must be shown that libertarianism is compatible with their instinctive opportunism. They cannot be taught to free themselves from the state; they must first be set free. Then, "with no State there to rule and enslave them the gradual freeing of their minds is inevitable. Abolish the Master, the State, and finally everyone will become supermen: where there is no shepherd, there can be no sheep" (Halbrook, 1970:35). In spite of the ultimate anarchist vision, the revolutionary strategy contradicts the typical Libertarian emphasis on social rather than political revolution. The revolutionary strategy has not, therefore, escaped rebuttal (Machan, 1970).

The revolutionaries are convinced that the movement itself must effect the change (in contrast to the educative and disruptive strategies, which imply that ultimately the larger society will effect the change). Those Libertarians who share the conviction that the movement itself must effect change in the structure of society, but who renounce violence as a means of effecting change, adopt a fourth strategy—separation. The separatists, like the nineteenth century utopians and twentieth century communal groups, seek to establish their own communities, and to maintain those communities as autonomous entities. One kind of separatist strategy is the nomad, and another is that of establishing free-trade, laissez faire communities.

The nomads have been further categorized into "clandestine urbanites," "remote homesteaders," and "land or sea-mobile nomads" (Ray, 1969). The clandestine urbanite refers to the individual who seeks to be anonymous and mobile in an urban area. He rents furnished apartments and adopts an assumed name. The remote homesteader lives at some distance from the city, but commutes when he is compelled by financial need to secure a job. And the land- or sea-mobile nomads are those who live in campers or yachts or houseboats. The land-mobile nomad travels around the country either alone or in a caravan, occasionally settling for a time in a "squat spot," which may either be a city street or a rural area. If questioned by authorities, the nomad may simply reply that he is a tourist on vacation. The sea-mobile nomad sails from one port to another. In either case, the basic purpose is to live apart from the coercion of the state, and to avoid the varied demands of the state.

The second category of separatists are those who establish laissez faire communities which are geographically separated from the political domain of existing states. One such effort is represented by Operation Atlantis, an attempt to acquire a West Indian island for the purpose of creating a free community. A number of other projects have been initiated which have similar goals. Some have even entertained the possibility of creating an artificial island in the ocean, or using a body of ships, to establish a free community.

A TYPOLOGY OF CHANGE STRATEGIES

The above discussion has already suggested a number of relevant points for developing a typology of strategies. Indeed, one of my purposes in examining the Libertarians has been to gain insight into the bases that underlie the choice of strategies, and to use that insight in order to construct a typology of strategies which will be applicable to other social movements. We have noted, then, that one basis for differentiating strategies is the matter of who implements the change. Revolutionaries and separatists assert or imply that the movement itself must make the change, while educationists and disrupters assert or imply that the larger society will effect the change under the tutoring or pressure of the movement. A second basis that we have pointed out is the amount of force required for the change. Some advocate violent or coercive methods; others insist on nonviolence.

A third basis for differentiating strategies was also suggested: the focus or target of the change. Coleman (1971) has pointed out that theories of change are primarily distinguished by whether they begin with "changes in the social conditions in which individuals find themselves" or with "changes in individuals." [3] Libertarians advocate strategies which also may be distinguished in terms of those that basically seek to change individuals and those which seek to change the social structure. That is, educationists stress the need to change the beliefs of individuals, who will then form a new social order; but the target of change—at least the proximate target of change—is the individual. The other strategies focus directly on the social structure, and aim at either changing that structure by direct action of the movement or forcing the larger society to effect structural change.

This threefold basis for distinguishing strategies (proximate target

of change, force required, and who implements the change) impl⌐
six types of strategies as follows:

TYPE	TARGET	FORCE	WHO IMPLEMENTS
Educative	Individuals	Nonviolent	Society
Small Group	Individuals	Nonviolent	Movement
Bargaining	Social Structure	Nonviolent	Society
Separatist	Social Structure	Nonviolent	Movement
Disruptive	Social Structure	Coercive/Violent	Society
Revolutionary	Social Structure	Coercive/Violent	Movement

Four of these strategies, as we have seen, are advocated by Libertarians. The use of small groups may be seen in "thought reform" in
China (Lifton, 1967), and in the effort to convert individuals in the
Pentecostal movement (Gerlach and Hine, 1970). Bargaining, like the
educative strategy, assumes rationality and self-interest, and is probably more often used in combination with other strategies (the disruptive and bargaining strategies have often been employed in the civil
rights movement), or in later phases of the movement (labor's shift to
bargaining as it gained legitimacy).

IDEOLOGY, INTERACTION, AND STRATEGY

The strategy or strategies employed by a social movement, then,
imply decisions about three factors: whether the individual or the
social structure is the proximate target of change; how much force is
necessary in order to effect the change; and whether the movement's
role is that of effecting the change itself or of somehow getting the
larger society to effect the change. But what determines how the
decisions about these factors are made? Let us first consider the role
of ideology.

Social movement ideologies perform a number of functions, including recruitment of members, facilitation of radical action, provision of a sense of worth and power to members, and so forth (Pinard,
Kirk, and Von Eschen, 1969; Wolf, 1971; Gerlach and Hine,
1970:160 ff.). They also narrow the strategic alternatives. As Wilson
(1973:245) points out: "The true believer finds in his ideological beliefs not only the promise of a better future but a new set of values by
which his present conduct is governed. Contained in the teachings of
most social movements is a set of statements about which means are
appropriate for the achievement of a given set of goals."

The extent to which ideology defines the appropriateness of means
varies of course. In some cases, the narrowing of alternatives is con-

siderable. The Pentecostal movement, for example, insists upon the individual as the proximate target of change. Furthermore, it is the movement itself that must effect that change, since only the saved can convert others. The small group—church meetings, home gatherings, luncheons, and so forth—is the only viable strategy.

In others, narrowing is minimal. This is true of Libertarians. Some, perhaps most, Libertarians argue for an educative strategy, pointing out that revolution and disruption are both unacceptable because they would result in the destruction of life and property of innocent people (Hospers, 1971:460–62). Others, however, insist that more force is required. Education, polemics, and the vote are not adequate to the task: "stronger, more militant methods can also be morally justified in terms of libertarian principles. They not only can but *must* be employed *now* if we are to achieve anything close to a true libertarian order within the next fifty years" (Tuccille, 1970:80). This latter argument is based upon the individual's "natural right" to resist anything and anyone seeking to coerce him.

Thus, a plurality of strategies or a single strategy may be demanded by the ideology. Whether strategic alternatives are minimized or maximized is a function of what Gerlach and Hine (1970:165) call the "split-level" nature of ideologies. This refers to the fact that the ideology of any movement contains one level composed of consensual beliefs, and others containing variations and diversity. To contrast Pentecostals and Libertarians again, the former have an ideology with a much larger consensual level. Pentecostals agree on what society needs and how to achieve it; Libertarians agree on a fundamental belief in individual rights, but differ on such matters as how much force is necessary to achieve those rights, what is the appropriate target of change, and who it is that will effect the change.

The movement ideology, then, will more or less limit strategic alternatives depending partly upon how much of the ideology is consensual. The limitations will depend partly also on the centrality in the ideology of the three factors differentiating strategies. That is, the target of change may be a dominant factor in some ideologies as it is in the Pentecostal which demands change in individuals. Or the ideology may be focused on the force required for change; in the Nazi movement, the ideology included the conviction that change demanded the continual application of intense force, and other elements of the ideology changed in order to pursue the strategy of force (Turner and Killian, 1957:327). Or, finally, the ideology may be inflexible at the point of who it is that will implement the change; in the Bruderhof, a communitarian movement, the ideology emphasizes the need for the movement itself to set the example in a nonviolent way for a new world (Zablocki, 1971:21).

Where none of the three factors is central to the ideology (and none is among Libertarians), we may expect a plurality of strategies being advocated. But strategic considerations depend upon more than ideology, and a factor of prime importance is the interaction of the movement with the larger society. Indeed, both the ideology and the program of the social movement are shaped and to some extent transformed through movement-society interaction (Lauer, 1972). We are likely to find not only diversity in number of strategies across movements, but also an "evolving strategy" within movements; the evolving strategy depends upon "the nature of the values as initially formulated" and upon the "sort of reception the movement gets as it proceeds" (Killian, 1964:449; Smelser, 1962:358–59). That is, interaction with the larger society tends to effect change over time in both ideology and strategy or strategies. But again, the amount of change will depend upon how central and consensual the three factors are in the ideology. Where there is centrality and consensus, interaction with the larger society is less likely to effect change. In the Bruderhof, and among Pentecostals and Nazis, for example, strategies remained stable through both adversity and success. Indeed, the mentality of such groups is well captured in the horse, Boxer, in Orwell's *Animal Farm;* Boxer's solution to all difficulties was to simply work harder (Orwell, 1946). Similarly, some movements assume that both *what* needs to be done and *how* to do it are unalterable; if success is elusive, the movement members must simply work harder.

But in movements where there is neither consensus nor centrality, we may expect both a diversity of strategies and changing strategies over time as a result of interaction with the larger society. This is exemplified in the black movement, which has gone through four phases of changing ideology and strategy in the twentieth century (Meier, Rudwick, and Broderick, 1971). There has never been consensus among black leaders on how much force is required to effect the desired change, on the target of change (the white man's thinking and feelings or the social structure), or who it is that must effect the change (the NAACP opted for society while black nationalists opt for the movement itself). Consequently, interaction experience with the larger society has resulted in successive ideological and strategic phases in the movement.

A similar process has occurred among some Libertarians. The movement as a whole is too amorphous to identify phases, but the process of shifting strategic positions is strikingly evident in certain individual Libertarians who have been characterized as moving from the extreme right to the extreme left. Actually, they have held consistently to the core ideology of belief in individual rights, but interaction with the larger society has convinced them that certain strategies which they once considered viable are in fact useless. Karl Hess moved from writing speeches for Barry Goldwater to advocating disruption and revolution as a result of his experiences in government; Vietnam helped convince him he was wrong about effecting change through politics: "We trusted Washington with enormous powers to fight global Communism. We were wrong. . . . We forgot our old axiom that power always corrupts the possessor." [4] Hess and other Libertarians came to believe that Conservatives were hypocritical in their espousal of individual rights and, at the same time, support of governmental coercion. Disillusionment born of interaction led to an abandonment of an educative strategy and an advocacy of more forceful methods.

In sum, I have identified three factors in movement ideologies that are crucial in determining strategic decisions. The effects of these three factors depend upon their centrality in the ideology and the extent to which they are consensual among movement members. High consensus and centrality means they are likely to be stable and determining for strategies; low consensus and centrality means that interaction with the larger society will result in shifts in strategy over time.

Thus, the typology enables us to understand the assumptions that underlie the choice of particular strategies, and a knowledge of the ideology enables us to anticipate whether a movement will doggedly pursue a single or limited number of strategies or shift among the various types as a result of interaction with the larger society.

Finally, the typology should serve another useful purpose in enabling us to identify internal contradictions in movements that will generate change in the movement itself. For example, the Libertarians represent a radical perspective in the sense that they advocate drastic structural changes in American society. But this is inconsistent with their dominant stragegy—the educative. Logically, a radical ideology demands commitment to radical strategies; I would predict, therefore, that the movement will either stagnate or decline, or move in the direction of the minority like Tuccille and Hess who advocate more militant methods.

NOTES

1. Quoted in Reichert (1967:865).
2. Russell Blackwell, quoted in Reichert (1967:864).
3. See also Killian (1964:448); and Turner and Killian (1957:33).
4. James Boyd, "From Far Right to Far Left—and Farther—with Karl Hess," *New York Times Magazine,* December 6, 1970, p. 49.

Social Change and Psychopathology in the Emotional Climate of Millennial Movements

GEORGE ROSEN

The victory of Alexander the Great over the Persians at Gangamela in 331 B.C. virtually brought to an end native Iranian rule and initiated a period of widespread political upheaval and painful social adjustment for the peoples of the Near and Middle East. With the aim of consolidating his conquest, Alexander began settling Greek and Macedonian veterans at various points in his empire, and his successors continued the process. Greek rule also meant the suppression of native law and the elimination of native functionaries—a policy which was intensified by the Greco-Macedonian kingdoms that arose after Alexander's death.

The response to Greek imperialism was resistance in various forms (Eddy, 1961). Almost everywhere, whether in Egypt, Judea, or Persia, resistance was justified in religious terms, though the grounds for opposition to Greek rule were not only religious but also political, economic, and social. Resistance movements were efforts to reestablish native rule, to protect native religion and law, and to end economic exploitation and social upheaval. Since the former kings were vice regents of divinities, and in some cases even the gods themselves,

"Social Change and Psychopathology in the Emotional Climate of Millennial Movements," by George Rosen is reprinted from *American Behavioral Scientist* Vol. 16, No. 2 (Nov/Dec. 1972) pp. 153–167 by permission of the author and the Publisher, Sage Publications, Inc.

religion, law, and social organization were believed to be the results of divine revelation. Hence, Greek imperialism was not just a political or an economic problem, but an attack on a fundamental basis of the social fabric.

THE MIDDLE EAST

Resistance to domination by an alien culture which threatened to alter radically or to end the old erupted at various times in military action, as, for example, in the Hasmonean revolt of 167–166 B.C. and in rebellions among the Egyptians. Very often messianic or millennial prophecy was associated with such militance as a means to encourage revolt, or as the response of beaten men where violent resistance was broken or was not possible. For example, a Persian prophecy that the detested Greeks would be expelled from Iran and Asia by divine intervention circulated throughout the Near East and is known in several versions. This idea is best known to us through the book of Daniel in the Hebrew Bible, with its prophecy of a progression of four monarchies which would culminate in a divine monarchy, when the alien oppressors would be cast down. This denouement would be accomplished by the advent of a savior who would lead the army of the good in an apocalyptic battle of annihilation of the sons of darkness and evil (Paterculus, 1924:14–15; Swain, 1940; Yadin, 1962).

Chapters 9–14 of the book of Zechariah, written probably in the third century B.C. elaborate messianic and eschatological themes found in the preceding sections of the same work and predict that God would send a savior-king who will defeat the Greeks in battle and establish a state of happiness forever.

The doctrine of the millennium, the idea of intervention by a divine leader who would deliver his people from oppression and usher in a promised age of peace and plenty, is an attempt to find solace in present misery. It is the response of people who, when ordinary means fail to ameliorate their condition, look to religious developments for salvation. Future salvation becomes a consequence of present misery, but it can also act as a stimulus to try to supplant the abhorred present with a more desirable future.

Similar responses have occurred among different peoples and at various times throughout history. Common to such peoples and groups are the kind of situation in which they find themselves, the conditions under which they live, and the attitudes, aims, and forms of behavior which they develop in consequence. At times when the social and moral framework of a society, or of a group within it, crumbles—when the world seems out of joint—at such times, the tension between outer experience and the world within, between social reality and emotional disarray, leads to the development of a type of sensibility and an emotional climate in which fear, insecurity, and anxiety tend to become pervasive and dominant elements (Rosen, 1967). Various factors are involved in producing such an atmosphere, and their importance will vary from group to group, time to time, and place to place. In making comparisons, therefore, it is important also to recognize diverse historical traditions and differing levels of culture. The vision of the Guarani Indians of a land without evil and the need to search for it because their inspired leaders, the medicine men, had prophesied the imminent destruction of the earth as a precondition for this achievement has similarities with the apocalyptic visions of Jews in the period before the revolt of A.D. 66, but clearly there are differences in local conditions, cultural concepts, historical traditions, and the like between Brazil and Judea (Nimuendaju, 1914; Ribeiro, 1957). With these cautions in mind, however, useful comparisons can be made.

So long as men live within an accepted structure of action, feeling, and value, as long as the majority of the individuals follow customary lines and continue to think and feel as they had always thought and felt without raising fundamental questions, human energy flows without hindrance into activity. But what happens when this energy cannot be released in the usual or expected manner?

Under such conditions, the need for ways of supporting and dealing with them brings forth attitudes and behavior patterns which derive from the historical experience of the group and from the internal and external cultural influences to which it has been exposed. The desire to overcome the present may lead to revolt stimulated and inspired by apocalyptic visions of a millennium. An example is the revolt of the Yellow Turbans in China, headed by Chang Chüeh (A.D. 184), which was preceded by a rumor that the Blue Heaven, having ceased to exist, would be replaced by the Yellow Heaven, and "that in the year of *chia-tzü* [184] the world would experience great happiness." Moreover, the rebels believed that at this time a great ruler would appear through whom a widespread peace would descend upon the earth (Purcell, 1963:141 ff.). An analogous phenomenon may be seen in the conflict between Latin and native cultures in the Western Mediterranean as expressed in the Donatist church in North Africa, especially in its strange revolutionary fringe, the circumcellion movement (Freud, 1952:112–15, 171–77, et passim).

EUROPE

Europe at the end of the Middle Ages exhibits similar developments. When the tensions and conflicts at work in late medieval

Europe split the Catholic church in the early sixteenth century, the popular undercurrents of religious emotion and faith erupted as a multiplicity of strange sects espousing radical beliefs and revolutionary aspirations. This movement, which has been described as the "Radical Reformation," stretched geographically from London to Lwow and from Flensburg to Ragusa (Williams, 1962). Many of those who held the sectarian faiths which proliferated among these groups were religious fanatics, obsessed with mystical speculations, millenarian fantasies, and only a small sense of worldly reality. As they threw off the burden of ecclesiastical domination and undertook to prepare for the Kingdom of Heaven, they seized avidly on texts from the Bible, frequently from the Old Testament, interpreting them in the most literal terms. The emotional climate among the more ardent sectaries is perhaps best described in the words which John Pell, English ambassador to the Swiss Cantons, applied in 1655 to certain of his contemporaries:

Men variously impoverished by the long troubles, full of discontents, and tired by long expectation of amendment, must needs have great propensions to hearken to those that proclaim times of refreshing—a golden age—at hand, etc. Nor is it a wonder that some should willingly listen to those that publish such glad tidings, under the name of the kingdom of Christ and of the saints; especially when so many prophecies are cited and applied to these times. [Vaughan, 1838: I, 156]

Given such environments, it is not surprising to find behavioral extravagances, some of which are comparable to those of later Protestant (Methodist, Baptist) revivalism. One of the most striking examples is the Camisard revolt of the Huguenots of Southern France, after the revocation of the Edict of Nantes in 1685, a movement characterized by religious exaltation, prophetic utterances, and bizarre physical acts (Knox, 1950:356–71; Ahneras, 1960:41–59; Cutten, 1927:48–66). Such phenomena may be psychopathological in nature, but they may also serve a social purpose as the means for generating superhuman efforts required to change certain conditions. Groups that wish to revitalize their societies and to create a more satisfactory world in which to live, groups that wish to arrest a process of disintegration which they know will lead to their disappearance, groups that are fighting against overwhelming odds—all require a belief and conviction that they are under some sovereign guidance and protection which will enable them to attain their heart's desire, and they need evidence, physical or psychological, to support their faith.[1]

But what happens if these efforts fail? Clues to the nature of the psychic process in such situations and some of the consequences have been provided by observers and investigators of revolutionary movements. The physician Rudolf Virchow tended to view the psychological reactions observed during and after the German revolution of 1848 as a psychic epidemic caused by interference with the historical process. What Virchow implied was that if the revolutionary process had proceeded normally—that is, to its desired end—the energies generated in the course of events would have been expended in achieving victory. However, the defeat of the revolution blocked the expression of these energies and led to their discharge in aberrant and abnormal ways (Virchow, 1851).

There is no indication that the sociologist Karl Mannheim knew of Virchow's views, yet his discussion of revolutionary chiliasm amplifies the latter's ideas on the psychological deformities of the defeated and the hopeless. "For the real Chiliast," he says, "the present becomes the breach through which what was previously inward bursts out suddenly, takes hold of the outer world and transforms it" (Mannheim, 1936:193). But when the revolutionary impulse is stifled and a contradiction arises between individual or group goals and the institutional means to attain them, a contrary situation with corresponding attitudes may develop. Revolutionary optimism and hope give way to resignation and quietism, apathy and despair. But as Mannheim also notes: "Chiliasm has always accompanied revolutionary outbursts and given them their spirit. When this spirit ebbs and deserts these movements, there remains behind in the world a naked mass-frenzy and a despiritualized fury" (Mannheim, 1936:195–96). These repressed, undischarged, often inchoate emotions—these energies thwarted of effective outlet in an anticipated, new social order—create tensions which seek and find release through aberrant, often bizarre channels. Intense yearnings and frustrated social impulses are transformed into pathological aberrations. Such periods of crisis and transition, when familiar worlds are broken and anxiety is diffused in society, bring forth individuals who reach the wilder shores of sanity where some are able to maintain themselves, even though precariously, while others lose their hold and are submerged in the dark and swirling depths of unreason (Dodds, 1965:37–68; Schechter, 1908; Zeller, 1877: II, 154–88).

In the course of the sixteenth century, the sects of the Radical Reformation in Europe were suppressed with extreme ferocity, and their doctrines were regarded with horror as subversive of the established order. But while the radical impulse was stifled, the mystical, millenarian ideas of the sectaries were not extinguished. They went underground, lingered on among tiny fringe groups, and reappeared from time to time, welling up from obscure levels of response under propitious circumstances.

Throughout the seventeenth century, there was no lack of prophets and visionaries to proclaim the end of time and the imminent second coming of Christ to rule with his saints in his kingdom. Apocalyptic fears, millennial fantasies, and messianic speculations were spurred by social disorder and personal anxiety throughout most of the century, a part of the psychological price of living in a period of political and economic crisis, war, religious persecution, famines and plagues, moral disorder, and corruption. This situation affected both Christians and Jews (Silver, 1959:161–92).

Radical sects were particularly prominent in England in the mid-seventeenth century, reaching the peak of their activity and influence under the Commonwealth (Rosen, 1968). On the extremist fringe, among the Fifth Monarchy Men, Ranters, Muggletonians, Quakers, and others, there were religious zealots whose ideas and behavior were peculiar even to their contemporaries. Regarding their millennial speculations, one writer commented sarcastically: "In their lectures and conventicles you might have heard such raptures that you would have thought it were a reading on Astrology. . . . Months, weeks, daies, and half-times and such like chronology alwaies past away their mad hours of meeting" (Pagitt, 1662).

Whether or not one accepts the implication that excessive immersion in the dark arithmetic of speculation was a psychological aberration, evidently the behavior of these enthusiasts was at the very least odd and frequently extraordinary. This is not to be wondered at if one keeps in mind who these people were, and that they conducted their daily lives on preconceptions and premises which are strange to us and to which we cannot lend any credence. Moreover, some of them may have been individuals whose mental and emotional balance was precarious. The sectaries of seventeenth-century England were mainly from the lower classes of society. To the learned and wellborn, the preaching of obscure and ignorant men and women was an act of social presumption, a menacing intrusion into the preserves and privileges of people of position, and, in the broadest sense, evidence of social upheaval. In this sense, a pamphleteer of 1646 asked sarcastically: "Is it a miracle or wonder to see saucie boyes, bold botching taylors, and other most audacious, illiterate mechanicks to run out of their shops into a pulpit? To see *bold, impudent huswifes* to take upon them to prate an hour or more; but when I say is the extraordinary spirit poured upon them?" (Barclay, 1876:157; Thomas, 1967).

What the conservative elements of society saw as pretension, impudence, and cause for punitive action was something else to the members of the radical sects. They were in revolt against what to them was the burden of institutional and doctrinal authority. They wanted to break with a dogmatic ministry which appeared to limit salvation to a social elite, so that their sense of what to do and how to act was fueled by social resentment (Davis, 1943). In reaction to the ridicule, scorn, and abuse visited upon them by their social superiors, whom they considered God's adversaries, the sectaries esteemed what the others despised and stressed the virtues of ignorance and social obscurity. This attitude tended to encourage an uncritical acceptance of what were believed to be God's messages and commands as always true and right. Those who accepted the theory of divine inspiration also accepted the scriptural world of divine intervention, of creative miracles and signs, and of tasks imposed on the unwilling flesh by an inexorable deity. Unrestricted in scope or character, such intervention might manifest itself in the most varied ways, in cosmic prophecy, or in individual picayunishness. Anything, no matter how curious, which was considered a godly sign provided a basis for action, often of a symbolic nature.[2]

The pervasive atmosphere of excess manifested itself not only in wild prophecies and notions, but in almost every aspect of life. Those who felt the word of the Lord burning within them declared it in the most personal acts as well as by proclaiming it to all sorts and conditions of men. Thomas Holme's description of his marriage to Elizabeth Leavens is imbued with this spirit. In a letter to Margaret Fell, he wrote:

Upon the 16 day of the 8 month, being the same day we were set free from outward bonds, being in Chester at Edward Morgan's house, and she with me, and many other friends, I was immediately commanded of the Lord to take her to wife that day, having before seen it clear in the light eternal, and had a vision of it long before, as likewise she had. So in obedience to the command of the Lord, I took her to wife, contrary to my will. [Nuttall, 1948:54]

In an environment where ready acceptance of eccentric and extravagant behavior made it difficult to distinguish the godly from the mentally disordered, it is quite likely that the sectarian ranks included individuals whose mental and emotional balance was at the least precarious. Within a common emotional climate, the mad differed from the sane apparently only in their exaggerated manifestation of a sensibility shared by both. Walter Scott grasped this aspect with profound and energetic sympathy of imagination in creating the figure of Habakkuk Mucklewrath, the mad preacher-prophet in the Covenanter ranks (Scott, 1906:224). What Scott saw in the light of imagination was a matter of direct observation in seventeenth-century England. Thus, on August 9, 1650, the Commonwealth Parliament passed an act stating:

That all and every person and persons (not distempered with sickness, or distracted in brain) who shall presume avowedly in words to profess, or shall by writing proceed to affirm and maintain him or herself, or any other meer creature, to be very God . . . or that true God, or the Eternal Majesty dwells in the Creature and no where else shall suffer six months imprisonment for the first offence and for the second shall be banished. [Firth and Rait, 1911: II, 409–12]

All the radical sects had members whose conduct was in some measure a consequence of mental and emotional disorder. Some, such as George Fox or John Bunyan, have left an indelible imprint on our culture; others, such as James Nayler, John Rogers, or Lodowick Muggleton, have receded into the obscurity of the past (Nickalls, 1952:26, 48–49, 51, 63, 570; Royce, 1898:29–75; Brown, 1928; Walker, 1964:218–19). Nonetheless, in their own time, they were able to participate actively in their social environment. They could do so because the sects with their ideas and forms of social organization and behavior provided culturally constituted and in varying measure sanctioned systems which enabled psychologically aberrant individuals to remain within the limits of social toleration. It was possible for such individuals to function more or less adequately in society as long as their behavior was not considered evidence of undue psychological impairment and sociocultural distortion. In an age when the Bible was interpreted literally, when a belief in personal revelations was prevalent, when mystical experience was cultivated in group settings, as among the early Quakers, and a search for the keys to the Apocalypse preoccupied persons of high intellectual achievement like Isaac Newton (Manuel, 1963; Miller, 1956:228–30), the fantastic views and extravagant behavior of the wilder sectaries did not appear entirely alien or stand out quite as sharply in society as they might today, though this statement may perhaps require some modification in light of movements and phenomena observed in the later 1960s.

Moreover, the radical sectarians of England in the mid-seventeenth century participated in a subculture of their own, in which religion and politics were inseparable, combining the otherworldly with the things of this world in terms of a tradition derived from the millennial writings of the biblical prophets and their commentators. The Fifth Monarchy Men expected the direct intervention of Christ to bring about the rule of the saints, but they were also political activists who did not shrink from insurrection. Such action was presented in terms of earlier religious ideas and traditions, ideas which exerted a powerful attraction for people, often poor and uneducated, who felt themselves alienated from the prevailing dominant culture. Within their subculture, the radical sects in terms of their millenarian doctrines promised improvement in the condition of their members and provided for total emotional and social involvement.

Moreover, members of such groups were inspired with a sense of their own significance. Commenting on sectarian movements in nineteenth-century America, Alice Felt Tyler noted that "the leaders of these new sects emphasized their separateness and the need for the close association of all members. The more peculiar the tenets of their faith, the more necessary became the instruction, criticism, and supervision that community living could make possible" (Tyler, 1962:108). This sense of belonging to a chosen group with a special way of life was a source of strength and emotional support for the individual. Belonging gave life a semblance of meaning and a way of establishing one's identity and maintaining one's self-respect. Under these circumstances, emotional instability and pathologic religiosity were no hindrance to participation; in fact, these sects facilitated social integration on the part of such individuals.

Similar movements and reactions have been noted at other times and places. Among the Paris *sans culottes* of the Year II, demands for fraternization and equality appear to have expressed analogous needs, hopes, and aspirations (Cobb, 1965; Soboul, 1958:457–504, 549–80, 649–80). Messianic and millenarian responses to white expansion and domination among American Indians exhibit similar characteristics, including militance, social cohesiveness, behavioral excess, and the like (Voget, 1957). From time to time, northeastern Brazil has produced religious movements whose avowed aim was to establish a new Jerusalem and to wipe out the degradation and misery afflicting their followers. Euclides da Cunha, in his classic account of the movement led by Antonio Conselheiro and of its suppression in 1896–97 at Canndos, provides appropriate evidence on this point (De Queiroz, 1958; Da Cunha, 1902). The Mahdist movements in Africa in the nineteenth century may be seen in the same light.

No matter whether in Europe, Asia, Africa, North or South America, or Oceania, where a group of people is dominated by another, often with a vastly superior technology, or where groups of people see themselves as aliens and exiles trapped in a world which they want more than anything else to escape, either by destroying the old order and creating a new and better world or by withdrawing into a compensatory inner or transcendental world, deliverers appear who promise to remove hardship, prevent impending calamities, and in general restore the past age of gold. Such messiahs promulgate prescriptions, establish certain usages, and prohibit others. These messiahs and the movements they head can be seen as attempts to instill new or to revive flagging energies in such groups. In this sense, they are "revitalization movements" as the anthropologist Wallace (1956*b*) has termed them. Not infrequently, such movements attract attention through the bizarre behavioral phenomena exhibited by their members, such as frenetic group dances, trances, twitching, glossolalia, convulsions, and so forth that have led students of past movements and observers of contemporary ones to describe such occurrences in terms of abnormal psychology, as forms of mass psychopathology, neurosis, psychosis, or delusions.

There is no doubt that such movements can harbor among their participants individuals who may be mentally and emotionally disordered, some of whom may even be leaders. Indeed, as pointed out above, such individuals can even be helped to function adequately in such a context. But such phenomena are not evidence per se of psychopathology. They occur within emotionally charged and explosive situations, under circumstances where, as Merton put it, there is a contradiction between cultural goals and the institutional means to attain them. Under the stimulus of intense desire and of the tensions that build up, there is a need for emotional expression and action. Liston Pope (1942:86), in his study of religion and industrialism in Gastonia, North Carolina, from 1890 to 1939 pointed out that the mill workers of that town wanted a religion that "works" and "changes things," and this is equally true of messianic and millenarian movements. A psychological atmosphere of this kind has often been present when mass epidemics occurred, a situation vividly described by Manzoni (1954: chs. 21, 22) for seventeenth-century Milan, when the populace sought relief by hunting down so-called anointers, who were believed to have caused the plague.

Millenarian movements are reactions to stressful situations involving social, political, and psychological elements. They are actively or passively critical of the present and endeavor through a variety of behaviors to alter it—for example, through magical efforts to alter circumstances, symbolic validation or expression of frustrated goals and repressed guilt, transcendental compensation, or violent resistance. Recognition that in such movements we encounter great surges of human hope and despair may perhaps help to comprehend our own time and some of its bizarre features.

NOTES

1. The psychological character of such groups is well rendered in the play, *Le Diable et le Bon Dieu,* by Sartre.
2. An instance in point is John Bunyan's use of biblical texts to deal with personal problems (Bunyan, 1925:310 ff.). John Wesley often had recourse to "the oracles of God," that is opening the Bible and deciding what to do by interpreting the passage upon which he happened to chance, as in his journal entry of March 28, 1739 (Wesley, 1963:65).

7

Militant Ideologies and Organizational Contexts: The War on Poverty and the Ideology of "Black Power"

J. KENNETH BENSON

In recent years we have witnessed the emergence and widespread acceptance of a radical formulation of American racial problems—the black power ideology. The ideology first emerged in the mid-sixties as little more than a slogan. At that point the concept of black power was not clearly formulated and did not enjoy much support from Negroes. Yet, by the end of the decade a fairly coherent black power ideology had developed and gained a substantial following.

The late sixties also saw the implementation of the War on Poverty. The black power movement and the antipoverty program shared the same social space and developed a complex interactive relationship. Their association in time and social location led some observers to argue that a causal relationship existed, i.e., that the War on Poverty in some way caused the growth of the black power movement and its increasing militancy. Yet, the exact nature of the relationship is not well understood.

My purpose is to analyze the relationship between the War on Poverty and the emergence of the black power ideology. It is my thesis

Reprinted by permission of the author and publisher from *Sociological Quarterly* 12 (Summer 1971).

that the War on Poverty provided a necessary organizational context within which the militant ideology was refined and rendered plausible. The War on Poverty, I will argue, generated a series of conflicts rooted in its organizational structure. These conflicts radicalized the perspectives of participants and sympathizers and made them more receptive to the black power ideology. Furthermore, the conflicts generated by the War on Poverty produced evidence of basic contradictions in American social organization which was interpreted as confirmation of the ideology of black power.[1]

THE EMERGENCE OF BLACK POWER IDEOLOGY

In the first half of the 1960s the ideology of the civil rights movement was widely accepted among American Negroes. Positions rejecting significant tenets of that ideology were not only lacking support but also were subject to negative judgments by many Negroes. In his 1964 survey, Marx (1967:106–25) found few Negroes willing to endorse a series of statements mildly supportive of black nationalism. Furthermore, he found large proportions disapproved of the Black muslims and of Malcolm X (Marx, 1967:27). So minimal was the support for radical analyses that Marx (1967:41–48) chose to measure "militancy" in terms of the endorsement of a series of statements reflecting a moderate, civil rights consciousness. There is evidence that this consensus was already breaking up among civil rights leaders. Bell (1968) for example, reports the emergence of a more radical perspective within CORE in the early years of the decade. However, this perspective apparently did not gain much support in the larger Negro community prior to the period of massive ghetto rioting from 1964 to 1968.

The black power slogan was popularized in the mid-sixties by leaders of the Student Nonviolent Coordinating Committee such as Stokely Carmichael and Rapp Brown (see Grant, 1968:459–66; Killian, 1968:125–46). Although the idea of black power was ambiguously formulated, the slogan immediately generated strong reactions inside the civil rights movement. It was clear from the outset that the endorsement of black power signified a sharp break with the established goals and strategies of the civil rights movement. It clearly implied a rejection of the coalition tactics of the established civil rights organizations such as the NAACP and the Urban League. Furthermore, it appeared to mark a major departure from the goal of integration championed by those organizations. Civil rights leaders quickly recognized this departure (see Rustin, 1966a).

The black power slogan produced strong but relatively incoherent responses in the general public, white and black. Many were apparently unable to describe in any detail what the implementation of black power would produce. For many the term apparently implied nothing more revolutionary than traditional pressure group politics. For others it called forth images of a violent overthrow of the government (Marx, 1967:215–41).[2]

In recent years the black power position has become increasingly coherent and has gained a substantial following. The elements of this emerging ideology include the following:

1) The view that American social organization is an interlocking, self-maintaining system of white advantage. The advocates of black power appear to be committed to the notion that the major institutions of American society form a reinforcing pattern which tends to perpetuate the dominance of whites. Distinctions between white institutions, between regions, and between levels of government which held a prominent place in the ideology of civil rights activism are obliterated in the emerging black power ideology. The conception that the federal government will work in fundamental and enduring ways in behalf of blacks and against the opposition of state and local governments is generally rejected. The identification of white churches with the cause of black liberation is denied. The proposition that the white university is committed to racial equality is received with derision. Instead, these institutions are seen as perpetuators of the racial status quo. They enshrine the values of dominant whites; they provide necessary support for discriminatory practices; they fail to attack racism with vigor and determination. This point of view regarding white institutions is often expressed in the application of colonial models to the American case (Carmichael and Hamilton, 1967:2–32; Hayden, 1969).

2) The commitment to a coercion model of social order. Black power advocates generally espouse the position that when stripped of all of its ideological elements, the social order is held together by the capacity of some groups to control others and thereby to maintain a position of advantage. They are generally cynical toward appeals to common values; and they tend to interpret such appeals as attempts to legitimate the defense of vested interests (Carmichael and Hamilton, 1967:40).

3) The rejection of integration as a goal. The proponents of Black power generally reject the notion that integration is the primary goal toward which Negro organizations should strive. In so doing, they reject the focal concerns of the civil rights movement (Carmichael and Hamilton, 1967:53–56). In place of the integration concerns of the civil rights movement have come the demand for black control over

ghetto institutions (Altshuler, 1970), and the determination to build black pride and consciousness (Edwards, 1970).

4) The rejection of coalition strategies. The ideology of black power involves a thoroughgoing attack upon one of the basic tactical assumptions of the civil rights movement, i.e., that coalitions with white liberals and liberal organizations are necessary. The abandonment of coalition is based upon a straightforward analysis of vested interests. It is argued that white liberals—individually and collectively—will support the cause of black liberation only within the narrow limits set by their vested interests. If this cause demands the undermining of the institutional structures from which white liberals benefit, they will abandon it. Inasmuch as the black power advocate believes fundamental institutional changes to be necessary, he chooses not to trust white liberals or their organizations (Carmichael and Hamilton, 1967:58–84).

5) The legitimation of violence. The proponents of black power have studiously avoided the unequivocal disavowal of violent means. They reacted against the commitment to nonviolence which had characterized the civil rights movement. Thus, initially their position was not an endorsement of violence but a repudiation of nonviolence (Carmichael and Hamilton, 1967:52–53). Later some leaders of the black power movement have become advocates of violence as a means of defending ghetto residents against police brutality and as a means of forcing the attention of authorities to the problems of blacks (Meier and Rudwick, 1969; Killian, 1968:125–76).

In recent years the black power ideology has ceased to be merely the doctrine of an elite cadre. The ideas of the Negro masses have undergone a transformation in the direction of an increasingly coherent, widely accepted black power ideology. This assertion can be supported by the following kinds of evidence. First, several studies have shown substantial acceptance among Negroes of a "riot ideology." This "ideology" involves the justification of civil disturbances on the basis of Negro deprivation and powerlessness and on the grounds that such actions constitute an effective strategy for bringing the attention of authorities to Negro problems. In a study of the Los Angeles disorders of 1965, Tomlinson (1968) found that Negroes tended to view the Watts riot as purposeful. More than fifty percent saw it as a Negro protest; and almost forty percent described it in revolutionary terms, i.e., as a revolt or insurrection. McCord and associates (1969:78–104) found large proportions of Negroes in several cities willing to endorse violence and to justify riots.

Second, there is some evidence that the black power ideology as a coherent, developed perspective is accepted by many Negroes. Form and Rytina (1969) found the acceptance of a Marxian model of social power and the rejection of a pluralistic model more common among Negroes than among whites. Brink and Harris (1966:56, 264), although concluding that black power remains a "fuzzy doctrine" to most Negroes, report some evidence indicative of a trend toward a coherent ideology. Twenty-five percent of their Negro sample endorsed the idea of black power, and 34 percent thought riots had helped the Negro cause. Aberbach and Walker (1970) in a study conducted in Detroit after the 1967 riots found that favorability toward black power was associated with 1) the tendency to describe the Detroit riot as an insurrection or revolt; 2) the expression of sympathy with rioters; 3) the explanation of the riot in terms of poor treatment accorded blacks; 4) the endorsement of militant black leaders instead of moderates; 5) the anticipation of one's own participation in a riot; 6) the belief that integration will be long in coming. Conant with Levy and Lewis (1969) in a study conducted in 1966–67 found polarization of opinions between whites and Negroes on the pace of integration.

Third, reform movements in many cities have become oriented toward black power concerns. That is, specific proposals for reform which have become focal points of debate appear increasingly to be based upon black power assumptions. Demands and proposals based on such assumptions now occupy the center stage in many cities. Thus, it appears that the ideology enjoys sufficient support in the black community to provide the basis for effective political action. As an example, consider the continuing controversy in New York City over the issue of public school decentralization. The demand for community control of schools has been based to a considerable extent upon black power ideology. The demand mobilized extensive support in the Negro and Puerto Rican neighborhoods. As a consequence, decentralization became a political issue of major importance in New York City; and, the state legislature enacted a decentralization bill (Altshuler, 1970; Levin, 1970).

In sum, it has been argued that in recent years the black power ideology has become increasingly coherent and has gained a substantial following among Negroes, especially the residents of urban ghettoes. In succeeding pages the connection between these developments and the War on Poverty will be explored.

THE IDEOLOGICAL CONSEQUENCES OF THE WAR ON POVERTY

The thesis of this chapter is that the War on Poverty provided an organizational context within which the emergent ideology of black power was refined and rendered plausible. More precisely, it is argued that a series of social conflicts rooted in the organizational apparatus of the War on Poverty facilitated the refinement and acceptance of the black power ideology. I will examine this argument through the description and analysis of a series of such conflicts.

The provision for "maximum feasible participation" of the poor in the design and administration of antipoverty programs produced a set of stakes which drew divergent groups of people into conflict at the local level. The principle of "maximum feasible participation" led to the policy of giving preference to the poor in the hiring of staff and to the development of mechanisms for the representation of the poor in the process of program planning and implementation in local Community Action programs (Donovan, 1967:41–48; Moynihan, 1969:89–100; Kramer, 1969:1–20). Consequently, in many communities throughout the country conflict was generated between groups contending for control over Community Action programs. Control of the CAP was an objective of importance because 1) it conveyed influence over the distribution of a large number of jobs earmarked for low income people; 2) it provided a position of authority and legitimacy from which to disseminate a preferred point of view regarding poverty and minority problems; 3) it provided (or at least promised) an opportunity to influence public policy in directions deemed appropriate on the basis of a preferred point of view; 4) it provided an opportunity to demonstrate the dominance of one group and its ideology over others competing for leadership of the Negro cause (see Bachrach and Baratz, 1970:98–99, for a similar discussion).

The Community Action programs, because of these considerations, became a center of conflict in many communities. Groups with opposing interests and divergent ideologies struggled to control the CAPs. The bases of these conflicts appear to have varied from city to city. In some communities divisions along racial and ethnic lines were crucial. For example, Kramer (1969) describes one case, Santa Clara County, California, in which militant Mexican-American groups contended with Anglos (1969:68–107) and another case, the Mission District of San Francisco, in which Negroes were arrayed against Mexican-Americans (1969:41–45). In some other cases the conflict was apparently between competing factions within the Negro community. Typical were conflicts between the established, moderate civil rights organizations and the newer, more militant ones. Those conflicts were based upon opposed perspectives regarding the proper program emphases for the CAPs. In general the moderate groups such as the Urban League and NAACP have been oriented to the provision of services by the CAP while the more militant groups such as CORE and SNCC (and often locally based groups lacking a national counterpart) have emphasized community organization. This basic pattern is clear in Baltimore according to the study of Bachrach and Baratz (1970:67–103). In some cases, established civil rights groups became active collaborators with CAPs in the delivery of services (e.g., the involvement of the Urban League in employment programs), while the more militant groups pursued objectives of control over CAPs or, failing that, opposition to them.

The effects of these conflicts upon the development of black ideologies have not been well documented by social scientists. Nevertheless, it is possible to engage in disciplined speculation. It appears that the conflicts occasioned an enormous expansion of ideological thinking, of efforts to construct and propagate coherent and distinctive formulations of Negro problems and their solutions. Very important in this process was the tendency to formulate precisely the differences between the perspectives of various contending groups. Necessary connections between ideas and programs were carefully formulated and vigorously defended. Program proposals were not simply weighed on pragmatic or expedient grounds. They were weighed as the manifestations of specific theories, approaches, perspectives. Beyond this, the perspectives and proposals of major participants were often debunked by arguing that they grew out of the vested interests of their proponents. Thus, the ideological differences were heightened and intensified.

The conflict between moderate civil rights organizations and militant black power groups was nurtured in the struggles for CAP control. Militant leaders could point to the moderates' position regarding the CAPs as evidence for the contention that the established organizations were oriented to the concerns of the middle-class Negro and to the maintenance of their dominance over other Negroes and of their privileged relationship to the white majority. The debate over black power and coalition politics, then, came to have in the poverty programs a delimited, immediate organizational context. The proponents of the positions were locked in battle for control of a concrete set of stakes—programs, jobs, bases of power, and influence.[3]

A second persistent pattern of conflict was that between the staff members and the representatives of the poor. The Community Action programs generally maintained a dual orientation which led to this type of conflict. The CAP was to be an instrument for organizing the poor and expressing their concerns; but it was also to be a purveyor of services to the poor. The latter function led to the employment of professional and semiprofessional staffs skilled in the delivery of public services. The staff members then became contenders for control over the CAP and over the orientation of its programs. In many cases these staff members came into conflict with the officially designated representatives of the poor or with the leaders of militant factions within minority communities.

These conflicts seem to have revolved around a series of interrelated issues. First, there was a continuing dispute in many CAPs over the extent to which the program would emphasize the delivery of services of a somewhat traditional type (such as employment, schooling, counseling) or, as an alternative, the organization of the poor as a political force to exert pressure upon established institutions. (Kramer [1969:1–21] sees this as a fundamental dilemma confronted by all CAPs.)

Second, there were numerous disputes over the control of programs once established. The CAPs moved very rapidly toward the implementation of a bureaucratic-professional model. Staff members assumed positions of dominance vis-à-vis clients and target area representatives. Proposals were often developed by staff members and submitted for funding without opportunities for effective involvement of the poor or their representatives. Staff members were hired, promoted, fired without consideration of the preferences of the poor. Policies were implemented by the staff in ways unacceptable to the representatives. In general, then, the evolution toward a bureaucratic-professional model tended to consign the representatives of the poor to a narrowly circumscribed, powerless role. (See Benson and Allen, 1969; Kramer, 1969; Miller and Rein, 1969; Miller and Roby, 1968.) Furthermore, the services provided by CAPs soon came to resemble very closely the services rendered by established agencies. The same basic professional skills were placed at the center of activity. Contact work with low-income people, handled generally by indigenous nonprofessionals, was assigned a clearly ancillary and subordinate status. In organizational structure, too, the new CAP services came to resemble established programs. Bureaucratic rules, guidelines, restrictions rapidly proliferated. An elaborate system of record-keeping and a tendency to evaluate and fund programs on the basis of quantitative indices of performance led to rapid growth of a stultifying bureaucratic mentality.

Third, conflict developed in many CAPs over the decentralization of authority. At stake in these disputes was the degree of autonomy of neighborhood service centers (Kramer, 1969; Bensman, 1967). Were these centers to have authority to develop unique programs demanded by neighborhood residents? Were these centers to have authority to overrule policy decisions and personnel assignments made by the central administrative unit? These issues in many cases were elliptical ways of raising the issue of participation by the poor since control by their representatives was generally more firmly established at the neighborhood level.

The neighborhood-staff conflicts provided fertile ground for the nurturance of black power ideology. The conflicts were amenable to a straightforward analysis in terms of vested interests. The claims of the bureaucratic-professional reformers could readily be interpreted as the defense of vested interests. Their responses to these issues could be interpreted as exacting tests of the depth and sincerity of their commitments to the poor. Thus, the basic professional claims of the reformers—to expertise and a service ethic—were debunked as devices to maintain their dominance and to defend their interests. Their opposition to neighborhood control—a principle readily adapted to the separatist tendencies of black power—provided evidence favorable to the position that alliances with white liberals are unreliable in the face of conflicting interests and to the position that appeals to common values are to be rejected in favor of a coercion model of social order.

The third locus of conflict is that between the established public service agencies and the newly formed antipoverty agencies. The conflict centered around the following issues: 1) the resistance of the established agencies to the legitimation of the domain claims of the antipoverty agencies; 2) the opposition of established agencies to the technology (the techniques, approaches, strategies) employed by the antipoverty agencies; and 3) the refusal of established agencies to cooperate with the antipoverty agencies. These issues were often closely linked in the typical patterns of conflict. In general, the emerging agencies were confronted in most communities by a social welfare establishment committed to old technologies, resistant to the erosion of their domains, and thoroughly unresponsive to the needs of the new agency.

The conflict with established agencies grew in part from the critical stance of the poverty program toward those agencies. Part of the justification for the poverty program was that old agencies were rigid and unresponsive to the needs of the poor and uncooperative in their relations with each other (Donovan, 1967:17–48). The poverty agencies were supposed to force the old agencies to correct these deficiencies. The new program was met in most communities by a reservoir of distrust and resentment.

The conflict with established agencies often took on a highly public, demonstrative form. In many cases the conflict was expressed in contests between the representatives of the poor and representatives of the agencies on governing boards of the CAPs. The established agencies often attempted to use their positions on these boards to prevent the CAPs from threatening their independence and public support. They seem to have been intent upon imposing an established, non-controversial model upon the CAPs. The agencies clashed with the poor on a series of issues such as the number of seats allotted to the poor on the governing boards, the criteria for selecting representatives (e.g., must they be poor themselves?), the autonomy of neighborhood units and service centers, the control of appointments to executive positions, the minimal qualifications of employees, the involvement of the agency in controversial programs and attacks upon establishment organizations, the relative emphasis to be placed upon community organizing, and the duplication of existing services. (See Marris and Rein, 1967; Kramer, 1969; Clark and Hopkins, 1968.) In addition, at an operational level many antipoverty workers experienced firsthand the intransigence of the public bureaucracies. Attempts to get help for specific clients, to produce policy changes, and to enlist the cooperation of the agencies often led only to frustration.

The conflict with established agencies was superimposed upon the conflicts within the civil rights movement. Moderate civil rights organizations such as the Urban League and the NAACP often allied themselves with established agencies and their conventional technologies and opposed the more radical formulations of CAP directives. Some moderate groups were committed to cooperative efforts with established agencies which were clearly designed to compete with and circumvent CAP efforts. For example, the Urban League was drawn into the employment program of the National Alliance of Businessmen (NAB) which was closely linked to state Employment Security divisions. The NAB effort was based on a traditional technology involving the correction of deficiencies in the employment potential of the unemployed worker and the avoidance of an aggressive approach to potential employers. It stood in marked contrast to the stance adopted by many OEO-based employment programs. The latter involved a more aggressive stance toward employers and an institutional (as opposed to individualistic) analysis of the unemployment problem. The NAB program was clearly more consistent with a middle-class, business-oriented ideology, while the OEO programs were more nearly aligned with the perspective of militant, lower-class blacks.

The conflicts described above provided important support for the emerging black power ideology. The established agencies, despite their public rhetoric of support for the poor, were shown to have a limited commitment at best. They were shown to be defenders of a political order, a "mobilization of bias" to use Bachrach and Baratz's

(1970) term. It was apparent that those agencies would defend their domains and their technologies against the incursions of a new agency; that they would struggle to control and contain new sources of funds and authority; that they would actively oppose new formulations of the poverty problem. It was then easier to persuade the masses that established agencies are part of the problem, not part of the solution. The ends of the established agencies could be dramatized and demonstrated by pointing to concrete examples of their resistance to the interests of the poor as defined by militant leaders. The need for black power could be linked to the necessity to control the public agencies. The militant leader could depict himself as a "hero" in his opposition to the "villains" played ably by the establishment agencies. Furthermore, since the moderate civil rights organizations were drawn into these conflicts, often on the side of the agencies, they could be painted with the same brush. Their complicity in the defense of the status quo could be clearly demonstrated; their opposition to the "true interests" of blacks (especially lower-class blacks) could be dramatized in the concrete experiences of antipoverty workers and sympathizers.

The fourth basic conflict involved major state and municipal politicians. To many mayors and governors the poverty program appeared both as a threat and an opportunity. It was a threat in that it offered a new source of funds, authority, and jobs not necessarily controlled by established authorities. As such, the new program had the potential to undermine or dilute established concentrations of power. Beyond this, poverty programs often criticized other public agencies and thereby created political liabilities for elected officials. At the same time, the poverty program provided an opportunity for established political figures to extend and consolidate their power. For these reasons many CAPs went through periods of conflict in which mayors attempted to gain a significant degree of control over local poverty programs; and, state governors were involved in a number of concerted efforts to gain and to exercise veto power over certain OEO programs administered by CAPs. (Analyses of these conflicts are available in Donovan, 1967:43–57; Kramer, 1969:25–67; Bachrach and Baratz, 1970:67–103; Marris and Rein, 1967:208–23; Clark and Hopkins, 1968:133–204, 233–60; and Moynihan, 1969:128–66.)

The specific issues on which these conflicts turned included the following:

1) The degree of emphasis to be placed upon community organization as opposed to service delivery: established authorities generally supported service delivery; and where they gained control, community organization appears to have suffered.

2) The degree of threat to traditional agencies either through direct

criticism or invasion of domains: established authorities generally defended the operations and domains of the traditional agencies.

3) The degree of control to be exercised by the poor in the gover-
nance of antipoverty programs: established authorities tended to resist the efforts of the poor to gain control of CAP boards.

4) The degree of acceptance and implementation of radical formulations of the poverty problem: established authorities tended to support moderate or conservative ideologies and to resist the efforts of
more radical elements to implement their ideologies.

5) degree of involvement in "political activity": established authorities tended to resist efforts to use antipoverty funds or personnel for
organizing and sustaining protests against government programs or
policies, or for supporting political causes.

The state and local political figures who opposed the more aggressive, threatening tendencies of OEO programs were able to mount
successful attacks at the national level. Legislation limiting the representation of the poor on CAP governing boards to one-third and in-
suring a significant representation of municipal authorities and public
agencies was passed under the pressure of these attacks. Also, governors were granted limited veto powers over OEO programs, and the
support of the Johnson administration for OEO was seriously eroded.
A Head Start program in Mississippi was removed from an aggressive
organization and placed in the hands of a more conservative body.
These pressures appear also to have induced a new conservatism and
caution on the part of OEO leadership at the national level. Thus, the
established political leaders were able by a variety of pressures to
force a more conservative line upon Community Action programs.

There were occasions when the opposing officials were unsuccessful. In San Francisco a mayor failed in his effort to maintain control
of the CAP (Kramer, 1969). In Missouri a governor's veto of a CAP
budget was overridden by OEO without significant modifications of
the legal services component he opposed. Similar cases occurred
throughout the country as national OEO officials clung resolutely to
certain key principles and policies. Nevertheless, overall it is clear that
the opposition was successful in curtailing seriously the aggressiveness and militancy of CAP programs.

The conflicts with elected officials contributed to the growth of militant black ideology. High officials were shown to support the interests
of the poor only within very narrow limits. They appeared unwilling
to surrender control of programs or to countenance any erosion of
their authority. Their support for the poor was limited by their own
interests in maintaining and extending their power. Furthermore, the
joint reactions of officials—the coalition between governors, mayors,

congressmen, and others—provided validation for militant claims that there is an interlocking power structure which maintains the subjugation of the black poor. The pluralistic model of the power structure underlying the coalition politics of moderate civil rights groups was dealt a severe blow by these developments. It could then be argued that the power structure only appears to be pluralistic and to allow the effective participation of blacks as a pressure group and that its monolithic character becomes manifest when a serious and clearcut threat to the established elites is mounted. Thus, it could be argued, coalition strategies—the poverty program itself a major example—do not produce significant change in the position of blacks. Rather, such strategies draw blacks into the support of an established power structure which will ultimately frustrate their interests. Substantial social change, necessary from the point of view of the militant, will be impeded rather than facilitated by such coalitions (Hayden, 1966).

The War on Poverty was launched at a time when opposing interpretations of the plight of American Negroes were being advanced and evaluated. The ideology of the civil rights movement—a moderate, conciliatory, integrationist perspective—was being challenged by the proponents of a more aggressive and radical formulation—the ideology of black power. The War on Poverty, planned in the period of ascendancy of the civil rights movement, was implemented in a period of ascendancy of the civil rights movement, was implemented in a period of internal division within the movement and full-scale assault upon its dominant ideology. In this context the new program became a battleground and a potential proving ground for the opposing ideologies. The principle of "maximum feasible participation" made the program particularly vulnerable to this development, but it seems likely that with or without that principle any major federal attack upon poverty at that particular juncture would have been beset by similar problems.

In this context the poverty program provided an organizational setting which facilitated the emergence and consolidation of a coherent black power ideology. It provided a set of issues around which to mobilize low-income Negroes. The contradictions in its structure led to a series of conflicts which were readily interpreted as confirmation of black power ideology. The reiteration of these conflicts throughout the nation facilitated the nationwide diffusion of black power ideology. The outcomes of the conflicts, although not uniform throughout the country, provided data susceptible to a black interpretation; and everywhere leaders of the emerging movement were available to provide such an interpretation. The poverty program supplied events, concrete experiences to be analyzed and understood. Black power ideology supplied the analysis and shaped the understanding of the events. The program in the absence of the ideology probably would not have had the same effects. The ideology without the program probably would not have gained support so rapidly.

NOTES

1. This does not mean that black power ideology provided the only or even the most reasonable interpretation. Nevertheless, it was the most plausible of the ideologies readily available in the ghetto. Furthermore, it was being promoted by activists in the ghetto and was perceived as *the* alternative to the more optimistic ideology of civil rights advocacy.
2. Marx (1967) contended that the position remains incoherent in the Negro masses. Our position, to be spelled out in succeeding pages, is that for a substantial minority of Negroes the ideology of black power has become a reasonably coherent perspective.
3. Moynihan (1969:128–66) describes several cases fitting this argument in a general way. Altshuler (1970:33–34) argues that Moynihan's cases were unusual but acknowledges that data to settle the issue are not yet available. Miller and Rein (1969) contend that the program became linked to black power demands.

part 3

The Effects of Movements on Change

Introduction

By definition, a social movement seeks to impede or implement some kind of change. Here we will be concerned only with the latter, the effort to effect change. But what kind of change? Some typologies of movements are based upon distinctions in the kind of change advocated; thus, the revolutionary movement strives for radical change while the reform movement only seeks modifications in the social structure. But no typology adequately embraces all the variety of changes which may be effected by a movement.

In this part we will examine change at a number of different levels, beginning with changes in individuals. For all social movements, whatever else they do, effect some change in their members. Indeed, some movements have as their proximate target nothing more than the individual. But even those that aim beyond the individual will effect alterations in their members. In a study of recruitment for the American draft resistance movement of the late 1960s, Useem (1972) found that new members underwent a socilization process. Draft resisters who lacked a prior radical affiliation were politically radicalized and, at the same time, alienated from their prior social environments. The draft system was the target, but members were changed independently of any effects on that system.

Whatever the goals of the movement, then, social psychological changes in members form a part of the overall effects. The first selection details such changes in millenarian movements. As Lebra points out, the changes can approximate a psychiatric cure or the correctional treatment for a criminal. The changes occur through a process

123

of socialization that involves enlightenment, integration, and commitment.

The next level of change effected by a social movement is that of the status/role. In the selection by Lauer and Chen, the status/role of women in China is shown to have been altered through the Communist movement. The actual change is not as great as that predicted by and claimed by the Maoist ideology; nevertheless, it represents a substantial change over traditional China. Clearly, the contemporary Chinese woman is not equal to the Chinese man; just as clearly, she is in a far higher position than her counterpart of previous generations.

The lower status and subordinate status of women is common throughout the world, including the United States. American women are striving to equalize their status, but are doing so primarily through the typical American pattern of seeking legal change. Most movements in the United States have legal change as a primary aim, since most are reformist in practice whatever they are in ideology. The essay by Chasteen focuses on such change—the passage of a public accommodations ordinance in Kansas City. The ordinance was passed, but its passage generated a countermovement and a process of conflict before the legality of the ordinance was finally secured in a city-wide referendum.

Chasteen's analysis supports the basic perspective of this book, for he emphasizes the importance of the "nature of the opposition" encountered for our understanding of social movements. He shows that various changes occurred in the movement itself as it interacted with its social milieu, including changes in leadership, membership, strategy and tactics, and goals. Even the effort to effect a relatively minor legal change is not without its sweat, agony, and consequences for the movement as well as for the larger society.

The public accommodations movement in Kansas City was a phase of the larger civil rights movement. If we focus on a movement as a whole, rather than on a particular concrete expression of it, we are likely to encounter diverse and multiple effects. Thus, in the next essay Jackson describes the broad societal changes that seem to be associated with the civil rights movement. Both extra- and intrainstitutional changes have resulted. Jackson's essay is of value for at least three reasons. First, it points out the extensiveness of the changes associated with a large-scale movement. Second, it implicitly illustrates the difficulty of attempting to deal with the effects of an entire movement, since the movement may have, among others, political, economic, educational, religious, and extrainstitutional effects. Third, it follows that the charges wrought by a movement involve far more than those for which the movement strives, so that any analysis must search for subtle as well as the obvious areas of change.

Finally, one theme which recurs throughout our examination of movements and social change is that of unintended and unanticipated consequences of social action. Long ago, Dawson and Gettys (1929:710) noted that there are "frequent incidental consequences of social movements." They supported this by reference to the Puritan movement in England which facilitated "the parliamentary rebellion, the radicalism of the Levellers, the founding of New England, sectarian divisions, and an incipient bourgeois ethic, all effects hardly intended by the Puritan leaders" (Dawson and Gettys, 1929:710). The final selection in this part is another example of unintended consequences of a movement—"the emergence of protest as a legitimate activity for large groups of Americans" as a result of the civil rights movement.

In the final chapter of this part, Laue supplements the essay by Jackson in listing some of the changes effected by the movement, but more importantly he indentifies the unanticipated effects of the movement and speculates on the future consequences. He makes the point that the movement not only legitimized protest, but also gave people a sense that "things *can* be changed." Thus, "unanticipated" and "unintended" are not to be equated with "undesirable." "(Undesirable" here refers to the perceptions of movement participants, not to the observer's judgment.) Sometimes the unanticipated is the undesirable, as the next part will illustrate in the deradicalization of Marxist movements. But the sense of power generated in people by the civil rights movement has not only enlarged the membership of the movement but resulted in new movements as women and minorities other than blacks have begun to press for rights.

Whether we shall ever get to the point where no "unanticipated" results could occur is a question involving one's philosophy of social science. That is, it involves the question of whether the sociologist can ever attain sufficient knowledge and tools to predict and control the course of social life. At this point, however, there is little question but that every social movement will generate some unanticipated and unintended effects along with the changes for which it explicitly aims.

Social Psychological Change

Millenarian Movements and Resocialization

TAKIE SUGIYAMA LEBRA

This chapter attempts to throw light upon those aspects of millenarian movements which can be regarded as mechanisms for resocializing adult individuals. The underlying assumption is that the millenarian movement can induce a change in a behavioral system similar to a psychiatric cure for a mental patient or to a correctional treatment for a convict. However, it is not my intention to obscure differences and contrasts lying between millenarian movements and institutional agencies such as mental hospitals and prisons. Contrastive points will be noted.

INSTITUTIONALIZED VERSUS MILLENARIAN RESOCIALIZATION

First, the therapeutic or correctional institutions, as an integral part of society, are expected to serve the established order and thus to re-habilitate misfits, whereas the millenarian movement declares an apocalyptic annihilation of the existing world to be replaced by a God's kingdom and encourages or legitimizes a departure from the established order. Institutions like mental hospitals and prisons are, in other words, "processing systems" (Wheeler, 1966) which receive

"Millenarian Movements and Resocialization," by Takie Sugiyama Lebra is reprinted from *American Behavorial Scientist* Vol. 12, No. 4 (March/April 1969) pp. 8–17 by permission of the author and the Publisher, Sage Publications, Inc.

clients, modify their behavior, and, hopefully, on completion of treatment, release them into the external world. The millenarian movement receives its prospective members and indoctrinates them, but provides no exit; its success being measured, contrary to institutions, by its ability to retain as well as to increase its members. This first point should account for the intensity of the resocialization process characteristic of a millenarian movement.

Second, despite their instrumentality to the larger society, resocializing institutions as "total institutions" are ecologically set apart from the outside world by physical barriers like "locked doors, high walls, barbed wire, cliffs, water, forests, or moors" (Goffman, 1961:4). This ecological discontinuity symbolizes the coercive recruitment of the institutional inmates, bolstered by the outside structure of authority and power, and implemented by "supervisory staff." Except for isolated utopian communities built up by collective migrants, the millenarian cult does not segregate itself ecologically from the external world, and thus leaves its members simultaneously anchored in both spheres of life. Millenarian resocialization is initiated in either publicly open places like streets, parks, auditoriums and temples or in private homes. Candidates for resocialization are recruited and retained voluntarily rather than through coercion. All this requires an effective operation of an internal, social-psychological control mechanism to play the role equivalent to external authority. At the same time, there must be a certain degree of doctrinal flexibility which accommodates the "double life."

The third point draws upon Turner's distinction between "structure" and its opposite—namely, "liminality" or "communitas"—which serves, I find, to pull together the foregoing two points and illuminate their further implications. Institutionalized resocialization is an extreme function of a "structure," whereas millenarian resocialization is a product of a "communitas" which "breaks in through the interstices of structure . . . at the edge of structure . . . . and from beneath structure" (Turner, 1969:128). Ordinarily millenarism may claim no more than a latent existence but can manifest itself and even threaten to take over "structure" once the latter reveals its inefficacy and fragility. Open emergence of millenarian movements, then, can be taken as a sign of a critical turning-point in the evolutionary history of a macro sociocultural system. It follows that a millenarian movement interlocks two systems—a macro, sociocultural system, and a micro, individual behavioral system. It does so by sychronizing their respective turning-points—a historical/phylogenetic and a biographical/ontogenetic crisis. Cultural "revitalization" (Wallace, 1956*b*) may result from a millenarian movement at a macro level, while resocialization is a micro-level product. The individual's experience through millenarian resocialization may be considered a miniature mirror of societal turmoil and conflict. Furthermore, a movement as a communitas has its own life history, which is terminated either with death or with institutionalization; it may or may not outlive the individual participating in it. The resocialization process in the movement is subjected to and shaped differently by various "life" stages of the movement itself; the participant must share the "fate" of the movement. This dual interlocking of the individual career with the sociocultural evolution and the movement's life gives a dynamic character and special momentum to millenarian resocialization.[1]

These characteristics of millenarian resocialization in contrast to institutionalized resocialization should be further clarified and confirmed in the following analysis of specific mechanisms. Three mechanisms are differentiated: enlightenment, integration, and commitment. In conclusion, resocialization will be reviewed from the standpoint of adaptation to larger society. Supporting data, which are admittedly sporadic, are drawn from the literature on a number of arbitrarily selected movements, primarily on Cargo Cults in Melanesia, the Ghost Dance among North American Indians, the Handsome Lake religion among Seneca Indians, the Black Muslim movement among American Negroes, and the Jehovah's Witnesses. The scarcity of information on the inner experiences of individual participants in a millenarian movement, which is especially needed for this essay, will be compensated for by a heavy reliance upon my field work on a Japanese millenarian cult, called Tensho-Kotai-Jingu-Kyo (hereafter, Tensho), among Japanese-Americans in Hawaii (Lebra, 1967, 1969–70, 1970, 1972). Space does not permit a systematic empirical elaboration. Reference to specific instances, therefore, will be made only where illustrations are particularly called for.

ENLIGHTENMENT

Enlightenment refers to a drastic, intense form of cognitive reorientation which is often experienced as revelation. The millenarian message "awakens" its susceptible receiver to the ultimate "truth" on a universal scale, and provides him with a supernaturally designed coding system whereby everything he has experienced suddenly begins to make sense and everything he anticipates in the future begins to appear polarized. The "causal" and "teleological" conviction replaces the confusion and meaninglessness to which the susceptible audience is likely to have been subject. Enlightenment reorients one who has been drifting in the state of goallessness toward a fixed, imminent millenarian goal, and renders a breakthrough for one who has been locked up in "relative deprivation" resulting from the perceived blockage of his "legitimate expectations" (Morrison, 1971). The disintegrated "mazeway" becomes resynthesized (Wallace, 1956a). The elements of millenarian enlightenment are discussed below.

Dichotomization and Third Category

The millenarian prophecy eliminates the complexity of daily human experiences by a simple dichotomization of universal phenomena. Everything seen, heard, or otherwise experienced can be placed on a binary map: it belongs either to the "creative" process toward the millenium or to the "destructive" process toward the apocalyptic catastrophe; either to salvation or to damnation; either to God's world or Satan's; the divine benevolence or the evil conspiracy; the righteous or the degenerate; winning or losing.

The human population is dichotomized, generally, between believers and their enemies. This dichotomy is coupled, when the movement involves interracial or intercultural relations, with the dichotomy of "natives" and "aliens," or of "black" and "white." Those cults which sprang up among natives under European colonial domination, such as Cargo Cults or the Ghost Dance, inevitably include racial dichotomies in their messages. The color contrast of black and white stands out even more clearly in the Black Muslim movement.

The present world is understood as the arena where the two worlds are engaging in an escalated war, where the doomed are attempting their last desperate struggle against the inevitable, or where God is punishing disbelievers or sifting his children by giving increasingly severe tests. Once this message is accepted, every experience—whether good or bad, pleasurable or painful, serious or trivial—only confirms the millenarian prediction.

The simple dichotomization of the universe, however, is defied by the complexity of reality binding the movement participants as well as outsiders. The movement faces the need for admitting or creating the third category which either cuts across the original categories or belongs to neither. The third category, thus included, must be linked to the binary map with some consistency.

Even in a distinctly nativistic movement like the Ghost Dance, the native way is not to be revived in its totality, nor is the alien way to be rejected altogether. Selectivity is indicated in the moral code proclaimed by Wovoka, the messiah of the Ghost Dance, forbidding, for example, destruction of properties and body mutilation, which used to be part of tribal mourning customs (Mooney, 1965:24). On the other hand, when the prophecy is consummated with the return of native ancestors and the removal of the whites, it was believed, "the houses, cattle and other valuable property of the whites would remain for the Indians to inherit" (Linton, 1943:467). The acquisition of European goods is the essential component of the Cargo Cult prophecy, and this is combined with the Melanesian nativism by the rationale that these goods originally belonged to the natives and thus are to be brought back by their resurrected ancestors.

The Black Muslim movement presents an intriguing case of such accommodation. Its militancy against the whites rules out even a selective acceptance of the white world, and yet it also despises "so-called Negroes." The solution is sought in the third category, which is neither white nor black—namely, the Islamic, Arabic world. This third world with its own race and culture is claimed to be the original home from which American Negroes came and to which they expect to return. Allah is black, yet, at the same time, the "son of the platinum blonde woman and the jet black man" (Essien-Udom, 1962:126). The category of "blacks" shifts to that of "Asiatics."

Reversal and Reinforcement

Enlightenment further involves the realization that the structure of the existing world will be totally transformed. Transformation often takes the form of a reversal of the existing order. The typical millenarian message has it that those who are deprived now will have a privileged access to God's kingdom; that failure and misfortune in this world will lead one to success and blessing in the coming world. Members of the Establishment, whether a dominant class or race, are handicapped in receiving God's favor and more liable, when the prophecy comes true, to be swept away, drowned, buried, burned, poisoned, or otherwise killed. In the millennium, the hierarchy will be reversed so that, as prophesied in a Cargo Cult in Fiji (Worsley, 1968:20), whites will serve natives, and chiefs will be placed below commoners.

Reversal of the established hierarchy or belief is not only projected into the coming millennium but is applied to the past and present. Black Muslims assert the racial superiority of blacks over whites with the contention that "Black Man" is the "Original Man" and that the white race was "grafted" from the black (Essien-Udom, 1962:131).

Reversal of the established order joins hands with reinforcement of the familiar; resocialization thus involves not only replacement of the old by the new messages but a selective activation of stored memory. This may take the form of atavistic revivalism as shown by leaders of the Black Muslims or of the Jehovah's Witnesses quoting the Old Testament and displaying their version of scholasticism despite their denunciation of the established clergy. Another form of reinforcement refers to acceptance of the existing value hierarchy: cult leaders and members alike tend to take pride in converting "prominent" members of society (see, for example, Lofland, 1966:179; Essien-Udom, 1962:195). The foundress of Tensho would enumerate celebrities of Japan and America as her disciples, and ostensibly indulged a Pitts-burgh "millionaire."

Predestination and Voluntarism

Enlightenment may be triggered by the idea of predestination, the idea that whatever has happened and is going to happen is predeter-mined under a supernatural design. The millenarian prophecy not only declares the predestined future event but offers the chronology of the past and present which has been beyond human control. The founder of Jehovah's Witnesses came up with the "plan of ages" beginning with Adam's fall, passing through the Jewish Age and the Gospel Age, and ending with the Millennial Age. Each age is punc-tuated by specific dates, 1914 being the first year of the millennium (White, 1967:67).

The idea of predestination, while it may strengthen a chiliastic con-viction and thus eliminate the last remnant of doubt, is also likely to provide a consolation for and facilitate resignation to one's misery and misfortune. For the Black Muslims, enslavement of the Negroes by white Americans was predestined under a divine design; Japan's defeat in World War II was planned by God in order to make her the true world leader—the message consoling to those Tensho members who had counted on Japan's victory.

Predestination is counteracted or supplemented by the millenarian emphasis upon voluntaristic human intervention. Human action, such as performing a dance and other prescribed rituals is believed to hasten the arrival of the millennium. Furthermore, whether the gate of God's kingdom is open or closed to one depends partly on one's faith and dedication. Absolute voluntarism is reserved for God him-self: he is free and not bound even by his own plan. This freedom of God to change his mind is used for "dissonance reduction" when prophecy is disconfirmed (Festinger, 1957; Festinger, Riecken, and Schachter, 1964).

This-Worldly Preoccupation and Transcendental Agnosticism

The millenarian message refers to this world and this life, scoffing at otherworldly orientations of established religions. This-earthly preoccupation is significant in focusing one's attention on a specific, sensible referent in space and time, such as the promised land like Mecca or Jerusalem and the calendar of prophecy. Salvation will occur while one is still alive, with one's soul and flesh, and will assure material abundance and bodily well-being, as well as spiritual happiness. The dead will come back to this life. Most importantly, the millenarian message has come from a messiah, prophet, and living god whom one can see and hear and whose ability to communicate with the supernatural has been amply demonstrated.

This kind of "secularism" is balanced by extreme transcendentalism, which inhibits the believer from speculating on God's intention. "Only God knows" what is going to happen, and human claim to knowledge is sacrilege. Such pious agnosticism is also mobilized, when prophecy fails, to induce the disillusioned believers into collective amnesia.

The above analysis of enlightenment has paid attention only to positive conviction and neglected the problem of doubt and skepticism. The believer is not necessarily a total believer, and, in fact, it is often the case that the most committed believer is not free of doubt and ambivalence. Schwartz (n.d.) gives an insightful analysis of this problem with reference to Cargo Cults. Refuting the dissonance-reduction theory, he claims that ambivalence and dissonance are necessary for maintaining a belief, that "suspicion and credulity must be seen as a dynamic unity." Such a "contrapuntal dissonance of dual consciousness," whether or not it should be attributed to the "paranoid ethos" of Melanesia, seems to offer a convincing explanation for the persistent recurrence of Cargo Cults in the face of repeated disconfirmation of prophecy.

INTEGRATION

Whereas enlightenment involves transmission and internalization of the millenarian message, integration refers to the social engagement of the prospective convert with the community of believers. The resocialization process here is viewed from the standpoint of interaction between the socialized-to-be (the inductee) and the socializing agents (the cult members). Enlightenment and integration, although they affect each other, should, I believe, be treated separately. In sociological tradition, primacy is given to the "normative" or "symbolic" component of human action by "action theorists," whereas "interactionists" tend to emphasize the "social" component. This discrepancy alone justifies assuming the mutual independence of enlightenment and integration.[2]

Solidarity

The first to consider is the particular form of solidarity afforded by a communitas, which, in contrast to structure, is undifferentiated (Turner, 1969), The lack of differentiation leads to two bipolar forms of social interaction. First, while members of a structure, because of its differentiation, relate to one another within the limit of role-status occupancy, interaction in a communitas involves the "whole person" of each individual with all his emotions and idiosyncrasies. The millenarian inductee, who happens to be alienated from being a "cog" of a bureaucratic machinery in the larger society, is likely to be impressed by the warmth with which he is treated and accepted by the cult members as no less than a total personality. Extreme intimacy and personal concern is offered especially at the time of proselytizing through face-to-face interaction either in a dyad or in a small "study-group" gathering. The proselytizer can be effectively accommodative to the listener's need since he himself has gone through conversion and thus is equipped with empathy in "taking the role of the other."

The lack of differentiation of a communitas, second, entails that type of solidarity which is based upon submersion of individuals in a collectivity. While the structure requires each individual to retain his separate identity as a role incumbent, the solidarity of a communitas imposes elimination of individual boundary. Millenarian cults are noted for the frequency with which a mass gathering is held, and solidarity is acted out in collective rituals. Individual participants may be overwhelmed by the size and power of the group, aroused to the sense of belongingness, and drowned in the excitement of co-action. Collectivistic solidarity precludes not only individuality, but also sexual intimacy: this was pointed out by Kanter (1968) as "dyadic renunciation," which takes the form of either free love or celibacy. Furthermore, "domestic communism" with communal housing and commensalism may replace family cohabitation (Worsley, 1968:150).

Intimacy, mutual trust, and equality characteristic of cultistic solidarity are symbolized by the use of kinship terms—e.g., brother and sister or of peer terms like "comrades" for referring to fellow members.

Solidarity is not determined by interaction within the millenarian community alone but by its boundary vis-à-vis the outside world. On the one hand, the cult can strengthen its internal solidarity by exhibiting its existence and power to external spectators. On the other hand, solidarity is further intensified by secrecy held by the cult from its enemies or "spies." The latter is interesting in connection with conspicuous secrecy or ritual skepticism attributed to Cargo Cults by

Schwartz. Secrecy is in reaction to the "persecution" which the cult activists have undergone or anticipate. The shared experience—direct
and vicarious—of persecution as well as shared secrecy may be a necessary part of solidarity. This explains, in part, why some cults ritually
expose their members to a humiliating situation, as in the collective
dance imposed on Tensho members in front of curious spectators or
the door-to-door campaign for selling the *Watchtower* messages.

Leadership

The millenarian cult, while its members are equal, is usually headed
by an extraordinary leader who appears as the second Christ, the
messenger of Allah, the vessel of God, and so on. Resocialization of a
convert thus may be carried out under the personal influence of such
a charismatic leader. Charismatic influence may be analyzed in conjunction with the three processes of attitude change suggested by Kelman: compliance, identification, and internalization. Compliance is
motivated by the power of the influencing agent, identification by his
attractiveness, and internalization by his credibility (Kelman, 1958).
The charismatic leader may be said to have a maximal command over
all three: power is derived from his supernatural sponsor, attractiveness attributed to his "magnetic" or parental appearance, and
credibility demonstrated by his performance of miracles. The leader
can thus trigger a cure of an "incurable" illness by touching the afflic-
tion, stop drug addiction overnight simply by a few utterances, and
effect other kinds of behavior change.

Cochrane's (1970) explanation of Cargo Cults with reference to
"big men" is suggestive in the present context. The cargo prophecy
has had a receptive audience, in his view, where natives were deprived
by European contact of the traditional big men whose leadership enabled them to enjoy manhood. Implications are that Cargo Cults are
aimed at the restoration of the traditional relationship between big
men and the rank and file.

If the role of follower and disciple facilitates resocialization, assumption of leadership is as effective, if not more, in self-transformation. Charismatic leadership itself emerges in conjunction with the
identity-crisis and self-transformation on the part of the leader-to-be.
One can save oneself by a successful recruitment of followers.

Leadership is not merely a by-product of a movement, but its acquisition could be the very end of the movement, and starting or joining
a movement could be instrumental to this end. The structural ladder
for attaining a leadership position lacking, the potential leader must
exhibit his ability through performances which are taken by his po-

tential followers as dictated by the supernatural. Among such "supernatural" performances are an extemporaneous speech, telepathic utterances, dancing and singing while appearing to be in a trance, and even convulsive seizures in front of the congregation. The apparently abnormal or sick behavior of spirit possession is not necessarily pathogenic but possibly, as Schwartz (n.d.) puts it, "pathomimetic" of the role of the possessed, so that one can acquire or retrain a leadership position. A remarkable case of such a pathomimetic trance was observed in the flying saucer cult, as reported by Festinger, Riecken, and Schachter (1964:124); at a gathering of believers, a woman, in the voice of the Creator, declared herself as elected to bear the Christ child. "Status inversion" does take place through cult involvement, as when women or adolescents become Cargo Cult leaders (Schwartz, n.d.).

Leadership within a movement further relates to what Turner calls a "pseudo hierarchy"—a symbolic replication of a structure—created in a communitas. As a movement matures, an elaborate system of formal hierarchy becomes developed, although the status tends to be only nominal particularly as long as a charismatic leader controls the whole organization single-handedly. Tensho followers, closely bound by charismatic leadership, recognized a loose hierarchy in accordance with the leader's favor, differentially distributed among them. The favor ranged from personal attention to commendation in public to the privilege of co-eating and, exceptionally, co-sleeping with the leader.[3] For Jehovah's Witnesses, baptism initiates the novice into the status of "full-fledged minister."

The degree of integration can be measured by the frequency, duration, and intensity of interaction within the millenarian community. Another measure is the extent to which a believer is sensitized to sanctions within the cult, whether from a fellow member, a leader, a follower, or from the whole group. The most severe punishment would be excommunication or ostracism. Conformity to cult norms is spurred by the desire to gain approval and to avoid disapproval from other members of the cult. This corresponds with the degree of deafness and blindness to sanctions from outside.

COMMITMENT

Enlightenment and integration are accompanied by commitment for full resocialization. A comprehensive analysis was made of the concept of commitment by Kanter (1968). By commitment, I mean in a much narrower sense, a series of overt actions which are irreversible. This may be said to come closest to Kanter's "continuance" and yet also cuts across the other two types of commitment—cohesion and control. The individual is no longer conceived of as a passive receiver of symbolic messages or social cues, but as an active participant who finds himself bound by the result of his action. The importance of such commitment for change of a behavioral system has been noted by revolutionists subscribing to the synthesis of theory and practice or learning and activity. (For the contrast between "individualist" and "revolutionary" schools on personality change, see Coleman, 1971.)

Commitment will be discussed from two points of view: abandonment and involvement.

Abandonment

Abandonment refers to a combination of disposal, renunciation, or destruction of material possessions with departure from the old social system. The imminence of a millennium demands disinterest in the wealth belonging to the existing world and may even urge the removal or destruction of such material possessions. This is either because the wealth stands in the way of one's salvation or because it appears worthless in comparison with the abundance of the coming millennium. As in some Cargo Cults, certain tools and goods—such as tin matchboxes and pocketknives obtained from white men—were discarded, houses were burned down, pigs were killed, food eaten (Worsley, 1968:52–53); European money was spent or hurled into the sea; an "orgy of consumption" thus prevailed (Worsley, 1968:154–55).

Along with economically valuable properties, symbolic objects are also abandoned. Tensho followers burned, destroyed, or threw away the most sacred symbols of their ancestors and departed kin—namely, the household altars and the ashes and mortuary tablets.

Material abandonment is coupled with social abandonment—that is, departure from the social system where the convert has belonged. The role of wife, relative, friend, neighbor, employee, student, or the like is redefined, neglected, or, if necessary, completely vacated. Such role departure by one member of the system can result in disintegration of the particular social system in question, as when the open rebellion of some Tensho women against their "godless" husbands eventuated in dissolution of families.

Believers are urged to renounce public duties. Jehovah's Witnesses under the leadership of Rutherford "refused to render military service, vote, hold public office, buy government bonds, salute the flag," and withdrew membership in unions, PTAs, social clubs, and lodges (Whalen, 1962:63). Black Muslims are supposed to boycott white-owned shops. Perhaps a more severe role-departure is insisted upon from other religious groups, which often are identified as the worst enemy of God. Collective migration of cult followers, as has happened among the Mormons, represents an extreme case of abandonment.

Millenarian commitment may challenge the mainstay of a given social structure through invalidation of principal norms—e.g., clan exogamy or an exchange system. Brunton (1971) argues that, in those areas of Melanesia where the exchange system had been disrupted under European contact, the promise of cargo could induce the natives to abandon the traditionally sacrosanct system completely. Tensho members were enjoined to discontinue, and thus became liberated from, reciprocal exchange with the "maggot" world.

Involvement

Since the millenarian world is dichotomous, commitment is dual: while abandonment refers to commitment away from the damned sphere, involvement means commitment toward the millennium.

First, material involvement, which may be viewed as investment, should be considered. Preparation for a millennium involves investment with material resources. Churches and temples must be built on purchased lots of land, and, as the movement expands, the administrative headquarters becomes necessary. Cult publications must be financed; full-time personnel must be provided with room and board; expenses for worldwide missionary travels, as well as for mass assemblies, must be funded. Cargo Cult followers, in preparation for the expected arrival of cargo, constructed airfields, wharves, storehouses, customhouses, and so on.

The source of revenue is sought in the pocket of every member. The millenarian cult, instead of imposing fixed membership dues, takes pride in relying upon "voluntary" contributions alone. What happens, in fact, is that one is pressured, either subtly or bluntly, to donate every penny available in order to prove one's faith and devotion. One of the Tensho euphemisms illustrates this point eloquently: a contribution in cash was called *magokoro*, a true heart or sincerity. Besides cash, contributions are made in labor and skill, as in construction of a church building or management of a cult store or school; wealthy members would donate real estate, automobiles, and other expensive commodities needed by the cult organization. These are savings kept at the millenarian bank or investments in the millenarian enterprise which would generate an unprecedented interest or profit.

Such economic investment is coupled with social involvement. Social involvement, first, refers to exposure and display of the convert's new identity in front of other cult members as well as outsiders. Commitment in this sense is made at various stages of entry and postentry. A prospective convert may expose himself by agreeing to buy a cult publication, attending a cult gathering where the public is invited, and disclosing his name and address under the pressure of cult activists. When he goes as far as to show up at a regular cult meeting and finds his presence conspicuous enough to draw the attention of the entire congregation, he will feel his self-exposure irreversible. The eager hosts of the assembly may point him out and persuade him to register as a member at that very time. Meanwhile, all the social support (discussed under integration), which may be irresistible, is lavished upon him. The membership identity, thus acquired, may involve the obligation to display it in public such as wearing a badge or a native costume. The Black Muslim convert erases his slave identity by replacing his old name by the "original" name given by Allah: a new first name and X.

Further exposure and display is made as the convert becomes a regular participant. He will make a testimony or confession which is heard and remembered by the congregation; he may exhibit the behavior which is indicative of membership commitment but looked upon as crazy or indecent by outsiders such as glossolalia (Hine, 1969), twitching, shaking, convulsions, and other forms of motor communication (Talmon, 1962). The outdoor dance of Tensho—which originated the popular name of this cult, the Dancing Religion—exposed the members to the jeering spectators among whom there might happen to be a member's neighbor, friend, or relative. The door-to-door salesmanship of Jehovah's Witnesses offering the publication *Awake* also gives them the opportunity to display membership identity to outsiders.

While display of the new identity vis-à-vis outsiders completes abandonment, display to fellow members binds one to meet their expectations by appearing consistent with the displayed identity. It becomes a matter of losing face not to present oneself as a devoted member. In order to protect his reputation as a trustworthy member, the convert will stay on and continue to display his devotion, thus committing himself even further. This is particularly true when the convert has already taken a proselytizer's role and succeeded in gaining converts; he must live up to the responsibility of a socializing agent and play an exemplary role for his followers. His reputation with the cult community corresponds with the side bets which, according to Becker (1960), explain commitment.

Social involvement through exposure and display is further intensified through accumulation of social debts incurred by receiving favors and benefits from the cult leader or fellow members. Among the received benefits may be a "miraculous" healing, recovery of marital harmony, avoidance of starvation, and so forth. The sense of indebtedness becomes reinforced, exaggerated, and communally registered as the convert acknowledges his gratitude in his testimony at the meeting. Once the leader succeeds in convincing his followers of his omnipotence, he can create debts and credits at will. The leader of Tensho convinced some of her followers that they had been saved from death by following her; many felt they owed their lives to her. Such a sense of debt keeps one committed to the cult chosen, since being a member in good standing is the best way of repaying the debt.

It is clear from the foregoing that commitment is inseparably tied with integration, so that one reinforces the other in a spiral fashion. The same is true with enlightenment, in that, in the course of commitment, the ideational conviction becomes stabilized and strengthened and vice versa. Firth (1956:113) illustrates this point when he says that the work involved in Cargo Cults—constructing the airstrip, wharf, and so on—is "part of the symbolic validation given to the idea that the things wanted are morally justifiable," or "part of an affirmation of native claims, native community solidarity, native values, in the face of what is conceived to be an impassive, unsympathetic or hostile outside world."

ADAPTATION: CONCLUDING STATEMENT

As stated at the outset, the millenarian movement differs from the institutionalized resocializing systems in that it tries to change the behavior of individuals *against* the normative expectations of larger society. The three mechanisms delineated above do operate at the expense of the outside world. Nonetheless, there are indications that the individual often finds himself, through millenarian conversion, better adapted to the larger, secular social environment. In fact, many potential converts are attracted to one movement or another in the hope of improving their life conditions here and now; the movement, for its part, also promises the realization of that hope. This is supported by the emphatically this-worldly orientation of millenarianism. If participation in a millenarian cult indeed facilitates adaptation to larger society, one can conclusively justify viewing millenarian movements as resocialization mechanisms.

Adaptation can be seen from two analytically divided points of view: change in the behavioral system of the individual actor and change in his social environment.

Behavioral Change

Millenarian resocialization compels the actor to internalize a rejuvenated self-image armed with dignity and self-respect and thus to be relieved from the old, miserable, stigma-attached self-identity. Pride is derived from a variety of sources: the conviction of being chosen and destined to enter the millennium, the ability to understand what is going on in this world while most people are lost in the unfathomable complexity and flux thereof, the sense of nearness to the supernatural, being accepted and trusted as a full-fledged member of the cult, and so forth. The reversal of the existing value order as promised in the millenarian message makes the convert proud of being a black, native, Indian, or Japanese American. Self-respect thus aroused goes with contempt, pity, or patronizing condescension toward the presently dominant class or race.

Along with the elevated self-image is self-confidence based on the social technique which has been acquired in the course of intensive face-to-face interaction within the cult community, as well as through proselytizing engagement with outsiders. A bashful, withdrawn novice is forced to talk in front of the congregation and to address a missionary speech to a group of indifferent or hostile strangers, until, to his surprise, he finds himself a skilled, fluent speaker. A mute, docile house-servant may turn into a confident worker who can articulate his rights vis-à-vis his employer. Self-confidence escalates as the proselytizer succeeds in converting his audience, since this is the most unequivocal proof of his social ability to influence people.

Both self-respect and self-confidence are intertwined with the cult-imposed moral discipline which is defined in terms of specific dos and don'ts. The preconversion indulgence and license give way to severe abstinence and self-control. Oral indulgence is to be replaced by vegetarian or other forms of food taboo, sexual promiscuity terminated by strict monogamy and sexual segregation as among Black Muslims, indolence and prodigality converted into diligence and frugality, alcoholic and narcotic addition, as well as criminal proclivity, overcome. Such discipline can result, one may note, in transforming the former deviant into an embodiment of the moral ideal of the dominant culture. Indeed, Malcolm X boasted that even a convict, once converted, would become a model prisoner (Lincoln, 1961:83). It appears as if Black Muslim discipline, whether intentionally or not, aimed at turning Negroes into classic, white American, middle-class puritans. The same point was made by Johnson (1961) with regard to Holiness sects.

Behavioral discipline impinges upon structural change. Sexual discipline for Black Muslims ties in with the desired change of kinship structure from matri- to patrifocality with the emphasis upon the husband's responsibility as protector and provider. A similar change was noted by Wallace (1961) in the Handsome Lake religion, where the sex role was so redefined that the traditional matrilineal structure would be transformed into a nuclear-family structure—a radical step in acculturation toward the white American standard.

Environmental Change

The proud, confident, disciplined convert exerts influence upon his social environment so that the latter begins to change to his advantage and react to him favorably. First, he can impress his family and friends, who know what he was before, with his remarkable change; his reputation for being disciplined and reliable may spread over and beyond the intimate circle. At a certain point, cult membership ceases to be a barrier and becomes a credential to make its holder desirable as an employee or customer—the anti-unionism of the cult certainly contributes to the attractiveness of the member as an employee.

Organized discipline is ostensibly demonstrated in a mass assembly to make an everlastingly favorable impression upon its outside audience. The Yankee Stadium assembly of Jehovah's Witnesses in 1961 was a case in point: "A squad of 6,000 cooks and kitchen helpers prepared meals for as many as 68,000 diners an hour; a cleanup crew of 2,500 picked up every scrap of paper, every apple core, and every candy wrapper at the end of each day's session." Park managers were "frankly amazed" (Whalen, 1962:135).

Further environmental change results from the new network discovered and developed through conversion, which opens the "opportunity structure." A jobless member may find an employer either among fellow members or, through this connection, outside the cult; likewise, a shopkeeper expands his clientele; the unmarried gain an easy access to a prospective spouse; the childless can adopt a member's child, as did some Tensho followers. The network may be widened into the Establishment through the proselytizer's eagerness to have contact with prospective converts.

Finally, as it penetrates the secular social structure, the movement becomes recognizable as a pressure group challenging the central authority and power. The initially religious movement thus may develop into a political movement, while development in a reverse direction is equally possible. A Cargo Cult under secularly minded leadership may become a revolutionary or reformist movement which the administration cannot ignore too long; the Black Muslim movement can and does turn its millenarian dream for a return to the "original" home into a separatist movement which alarms ordinary United States citizens and the authorities. The millenarian cult as a political pressure group can make the environment less resistant and more congenial to its members, since their voice is now heard and heeded.

It is concluded that the millenarian movements can resocialize the individual involved through enlightenment, integration, and commitment, with the result of better adaptation to the larger, secular society.

NOTES

1. These points of contrast hold true only in relative terms. Institutional clients, for instance, may keep coming back as if they could no longer live outside the institutions, whereas millenarian believers may become processed into the outside world, as will be seen at the conclusion of this essay.

2. Further inference along this line can be made from Schein's study of the Chinese brainwashing of American war prisoners. He found two types of reaction to indoctrination—ideological change and collaboration—which do not imply each other (Schein, 1956:164). "It was possible for a man to collaborate with the enemy without altering his beliefs, and it was equally possible for a man to be converted to communism to some degree without collaborating." Likewise, some millenarian converts may be resocialized primarily through social integration, and others more through enlightenment.

3. This should not be taken as implicit of sexual intimacy since the Japanese are accustomed to co-sleeping as a matter of simple, nonsexual togetherness.

Ideology and Role Change: Women and the
Chinese Revolutionary Movement

ROBERT H. LAUER AND KATY CHEN

In Marxist thought, women have been in as degrading a bondage as
men in the capitalist system. And like men, women would only gain
their freedom (and their equality with men) when the capitalist order
was shattered. As Engels (1968:158) put it, women's freedom and
equality are not possible "as long as women are excluded from socially
productive work and restricted to housework, which is private." The
Chinese Communists agreed with this assessment, and sought from
the beginning to change the female role in Chinese society. The constitution adopted in 1949 asserted that the feudal system which had
enslaved women was abolished: "Women shall enjoy equal rights with
men in political, economic, cultural, educational and social life." And
the mass media continue to emphasize the new role of women. In a
comment on International Working Women's Day, the *Peking Review*
pointed out in 1973 that Chinese women are equal with men both politically and economically. Men and women receive the same pay for
equal work. Furthermore, husbands have assumed some household
duties in order to facilitate the process of incorporating women into
the work force. In sum, "equality has brought real democracy, harmony and happiness into the family." [1]

In brief, Chinese Communist literature repeatedly asserts the
equality of women in the sense that women have equal status and may
assume equal responsibilities with men, and receive equal rewards.

This implies that in any context—industrial or political—women should not cluster at the lower levels. In a factory, for example, if 70 percent of the work force is female and only 20 percent of management is female, the situation is not one of equality. Rather, there should normally be roughly equal proportions of the sexes at all levels—or at least a tendency in that direction. This, at any rate, is the view of equality that emerges from the literature.

All of this of course represents a break with traditional Chinese society. For despite the occasional appearance of a woman ruler such as the Empress Dowager in the Ch'ing period, women were not a normal part of Chinese political life. In fact, political activity was neither encouraged nor approved of by the traditional norms for female behavior. There were some efforts to change the female role even prior to the Communist revolution, but it was not until that revolution had succeeded that the changes were declared both appropriate and legal.

By 1955, a few years after the Communist movement had established itself as the legitimate government of China, the female role was defined in terms of building a democratic and harmonious family which would be bound together in productive efforts and social reconstruction. Since the new constitution guaranteed the equality of men and women in political, economic, cultural, social, and family affairs, and since the state was committed to the protection of female rights and the welfare of children, "women no longer need to initiate a militant struggle for such things." [2] Rather, women were to be united with men in a joint effort to build a socialist society.

To what extent has this goal of the equality of women been realized? To what extent has a revolutionary movement succeeded in one of its major goals after it has obtained the power to effect basic changes? In this chapter, we will examine the extent to which the role of women has changed in Chinese society, and the extent to which that change measures up to the ideology of equality. Unfortunately, sufficient data are not available to examine fully the dynamics of status-role change in relation to ideology, but we are able to compare the extent of change with one facet of the ideology—the notion of equality. This provides us with some indication of the impact of the movement upon the female status-role.

As our indicator of change, we will employ the political role of women. For although woman's role has changed in numerous ways in China, the political aspect of that role is crucial; in a society where politics is supreme, political participation is an excellent measure of equality. The Chinese themselves have paid particular attention to the political role of women. In 1955, a newspaper pointed out that women in government was once an unthinkable phenomenon. But

the "Communist Party and the People's Government make special efforts to bring out and develop the talents of women and encourage
them to take part in the government of their country" (Croll,
1974:79). By 1972, it was acknowledged that women had not yet
achieved political equality. Nevertheless, the "Communist Party and
the women's movement have played a mutually supportive role in
creating the foundations of the emancipation of women" (Croll,
1974:103). And in 1973, a newspaper article pointed out that while it
was true what women had not yet entered into the building of a socialist society in sufficient numbers, the revolution had made it "possible
for them to raise their political consciousness, increase their ability
and bring into play their talent and wisdom in concrete struggles, and
exercise the right to run state affairs" (Croll, 1974:106).

In other words, there exists the recognition in China that women
are equal in theory and in law, but not yet in reality because of the
lingering effects of the old social order. Still, the Communist party
has worked to make women equal, and we would expect that it would
take the lead in bringing women into the higher echelons of the state.
If the official statements are correct, we should find the greatest
amount of political participation by women in those areas when the
party has the most control.

ORGANIZATION OF WOMEN

Prior to the Communist revolution, Chinese women engaged in
what were primarily unorganized and sporadic efforts to change the
traditional, oppressive role of women. Moreover, those efforts were
exerted by urban, educated women and not by the working or peasant women. The Western challenge of the late nineteenth century
gave considerable impetus to a shift away from traditional patterns,
however. In the first decades of the twentieth century the traditional
patterns were being swiftly eroded; women and youth gained a
greater voice in the social order, ability became increasingly important, and the rights of the individual began to displace the traditional
loyalty to the family (Townsend, 1968:21).

But it was only after the revolution had succeeded that the efforts
to organize women were "persistent, systematic, and extensive, affecting an increasing proportion of the female population" (Yang,
1959:128). Not only the urban women, but the entire female population was to be organized in order "to help transmit and execute government orders and policies, and to bring women's demands and
opinions to the attention of the government" (Yang, 1959:129).

The fact of this organization and the consequent political participation of women has been repeatedly emphasized in the Communist

press. For example, during the 1950 battle for Hainan Island (in the southern area of Kwangtung Province), women were organized to help the troops which were passing through that country. Food, carrier, and service corps of women were formed for the purpose. In two villages alone, over twenty thousand mosquito nets were laundered for the army and numberless clothes were washed. Women carried rice to troops throughout the night and encouraged their husbands to join the battle.[3]

Other accounts tell of women who helped capture and kill counter-revolutionary bandits,[4] of women who participated in guerrilla activities prior to the success of the revolution, and of women who joined the People's Militia and encouraged their husbands to follow suit.[5] Other examples of women who performed notable deeds are:

Kuo Shu-chen, 64 year old Secretary of the General Communist Party branch of a production brigade, led the other members of her commune in building a model socialist unit. Her revolutionary spirit has been praised by the peasants.[6]

Lung Tung-hua, 41 year old peasant woman, serves as a model of the peasant, keeping in close touch with the masses and serving on the provincial revolutionary committee.[7]

Ahyimuhan is a model woman cadre. She is party branch Secretary of a production brigade and has been praised by the masses as a cadre who zealously defends Mao's revolutionary line.[8]

These examples serve to illustrate the fact that the Chinese press pointedly emphasizes the role of women in the revolution, both in the time prior to the success of the revolution and in the postrevolutionary task of building a socialist nation. It is obvious, then, that the Chinese accept the Marxist notion of equality of the sexes, and are at pains to try to demonstrate that such equality is in the process of realization in the People's Republic.

Nevertheless, the party has recognized that "women are perhaps the only 'underprivileged' group in China" (Townsend, 1968:156). The revolution did not succeed in extirpating all of the traditional notions about the subordinate status of women. Furthermore, the oppression of women in traditional China was greater than that of men. Mao noted that while men had been subject to political, clan, and religious authority, women had been subject to all of these plus the authority of their husbands. Women therefore need not only to be organized; they also need an organization of their own that will press for the full realization of their equality. Consequently, the All-China Federation of Democratic Women serves the dual function of mobilizing women for the task of building a socialist nation and of pressing for full equality for women.

The federation was founded in April 1949, with the explicit purposes of mobilizing women for the increase of production both in industry and in agriculture, and of gaining women's freedom from their pre-Communist oppression. In accord with these aims, the federation has often acted as an auxiliary branch of the government. For example, it aided in the drafting and subsequent administration of the new marriage law.

Membership in the federation was reported at 76 million by 1953, an increase of 46 million from the 1950 figures. The leadership has involved both members and nonmembers of the Communist party. Prominent among nonmembers is Sung Ching-ling, the widow of Sun Yat-sen, who has served as First Honorary Chairman. Ho Hsiang-ning, Second Honorary Chairman, is the widow of a Kuomintang leader. But both of these nonmembers of the party have been noted for supporting leftist causes.

The federation has thus sought to represent all Chinese women, and has striven to gain equality for all women in government and industry. Among its activities in pursuing these aims are: the training of women cadres for the work of the party; the encouragement of female participation in all kinds of production; the establishment of day-care for children so that mothers may work; and the linking of Chinese women with other women of the world in order to support international peace and friendship.

Thus, both the ideology and the organization of the Communist movement in China should facilitate the attainment of equality of the sexes. But to what extent has the role of women changed in actuality? As noted above, political participation is a crucial indicator of equality. In the next section, therefore, we will attempt to show the extent to which women actually participate in the Chinese polity.

WOMEN AND POLITICAL LEADERSHIP

To be truly equal, women must not participate in politics only at the lower levels; they must share equally in political leadership. Moreover, as we noted above, we would expect that women would make some of their greatest gains in the top echelons of the state since the party itself presses for their equality. (One of the consequences of federal commitment to equal rights for blacks in the United States is a high proportion of them working for the federal government.) The question we are raising, therefore, is to what extent do women actually engage in political leadership? We will explore this question along two dimensions—the proportion of women who engage in political leadership, and the influence exercised by those women who are political leaders.

When we turn from the ideology and the statements of the Communist press, we discover immediately that the proportion of women in the political leadership of the nation is quite small. In the great majority of instances, it is men who are elected as ministers, as members of party congresses, as high-ranking civil servants, and as leaders of the various levels of the polity. There are very few women in those units which make political decisions and direct the state. Women normally exert only indirect influence on those units, either through elections or through organized groups such as the federation.

The relatively small proportion of women who are leaders is evident even in those writings which are designed to show the great gains women have made. For example, Teng Ying-ch'ao, the wife of Chou En-lai and the vice-chairman of the federation, made a long report in 1952 detailing the enhanced political role of women (Snow, 1967:64). The proportion of women participating in the people's representative conferences increased from about 10 percent in 1950 to 15 percent in 1951, and in some areas it reached the level of 30 percent. Teng Ying-ch'ao also pointed out that 36 women held leading positions in the Central People's Government, that 4.7 percent of the members of provincial and municipal people's government councils were women, and that 16 percent of the members of the municipal district government councils of Peking were women.

These proportions undoubtedly represent considerable change from the traditional pattern, but they also clearly represent considerable inequality between the sexes. Moreover, more recent reports continue to indicate much inequality. In their study of a Chinese village, Myrdal and Kessle (1970:134) note the discussion that led to women gaining political rights. The women quoted Mao to back up their claim for participating equally in political work, and the brigade finally decided that when women attend political meetings their husbands should stay home and care for the children. Nevertheless, political participation is not necessarily political leadership, and the authors note that only three of the eleven members of the Revolutionary Committee are women. This again represents a gain from the situation of 1962, when there was one woman member among the twelve-person brigade management committee; still, three out of eleven is not equality.

Even in the Communist press itself, the articles of praise contain the evidence of considerable inequality. An article in the *Peking Review* on March 9, 1973, contrasted the oppressive state of women in prerevolutionary China with the present status of equality. Nevertheless, the article also stated that, in the 37 textile mills in Peking, women comprise 70 percent of the workers and staff and 37 percent of "all responsible positions from section leaders, technicians and cadres on up to the mill level." [9] Equality in this case would demand somewhere around 70 percent of the responsible positions to be held by women.

There are, of course, exceptions to this general situation of inequality. And the party recognizes at times the inequalities and the difficulties of changing the traditional ideas about women. For example, when certain villagers resisted the idea of a woman being trained as a cadre, the party branch began a campaign to teach equality between the sexes and organized a public discussion of the question of female political participation. [10] That such stories appear in the Communist press along with flat statements about the equality of men and women is evidence that there is awareness about the persisting problem of the female role.

Thus far we have offered scattered pieces of evidence that the political role of women is considerably better than in traditional China but considerably short of equality with men. We will now offer more systematic evidence in the form of an examination of the composition of important political units, namely, the proportion of women in political assemblies, the government, and the higher civil service. Specifically, we will look at female participation in the Central Committee of the Chinese Communist party and in the central government.

In order to show the significance of female participation in the Central Committee and the central government, we will briefly review certain aspects of the structure of the Communist party. [11] The Central Committee of the Chinese Communist party is elected by the National Party Congress, which is the highest though not the most powerful organ of the party. The party constitution of 1956 specified a five year term and annual sessions for the congresses, but only nine congresses have been held from 1921 to the present. In some ways the congress serves purposes which are similar to a political convention in the United States: party members are infused with enthusiasm and make contact with leaders, but policy declarations at the congresses have normally been decided beforehand. The congress, therefore, usually formalizes decisions and generates commitment towards the support and implementation of those decisions.

The Central Committee has a number of important functions. It convenes the congress, generally directs the work of the party, elects important organs and officials such as the Politburo (the policy-making body), maintains control over the army, and ratifies and implements policy which has been established by the Politburo. Since the Central Committee is elected by the congress, there have been nine Central Committees, and they have varied considerably in size in terms of the number of both full and alternate members. The latter attend the sessions, have the right to speak at the sessions, and fill vacancies. But only full members have the right to vote.

With respect to the central government, the legislative function is vested in the National People's Congress. But the congress is too large and meets too little to be other than a formalizing unit for decisions made elsewhere. Along with its Standing Committee, the National People's Congress has generally approved policies which have been set by the Communist party. More important in terms of power is the State Council, which is a kind of cabinet headed by Premier Chou En-lai. Included in the council are the heads of thirty ministries and five commissions. The council has been described as "the leading executive agency of the government, responsible primarily for economic management through its command of the various ministries and commissions under it" (Waller, 1970:97).

Let us now examine the participation of women in these high-level party and governmental units. First, the number of women in the nine central committees of the Chinese Communist party are as follows: [12]

(1)　First Central Committee
　　　　　　　Members:　140　　　Female:　7
(2)　Second Central Committee
　　　　　　　Not available
(3)　Third Central Committee
　　　　　　　Members:　144　　　Female:　8
　　　　　　　Alternates:　36　　　Female:　5
(4)　Fourth Central Committee
　　　　　　　Members:　118　　　Female:　3
　　　　　　　Alternates:　42　　　Female:　2
(5)　Fifth Central Committee
　　　　　　　Members:　73　　　　Female:　5
　　　　　　　Alternates:　29　　　Female:　1
(6)　Sixth Central Committee
　　　　　　　Members:　34　　　　Female:　Not available
(7)　Seventh Central Committee
　　　　　　　Members:　44　　　　Female:　1
　　　　　　　Alternates:　17　　　Female:　1
(8)　Eighth Central Committee
　　　　　　　Members:　88　　　　Female:　4
　　　　　　　Alternates　89　　　　Female:　4
(9)　Ninth Central Committee
　　　　　　　Members:　170　　　Female:　13
　　　　　　　Alternates:　109　　Female:　10

From the First Central Committee, with its 5 percent female representation, to the Ninth Central Committee, with its 7.7 percent repre-

sentation (or 8.25 percent if we include both full members and alternates), the representation of women in this important party organ has
been minimal. Furthermore, of the women in the Ninth Central Committee, five were wives of important political figures, including the
wives of Mao, Lin Piao, and Chou En-lai. Obviously, the Communist
movement's goal of equality of the sexes has not been achieved in the
membership of the Central Committee.

With respect to the central government, the 1966 *Directory of Chinese
Communist Officials* gives female names for the following positions
among others: [13]

(1) Vice-Chairman of the People's Republic;
(2) State Council: Deputy Secretary General, Deputy Director of
    the Premier's Secretariat, and Agriculture and Forestry Staff
    Office Deputy Director;
(3) Ministries of the State Council: Vice-Minister of Commerce,
    Vice-Minister of Finance, and twelve other posts of varying
    kinds;
(4) Commissions of the State Council: Deputy Director of the Sec-
    ond Department (Afro-Asia) and Deputy Director of the Pro-
    paganda Department of the Commission for Cultural Relations
    with Foreign Countries;
(5) Special Agencies of the State Council: None;
(6) Supreme People's Court: President of the Higher People's
    Courts in two provinces.

In other words, there are 22 women who hold positions. It may be
noted that none of these are among the highest positions, and that the
22 women represent only 1.9 percent of the total number of officials
listed. A number of women also hold positions in various provincial,
autonomous region, and municipal governments. But again the
number is small, and the positions are associate or less (e.g., deputy
director rather than director, vice-chairman rather than chairman,
and so forth) for the most part. Finally, of the 591 individuals serving
in the diplomatic and consular corps in 48 foreign countries, none are
women.

It is true, of course, that women did hold political office at high
levels in the Kuomintang structure as well as the Communist government. Yang (1959:130) points out that such women were exceptions
and argues: "That common women such as laborers and peasants
now hold responsible positions as a regular part of the political system
is striking evidence of the new situation brought about by the changed
social status of women under Communist rule." We would not quarrel

with the statement, but would point out that the actual number of women is still quite small, particularly if the goal is equality. Furthermore, the positions held by the women are normally not the highest in any particular political unit, whether that unit be a province or a ministry of the central government. And finally, as Yang himself recognizes, the reason that "common women" are holding positions is because social class origin is used to determine qualifications for political office; women from the landlord or rich peasant strata of Chinese society are normally excluded from political positions.

Where women do not have the appropriate social class background for high political office, their presence in that office usually entails extenuating circumstances. For example, the Vice-Chairman of the People's Republic, Madame Sung Ching-ling, is wealthy and a member of a family that helped finance the emerging Kuomintang. But she has supported leftist causes, and, more importantly, is the widow of Sun Yat-sen. She thereby has symbolic significance for the Communist movement, giving it continuity with Chinese tradition.

William Goode (1963:304) is correct in his general assessment of the role of Chinese women in the Communist nation: "Without any doubt, Chinese women have been given far more opportunity than ever in this history of their country to obtain political power, economic advantages, and educational growth." We have not examined areas other than the political in this chapter, but it is not difficult to find data that tend to support Goode's statement. Goode himself, for example, points out that by 1958 women comprised 20 percent of the students in institutions of higher learning and 42 percent of the students in higher medical and health schools. Indeed, the Communists began an immediate and intensive adult education program when they assumed power. More than two-thirds of the population between the ages of fourteen and forty are now able to read and write.

Lo Yu, a Chinese educator, has publicly decried the discrimination against women which has characterized higher education. Women, he argued, are half of the population "and form a great force in the socialist revolution and socialist construction," so that particular attention must be paid to "selecting girl candidates who are qualified for study in university."[14] Nevertheless, among the twenty-eight hundred freshmen enrolled in Ching-Hua University in Peking in 1970, 20 percent were women.[15] As in the political arena, woman's status is far short of equality.

In sum, there is little doubt that the ideological directives of the Communist Chinese with respect to the role of women have resulted in significant changes. Women have made gains in every area of their existence. They no longer need to live under the subjugation of husbands, parents, and parents-in-law. They have been freed from old discriminatory and restrictive practices so that they may fully share the responsibilities of the citizenry of the new state. Old customs based on differentiation between the sexes are now attacked as feudalistic. The division of labor based on sex, which confined women to working inside the home, has been discarded. Indeed, a premium is placed upon the training of a generation of assertive, independent-minded, achievement-oriented women.

Nevertheless, in the crucial area of political participation, the number of women is small. Moreover, the part played by those who are political leaders tends to be of a particular kind, namely, to lead in those areas traditionally defined as the concern of women. Thus, the women who hold administrative positions in government tend to concentrate on such matters as health, education, motherhood, family welfare, and housing. Furthermore, females tend to fill in the associate or deputy positions rather than the head positions.

Twenty-five years after the revolutionary movement had succeeded in acquiring power, therefore, the nation still struggled with the ideological directives and the traditional ways. Undoubtedly, the Chinese woman has risen greatly in her status. But the official claims are somewhat misleading:

Hundreds of thousands of outstanding working women in China today hold positions of leadership from the grass-roots level right up to the central authorities of the Communist Party and the state. . . . The tens of thousands of working women holding important leading posts and running state affairs prove most convincingly the steady rise in women's political status and testify to the superiority of China's socialist system.[16]

As our data have shown, Chinese women are still far short of the position in society called for by the ideology of the movement. We must wait to see whether the present situation is merely one of tokenism (as one might conclude in view of the subordinate positions held by women in the polity); one in which women have reached the apex of their status (in which case the ideology might be modified to fit the realities of the situation); or one which is transitional towards actual equality between the sexes (in which case we will see increasing numbers of women in higher and higher positions). A skeptical Westerner might conclude that after twenty-five years we could only have a case either of tokenism or of women at the apex of their status. But that would be to ignore the typical Chinese approach to the temporal process: "diplomacy, compromise, or just waiting for an opportunity—a half a century to wait is not too long according to Chinese concepts of time" (Callis, 1959:37).

NOTES

1. *Peking Review,* March 9, 1973, p. 15.
2. "How Should Family Women Better Serve Socialist Reconstruction," *Women of China* 10 (October 1955): 18–23.
3. *Nan-Fang Daily* (Canton), April 14, 1950, p.2.
4. *Shing-Tao Daily,* March 8, 1951, p. 2.
5. All-China Federation of Women, *The Stories of Brave and Model Women,* trans. Katy Chen (Canton, 1950).
6. Shu-Chen Kuo, "Fine Women Communist Party Member in Northeast China," *New China News Agency* (Chang chun), March 6, 1971.
7. "Chinese Model Peasant Women Maintains Close Ties with Masses," *New China News Agency* (Hofei), March 13, 1971.
8. "Woman Cadre of Vighur Nationality Firmly Defends Chairman Mao's Revolutionary Line," *New China News Agency* (Vrumchi), March 9, 1971.
9. *Peking Review,* March 9, 1973, p. 12.
10. Ibid., March 30, 1973, p. 17.
11. This review follows D. J. Waller, *The Government and Politics of Communist China* (London: Hutchinson University Library, 1970), pp. 50 ff., 95 ff.
12. The data concerning the first through the eighth Central Committee are taken from United States Government Committee on Intelligence Research Aid, *Directory of Chinese Communist Officials* (Washington, D.C.: Government Printing Office, 1966). Data for the ninth Central Committee are taken from *Peking Review,* April 30, 1969, pp. 47–48.
13. The data are taken from the *Directory of Chinese Communist Officials,* pp. 111–74.
14. Yu Lo, "Pay Attention to Selecting Girl Students," *Current Background,* trans. United States Consulate, Hong Kong, December 30, 1970.
15. Ping-Chung Lee, "Editorial on Culture and Education in Mainland China," *Mainland China Studies* (Taipei, Taiwan: Institute of Mainland China Affairs, April 1971), pp. 27–28.
16. *Peking Review,* July 4, 1975, pp. 16–17.

Public Accommodations: Social Movements in Conflict

EDGAR CHASTEEN

Why did sociologists not anticipate the civil rights movement? Because they were tied to an analysis of collective behavior which emphasized life cycles, typologies, and natural histories—in short, to a static and universal series of stages. This system of analysis had effectively excluded the unexpected; it was a philosophy of evolution, not a sociology of revolution.

The study herein reported was concerned with the analysis of a social movement designed to achieve for Negroes equality of access to public accommodations in a large midwestern city. The intent was not to do a natural history analysis, as it was the author's belief that this approach was not the most fruitful one available. Thirty years' experience with natural historical analysis of social phenomena has demonstrated the difficulty of distinguishing stages and cycles. There is an ever present temptation to force data into preconceived and inflexible categories. Only the reputation of natural historians is enhanced by such a pursuit, and that only until their successors discover the relative debility of their method and the sterility of their conclusions.

Nor was the present study approached typologically. The ancient sage who held that there was nothing new under the sun had not

Reprinted by permission of the publisher from *Phylon: The Atlanta University Review of Race and Culture* 30, No. 3 (Fall 1969), copyright, 1969, by Atlanta University.

foreseen the fertile imagination of twentieth-century social scientists as it was to burst forth in novel semantic variations and syntactic combinations, i.e., typologies. The typological tradition is hoary and was a powerful tool in the writings of scholars such as Weber, Durkheim, Tonnies, Cooley, and Riesman.[1] But the methodology has become today more used than useful. Fresh approaches to the study of society are needed.

The comparative method did not seem in order here either. It would have been easy enough to compare the public accommodations movement with other similar episodes of collective behavior. Such an analysis is always an implicit part of sociological reporting, and the literature has been enriched by it. It seems to the author, however, that morphologically the study of society as practiced by sociologists leaves much to be desired. Social scientists were caught by surprise by the Negro movement following World War II. They are trying now to explain *post factum* what they could not predict. Until such times as they are certain what makes society "hang together," they are in a poor position to compare appendages of the social organism. They will establish a basis for comparison only when they have examined thoroughly and explicated each part of the whole. Only then will comparative study become classificatory rather than exploratory.

The approach to the study of a particular movement made use of in this study might be thought of as cross-sectional. The study is concerned with the effect on the public accommodations movement of an anti–public accommodations movement which developed at the time when the former seemed finally to have accomplished its objective.

Most studies of social movements have sought either to isolate and describe stages, cycles, and/or mechanisms, or to construct typologies. Very little attention has been given to the life history of a social movement as related to the nature of its opposition. Variables such as leadership, tactics, strategy, and membership have been viewed as concomitant characteristics of stages rather than as responses to changes in the nature of the opposition. This view of movements as following cycles rather than responding to challenges is an implicit contradiction of the common agreement that collective behavior is improvised rather than customary, noninstitutional rather than institutional. If social movements are characterized by a flexibility which enables them to reconnoiter, regroup, and reorient in response to sudden changes in the opposition, then to think only in terms of evolutionary processes is to miss the mark.

What happens to a social movement which suddenly finds itself confronted with another movement espousing contradictory values and objectives? How does the first respond to the second? What changes in organization, ideology, and strategy occur? Do the former leaders continue to function under the new conditions? What is the effect on the recruitment of new members? What changes occur in the public definition and image of the older movement?

These and related questions are not best answered through recourse to the evolutionary hypothesis. On the contrary, it seems to this writer that conflict theory affords a more powerful analytic model.

Drawing upon the knowledge of the effects of conflict upon group structure, one may predict certain changes in the organization of the public accommodations movement. Coser says that "conflict with another group leads to the mobilization of the energies of group members and hence, to increased cohesion of the group" (1956:95). One may hypothesize, therefore, that the appearance of an anti–public accommodations movement will unify the already existing public accommodations movement. One would expect the greater cohesion to be of two types: 1) the pro–public accommodations factions will seek a means by which their differences may be reconciled or overlooked and 2) individuals and groups which have been latent or passive supporters of the movement will be pressed into more active roles, and those who have maintained neutral roles prior to the challenge of the anti-movement will be forced to take sides.

A consequence of the change in the structure of the group will be a change in leadership. As factions are reconciled, new groups and individuals are incorporated into the movement and the character of the struggle is modified, old tactics must be traded for new. As the history of revolutionary and reform movements indicates so clearly, the leaders are usually so married to the definition of the situation as it existed at the time of their initial involvement that they are incapable of adjustment to the new conditions.[2]

One is led then to a second hypothesis: The challenge of the anti–public accommodations movement will result in new leadership for the public accommodations movement. Concomitant with the change in leadership will be a change in organizational tactics. Indeed, it is almost redundant to speak of leadership and tactics, for the two are but sides of the same coin.

No prediction may be made as to the tactics which will be adopted by the movement without a knowledge of those of the opposition. In this particular case, the anti–public accommodations forces called for a decision by the electorate of the city.

The public accommodations movement had succeeded, after years of effort, in getting a public accommodations ordinance passed by the City Council. The ordinance which was passed in the fall of 1963 was actually the second such legislation enacted by the city. The first one had been made law three years earlier, but it was restrictive in scope. The 1963 ordinance simply extended the coverage of the first.[3]

The realization of their objective would undoubtedly have resulted in the disbanding of the movement, or its redirection, except for the emergence of an anti–public accommodations movement on the heels of the second ordinance. The objective of the anti-group was the repeal of the ordinance. Toward this end, this group sought to pressure the City Council into rescinding its action. The council refused but was forced to submit the ordinance to city-wide referendum. Thus the public accommodations proponents found themselves faced with one additional task. Failure here would mean that their years of hard work had been an exercise in futility.

Certain predictions about the tactics of the public accommodations movement may be made in the light of this particular challenge. Success or failure will in this case hinge on the ability of the movement to persuade the public of the superior merit of its position. Prior to this time the movement had concentrated on individual appeal to city officials and owners of public facilities. Now it must find ways of inducing thousands of people to vote its way. And it must see to it that they vote.

Certainly mass propaganda will be a necessary tactic. Such propaganda will be aimed at the uncommitted white public and the heretofore apathetic Negro public. In content it will seek to convince its audience that the ordinance is in keeping with the values of democracy, and it will picture the opposition as alien to those values.

The public accommodations movement will be forced to enlist the support of the Negro community to a greater extent than formerly; now, pressure brought to bear by a relatively small number of Negro leaders will not suffice. Grass roots support is mandatory. It will not matter how legitimate the claim or how eloquent the speeches if the ballot box is found lacking.

Is it possible to predict the outcome of this conflict? As would be expected, both sides were claiming victory prior to the vote. It might be predicted that the direction of the vote will depend upon the behavior of the power structure, the demographic characteristics of the city, the percentage of registrants voting, the relative effectiveness of the contending organizations, and so forth. As it turned out, the ordinance was upheld, but by a very small majority. It is interesting, and fruitful, to speculate as to why the vote developed as it did.

On the one hand, there was the public accommodations movement. Its history in Kansas City dates back to World War II. It had successfully met several tests of strength. Yet when challenged by a hastily constructed opposition movement composed of a lower-middle-class business organization and an ultra-right-wing political group with Birch Society, ties, the public accommodations movement came within an eyelash of losing the day. Why?

This study is designed as a before-and-after comparison of a social movement. What was the movement like before an opposition movement appeared? What was it like afterward? The study also seeks to understand the reasons for the resolution of the conflict.

An intensive review of the historical materials of the public accommodations movement is the basis of the study. These include: 1) published accounts of the activities of the movement since its origin a quarter of a century ago; 2) partisan and antagonistic writings on the subject,[4] 3) organizational and public records; and 4) interpretative documents. A series of twenty-five unstructured interviews was conducted so as to fill in some of the data gaps characteristic of written documents and to provide a check on their reliability. Respondents were persons whose activities in the public accommodations conflict had been documented previously by the author from his study of the history of the movement.

A second method utilized in order to get at the meaning of the vote on public accommodations was an analysis of voting statistics in terms of demographic characteristics and political divisions within the city. The first step consisted of the construction of a map correlating census tracts and political wards. This was done in an effort to relate the vote as reported by the Board of Election Commissioners to such characteristics as race, income, education, occupation, and housing as reported by the Bureau of the Census (Chasteen, 1968).

From the local rebirth of the National Association for the Advancement of Colored People in 1939 to the strident demonstrations of the Congress of Racial Equality in the early sixties, the public accommodations movement in Kansas City was made up of a potpourri of diverse and sometimes conflicting organizations. It was not until 1958 that the newly created Community Council for Social Action focused the movement on securing a city ordinance forbidding discrimination in public accommodations.

It was only a little more than a year after the focusing occurred that the first public accommodations ordinance was introduced and passed by the City Council. Earlier efforts to secure enactment of such legislation had been made off and on since 1945,[5] with the first really serious effort coming in 1956. In 1955 the first Negro candidate had been elected to public office after having been endorsed and actively supported by the mayor elected at the same time. The Negro, an attorney and president of the local NAACP, became the first of his race to become a municipal judge in Kansas City history.

The mayor elected in 1955 was viewed by Negro leaders as a supporter of rights for Negroes who sought, with help from selected Negro leaders, to pressure the City Council into adopting a public accommodations ordinance.[6] He was unsuccessful.

In the municipal elections in 1959, a new political party came to power, and a public accommodations ordinance was introduced immediately. After much debate, a compromise version was substituted for the originally comprehensive ordinance, and it was passed by the council on January 15, 1960, by a vote of six to two.

The ordinance forbade discrimination in hotels, motels, and restaurants. Most hotels and motels had desegregated prior to the passage of the ordinance in response to pressure and the fear of pressure from Negro organizations. The ordinance was challenged immediately in the courts by the Restaurant Association of Kansas City,[7] and the Jackson County Circuit Court declared the ordinance unconstitutional. It was more than two years later (April 9, 1962) that the Missouri Supreme Court, acting upon an appeal of the lower court decision by the city and the NAACP, by a vote of four to three, held it to be a legal exercise of the police powers of the city. The ordinance was now law.

In August of 1963 a new public accommodations ordinance, authored by the NAACP legislative chairman, was introduced in the council by one of its newly elected Negro members. After a month's consideration and debate, an ordinance outlawing segregation in places advertising themselves as open to the public was passed. Specifically excluded from coverage were barber shops,[8] beauty parlors, and rooming houses.

At this point the public accommodations movement had accomplished its purpose. It is probable that a future attempt would be made to strike the exclusions, but for the most part public accommodations were now legally accessible. But an event was about to occur which would transform both the character and the activities of the movement and return it to action.

Prior to the passage of the 1963 accommodations ordinance by the City Council of Kansas City, the public accommodations movement had been reacting to a social condition—the existence of discrimination. This condition had taken on a multiplicity of forms and had worked its way into the very fiber of city life. The processes by which such a condition is opposed are necessarily many and varied, thus accounting for the divergent strategies and tactics characteristic of the movement's pre-crisis history.

Upon passage of the ordinance declaring that condition illegal, the movement found itself momentarily without a goal. Falling back upon the knowledge of the life histories of successful organizations, one may feel confident in predicting that a new goal would have been fashioned. For successful organizations never die; they simply take on new functions.

The immediately adverse reaction of a segment of the white community to the new ordinance made it unnecessary for the movement to seek a new opponent. For the ordinance served as the key to Pandora's box which, when unlocked, spilled forth the orthodox anti-Negro racial, political, and economic doctrines authored by a temporary and uneasy coalition of right-wing conversatism, reactionary Protestantism and extreme laissez-faire capitalism. The attention and energies of the city administration, the Kansas City "better human relations community," [9] the public accommodations forces, and the rapidly developing anti–public accommodations movement were thereby riveted upon the question of legal access by Negroes to public facilities. Thus began an eight-months'-long struggle between the opponents and proponents of public accommodations legislation.

The public accommodations movement, which all its life had fought a condition, now found itself locked in a struggle with an opponent. A condition is relatively passive and susceptible of manipulation. The initiative, therefore, resided with the movement. Being continually on the offensive affords tremendous tactical advantage, for it makes it possible to pick and choose from among several possible courses of action that one which seems best fitted for the occasion. The public accommodations movement lost that initiative with the appearance in 1963 of the anti-movement. Because the challenge issued by the opposition was specific, it in effect dictated the response of the pro–public accommodations forces. Unlike the opponents of the earlier ordinance, the new opposition did not play to the strength of the Negroes by choosing to make a court test of it. Rather, it chose to hit the Negroes at their historically most vulnerable spot—the ballot box.

Before examining the various maneuvers of the conflicting parties in this struggle, it is necessary to go back in time to the early stages of the public accommodations movement to look at its opposition. Obviously opposition to use of public facilities by Negroes was not confined to the 1963 ordinance. Had it not been for existing and continuing opposition, such an ordinance would have been superfluous. It was not the existence of opposition but its form which distinguished 1963 from any earlier year.

Prior to the passage of the first public accommodations ordinance in 1960, the city itself had led the fight for continued public segregation. The subject of an ordinance had been broached first by the NAACP in the late forties. The city administration responded that any public accommodations ordinance would be unconstitutional.

Shortly afterward the NAACP attempted to introduce an ordinance by petition and failed.[10]

In the mid-fifties the local NAACP undertook to research the legality of public accommodations legislation. Based upon its findings, the NAACP again asked the city to rule on the constitutionality of the proposed ordinance. Again the city's opinion was negative, despite the fact that the United States Supreme Court had already issued its 1954 school desegregation decision.

City opinion regarding the legality of public accommodations did not change until political exigencies in 1959 necessitated support by Negroes of the Democratic Coalition which was seeking to break the nineteen-year monopoly of city control exercised by the Citizens Association.[11]

This support was obtained by the victorious Democratic Coalition through three principal means. 1) There is in Kansas City a procedure, a legacy of the fear of partisan politics generated by the Pendergast machine, for cross-endorsement of a candidate by opposing political parties. Since the Citizens Association's incumbent mayor was popular in the Negro community, the Coalition chose to cross-endorse him rather than run against him.[12] 2) The first Negro had been elected to city office—municipal judge—in 1955 as an association candidate. This man, an attorney and local NAACP president, was also cross-endorsed. 3) The coalition entered into a gentlemen's agreement with Negro leadership prior to the election that if their slate of city council candidates was elected, a public accommodations ordinance could be expected posthaste.

Sufficient support was rallied for coalition candidates to be elected. A public accommodations ordinance was quickly introduced and, after several weeks of debate, it became law.[13] Negroes in Kansas City had come a long way since their naïve nonpartisan committee efforts of the early forties. And at last they had a trophy to exhibit.

That Negro leadership had learned its lesson well is attested to by the establishment in 1960 of the first political organization led by Negroes, the election in 1963 of two Negroes to the city council for the first time in history, and the passage in the same year of a more inclusive public accommodations ordinance. The Negro community was now conscious of the potential political power which its growing size made possible. It was soon to give a display of that power in response to the new ordinance opposition.[14]

The opposition to public accommodations legislation from 1940 to 1959 may be characterized as legalistic and exercised primarily by local governmental functionaries. The city administration made no attempt to rally public opinion for its position, and the average citizen of both races remained virtually oblivious to the struggle being conducted in the courts.

By choosing to engage in legal skirmishes, the city played into the hands of the public accommodations advocates. For the NAACP was geared for such a struggle. Thirty years' experience and the availability of excellent and dedicated legal talent gave the organization a decided advantage. The city also failed to recognize the meaning of the increasing percentage of the population which was Negro and the inevitable effect of it upon the balance of political power. And as political power shifts its locus, legal opinions are modified. The American tradition which sees democracy as a system of unchanging laws rather than a fluid state of compromise dependent on political considerations is a dangerous facade to maintain.[15] The city administration apparently mistook the facade for fact and adopted a tactic with which it could not sustain itself.

The opposition party which succeeded to power in 1959 reversed the city's position and assumed the constitutionality of the proposed ordinance. After passage of the 1960 ordinance, this constitutional attack was resumed by the Restaurant Association of Kansas City; but the restauranteurs' position was denied in 1962 by the Missouri Supreme Court. Thus the question of the constitutionality of such legislation was finally decided in favor of the Negro community.

When the public accommodations ordinance of 1963 was passed, a new counterattack was necessary if its foes were to contest it. The rationale for the eventual attack was laid even before passage of the ordinance. A local amusement park owner sought to cast the issue as one of property rights and to brand civil rights agitators as communists: "I've always had the privilege to discriminate," Mr. —— said. "Discrimination is a good word that's been kicked about by the Commies." [16]

The man who was later to become president of the most active anti–public accommodations organization attempted to state the question as one of the rights of whites versus those of Negroes. He decried the idea that "freedom of choice of the Negro must be sacrosanct over and above the freedom of choice of the white man." [17] On another occasion this person said the "ordinance was definitely in harmony with the furtherance of the Communist program to destroy the system of free enterprise." [18] The economic soundness of the proposed ordinance also was questioned.[19]

The anti-movement was a diverse collection of organizations with different philosophical rationales and operating procedures. Each opposed the public accommodations ordinance for its own reasons yet found itself forced into an alliance it could not live with easily but could not live without at all.

Of the four organizations active in the anti-movement, two were in existence and serving different functions prior to passage of the ordinance. The other two were created especially to oppose the ordinance. Of the four, two remained active in the Negro-white controversy after the referendum. The Tavern Owners withdrew from the movement and the Citizens Committee Against the Public Accommodations Ordinance ceased to exist; the leadership was absorbed by the Association for Freedom of Choice and the membership was disbanded. The association continued its opposition to all things favorable to Negroes. The Southeast Homeowners' Association, having failed in its efforts to maintain a segregated community or to append open housing legislation to the public accommodations ordinance, turned its attention to efforts designed to create a stable interracial community.

The anti-movement leadership was drawn from business and professions primarily. The business people were owners and/or operators of small establishments catering to a lower-class and lower-middle-class clientele which came under the terms of the ordinance. The professionals were lawyers and ministers. Only one person involved in the anti leadership could in any way be construed as a member of the city power structure. This one was the city councilwoman from the southeast section of the city and active in the Southeast Homeowners' Association.

The membership of the anti-movement was composed of working-class and middle-class individuals with three of the component organizations of the former type. The tavern owners who were active in the anti-movement were primarily those who owned taverns in the inner city, a number of which bordered on the Negro community. The patrons of these taverns were drawn almost exclusively from the working class. The Association for Freedom of Choice was composed largely of owners and operators of seasonal businesses which were recreational in nature. Citizens Committee Against was organized by a small Protestant church having working-class (nonprofessional, non-owners) members and a few lawyers and ministers. Only the membership of the Southeast Homeowners' Association approached that level of pecuniary sophistication, civic involvement, and democratic orthodoxy which social statisticians envision when they talk in terms of the average American.

The anti-movement did not seek the support of the established institutions of the city and it was not offered. With the exception of one of two mutant churches, the anti-movement was openly opposed by most of the economic, civic, and religious powers and institutions of the community.

With the exception of the activities of the anti-forces associated with the petition for referendum, there was little effort made to involve the public. All the reources of the anti-movement were concentrated in the propaganda campaign to influence a negative vote, but little energy was expended in registering voters.[20]

The anti-movement's public image also was poor because of the prominent part played by the Tavern Owners and the vicious racism of the Association for Freedom of Choice.

Because of the poorly organized state of the anti-movement and its even worse public image, the leadership of the pro-movement predicted a decisive victory for their forces. This feeling of confidence did not lull them, however, into a false sense of security.[21]

Earlier it was predicted that the internal organization of the public accommodations movement would undergo change as a result of the appearance of the opposition. From the prediction the following hypotheses were drawn.

1) The appearance of the anti-movement will unify the public accommodations movement, the unification to take two forms. a) The pro–public accommodations factions will seek a means by which their differences may be reconciled or overlooked. b) Individuals and groups who have been latent or passive supporters of the movement will be pressed into more active roles, and those who have maintained a neutral role prior to the challenge will be forced to take sides. 2) The challenge of the anti-movement will result in new leadership and organizational tactics for the public accommodations movement.

The following description of the post-crisis history of the public accommodations movement was intended as a qualitative test of the validity of the above hypotheses.

Three new organizations emerged some months before the referendum to champion the ordinance. The most publicized and best rewarded was known as People FOR Public Accommodations. Also active in the pro–public accommodations camp were two other organizations—Operation Public Accommodations and Operation Freedom.

Charles Evers, NAACP field secretary for Mississippi, was asked a few years ago on a nationwide radio network to name those who had done most for civil rights in the South. Without hesitation or sarcasm he named the mayor and police chief of Birmingham, Alabama, who had ordered the use of police dogs and tear gas to disperse civil rights demonstrators. Following the same reasoning, astute Negro observers of the public accommodations movement in Kansas City cited the value to their cause of the anti-movement.

The character of the organizations making up the opposing social movements has been noted. In the remaining pages, attention will be directed to those characteristics of the pro–public accommodations movement which initially it was predicted would be affected by the challenge of the anti-movement. These characteristics are: 1) membership, 2) leadership, 3) tactics and strategy, and 4) goals.

Dante wrote that the hottest places in hell are reserved for those who, in a time of great moral crisis, maintain their neutrality. Implicitly, Dante had recognized what Coser was later to explicate more fully in his *The Functions of Social Conflict,* namely, that external conflict leads to internal cohesion.

The pre-crisis membership of the public accommodations movement was almost entirely Negro, with a sprinkling of liberal but relatively powerless whites (in terms of community status). It is impossible, however, to know what the outcome of the public accommodations dispute would have been had not these whites participated in these early activities. Their role was quiet but not without importance in preparing the community for change. Negro membership during most of this time was small and fairly homogeneous in terms of social characteristics. One activist, grass-roots organization had appeared in the later fifties as part of the movement; but after its initial success with direct action tactics, it had fallen back into the traditional pattern and was maintained by only a small core of adherents.

Throughout the entire pre-crisis history of the movement, most of the white community had been busy elsewhere, though with important exceptions. The Kansas City School Board implemented plans to integrate the public schools soon after the 1954 Supreme Court decision. A number of hotels had desegregated voluntarily during the mid-1950s in response to requests by Negroes. For most of this period, local government and the courts had been the bastions of opposition to changes in Negro-white relationships. When political realities of the late fifties dictated an end to this official policy of opposition, the cudgel was taken up by a segment of the white community. Soon after this segment mobilized for action, so did the power structure of the white community and the whole of the Negro community.

Whereas formerly the nature of the conflict necessitated no mass identification with one of the principals, such identification was now required. The anti-movement stripped away whatever vestiges of neutrality and hesitancy remained in city government. The administration had committed itself already to the ordinance and had no honorable way out. (This is not to say it wanted a way out but to point out that it had no choice. "He who is not for me is against me.")

An examination of the membership rolls of the pro–public accommodations organizations arising after the challenge shows them to contain names of individuals and institutions never before identified with the public accommodations controversy. This fact demonstrates that a great number of individuals and organizations were associated with the public accommodations movement at this time, but it tells nothing about their degree of involvement. If judgment could be made on the number of persons mentioned in newspaper coverage of the movement's activities, the conclusion would be that few were actively involved. This conclusion would be supported also by the statement of a majority of the pro–public accommodations leaders who were interviewed.

Old leaders are seldom adequate for new situations. This timeworn observation was borne out in the crisis period of the public accommodations movement. As has been seen, the pre-crisis movement was made up of a number of distinct organizations. Yet when the challenge was issued, none of the existing bodies led the pro–public accommodations forces into battle. For this purpose three new organizations were formed, thus bearing out another truism, to wit: it is easier to create a new organization than to reform an old one.

The already existing organizations played a vital role in the creation of the new ones and, for the duration of the conflict, were absorbed by them. All three of the new collectives were led by individuals who were novices to the leadership role in the movement. In fact, the white leadership of People FOR Public Accommodations was selected primarily because, while sympathetic to the cause, it had never participated actively in the controversy permeating the issue. The top echelon leadership of Operation Public Accommodations consisted both of Negroes who had occupied lower positions in the leadership hierarchy of prior organizations and those who were behind-the-scenes manipulators of earlier efforts. In no case did the top leaders of an existing organization occupy a similar position in the new. This emergence of new Negro leadership is consistent with the recent findings of Thompson in New Orleans, Killian and Grigg in Florida, and Burgess in "Crescent City." The leadership of Operation Freedom, while not new to that position, had functioned heretofore in ecclesiastical and social welfare organizations. Continuity and coherence were lent to this succession of organizations by the NAACP, which functioned as the nucleus for the periodically expanding and contracting public accommodations movement.

This new leadership was made necessary by three facts. First is the fact that new problems (getting out the vote rather than legislating) call for new answers. And few people are intellectually and emotionally flexible enough to modify the accumulated thought patterns of a lifetime when suddenly confronted by a novel situation. So new leaders emerge. Their relative lack of experience in that position is more than offset by their adaptability. Just as underdeveloped nations enjoy a certain advantage over mature ones in responding to social change, so do individual leaders.

The second fact dictating a change in leadership was the need to unify the pro–public accommodations movement. The existing organizations, though working for a common goal, disagreed among themselves on questions of how best to achieve that goal. To have selected as the leadership of the new organizations those with comparable positions in the old would have been to create discord among those who disagreed with the old leaders and jealousy among their competitors. By choosing new leadership it was possible for the movement to close its ranks and to speak with, if not one, at least a minimum of voices.

The third reason for a change in leadership was that the existing leadership had a vested interest in the status quo. Their leadership position was in large part a function of the conditions then governing Negro-white relations. This made them suspect to the aspiring Negro leaders and put them at a certain disadvantage in bargaining with white leaders.

The public accommodations movement found it necessary in 1963 to respond to a challenge of its hard-won concessions. The nature of the challenge dictated that the tactics used heretofore by the movement (negotiation, litigation, social action) would not suffice. The issue would be decided at the ballot box. The only choice open to the public accommodations forces was whether to concede or to get out the vote.

Of course the Negro organizations could have chosen to concentrate on convincing the white electorate to uphold the ordinance in referendum. But they made no such mistake—and it would have been a mistake. For the ordinance was upheld by only 1,614 votes out of 89,902 cast. Of this number at least 20,000 votes were Negro.[22]

It is not difficult to imagine why the Negro leadership felt it could not rely on white support. For twenty years it had sought to integrate public facilities and for twenty years whites had opposed such a change. It is significant in this respect that nearly every Negro interviewed for this study made reference to the fact that, "white people just don't like Negroes." [23] Given the realities of the situation, then, the public accommodations movement had no choice but to take on the responsibility of getting out the vote.

This strategy was adopted also by that part of the movement active in the white community. But the tactics used in the attempt to get out the white vote were greatly different. The white organization made

extensive use of the mass media, formal meetings, and mailed literature, while its Negro counterpart relied upon a door-to-door canvass
of its area. Transportation of registrants and voters also played a
larger part in the activities of the Negro organization.

Of course the ultimate goal of the public accommodations movement remained after the crisis what it had been before—the elimination of racially segregated public facilities. If goals of a less general
sort are recognized, however, it is possible to argue that these were
modified in response to the anti-movement's challenge.

The pre-crisis history of the public accommodations movement had
been characterized by a succession of temporary goals. At one time
the goal was the integration of a public park, then of a swimming
pool. Somewhat later came the hotels, motels, and restaurants. Finally
came a public accommodations ordinance. The referendum presented an unexpected extension of that final goal. But this goal differed from earlier ones in that it was not an end in itself.

In retrospect, two ultimate goals can be seen in the effort of Negroes to mobilize the vote. The immediate one, of course, was to
uphold the public accommodations ordinance. The second and
longer range goal was to build a Negro political base from which to
deal with the white community in the future. In a very real sense the
ordinance served as a front for the really significant meaning of the
effort of the Negroes. Since the activity was undertaken in the name
of the ordinance, a great deal of white support which was given would
not have been extended in its absence. And out of the referendum activity rose a Negro power, the vitality of which is now being felt and
will continue to be felt both in the city and statewide.

The goals of the white proponents of public accommodations were
substantially different from those of Negroes. Whites could not let
anti–public accommodations win because of the poor national image
the victory would have given the city. A letter written by the president
of the Kansas City Chamber of Commerce to one of the People FOR
Public Accommodations chairmen on the day following the referendum contained this line, "at last, we can relax and say that Kansas City
will not have been disgraced in the eyes of the nation." Along with the
poor image would have come economic, governmental, and social difficulties. As Silberman wrote:

There is a fundamental difference in the situation of Negroes and whites
that leads almost inevitably to conflict over tactics and strategy; Negroes are
outside the mainstream of middle-class American life, whereas their liberal
allies are on the inside. Hence, the latter have a deep interest in preserving
the status quo, in the sense of maintaining peace and harmony.[24]

This difference in the goals of Negroes and whites was further substantiated by a study of racial voting attitudes in the 1960 presidential election. A random sample of 150 Negro registered voters and a like number of white voters was drawn and asked to rank twelve issues according to the importance of each in deciding their vote. The results were as follows (Middleton, 1962):

	Rank Order	
	White	Negro
(1) Keeping the nation prosperous and avoiding a depression	2	3
(2) Relation of church and state	6	9
(3) Maintaining the proper degree of prestige, power and leadership of the United States in the world	1	4
(4) Racial segregation and civil rights problems	5	1
(5) Corruption in government	12	11
(6) Keeping the nation out of war	3	2
(7) Labor-management disputes	8	10
(8) Inadequate medical care for old people	10	8
(9) Rising cost of living	7	6
(10) Prevent the spread of communism to other countries	4	7
(11) Farm problems	9	12
(12) Inadequate public schools	11	5

It should be noted that the greatest differences between attitudes of Negroes and whites were on issues number 4 and 12: racial segregation and civil rights, and inadequate public schools. Indeed, when all twelve issues are ranked by both races, Spearman's rank order correlation coefficient is only .65, which means that only 42 percent of the covariance is accounted for ($r^2 = .4225$). When items number 4 and 12 are excluded, the correlation coefficient becomes .85 and 72 percent of the covariance is accounted for.

The traditional perspective of social movement theory has been that of natural history, which sees all efforts at social amelioration as following the sociobiological process—birth, adolescence, maturity, and senility. Such an approach tends to impose an artificial rigidity upon social behavior. It seems more profitable to view social movements as response to a hostile environment and to couch the explanation of their character at a point in time in terms of the behavior of the "enemy" as defined by the movement.

This analysis of the public accommodations movement in Kansas City demonstrated a change in the movement's leadership, membership, tactics, strategy, and goals in response to a crisis induced by its enemy.

If sociology is to anticipate the accelerating tempo of social change in the last quarter of the twentieth century, it must expand its theoretical vistas to provide for the unexpected. Unless social movements can be viewed at given points in time as response to a specific enemy, sociology can never offer more than *post-factum* interpretation and *ad hoc* hypotheses.

There is no longer much place for societal theories drawn from sociobiological reasoning. Neither is the logic of sociopsychological action theory sufficient. Societal theories based on socioecological analogy are necessary. What types of social environments produce given types of social behavior? When that environment changes, what behavioral consequences follow? When a social environment is invaded by foreign and/or hostile elements, what response is the host likely to make?

This perspective on social movements would supplement the descriptive insights of biological analogy with the predictive powers of social behavioral ecology.

NOTES

1. See McKinney and Loomis (1961:557–82) for an excellent discussion of the more fruitful types.
2. Lecture by James Silver, author of *Mississippi: A Closed Society*, February 1, 1965. A professional organizer of student civil rights in the South has said that one of his most difficult jobs is convincing some of his old leaders that they must change their approach. If they will not or cannot, he has no choice but to throw them out of the movement.
3. The 1960 ordinance prohibited racial discrimination only in hotels, motels, and restaurants. The 1963 ordinance enlarged on those places which were required to operate without regard to race. The 1963 ordinance forbade discrimination in "places of public resort or amusement," and included such facilities as taverns, amusement parks, libraries, hospitals, and trade schools. Barber and beauty shops and rooming houses were not included in either ordinance.
4. For a discussion of the worth of such materials tempered with a word of caution relative to interpretation and use, see Selznick (1952:14–16).
5. Interview No. 6, October 6, 1964.
6. Interview No. 12 (white), October 24, 1964.
7. See *Kansas City Call*, July 8, 1960, for a list of the opposing restaurants.
8. While this ordinance was being considered by the council, barbers besieged City Hall en masse to protest their inclusion. See *Kansas City Star*, September 9, 1963.

9. See Dorothy Davis, "Changing Discriminatory Practices in Department Store Eating Facilities in Kansas City, Missouri" (Master's thesis, University of Kansas, Lawrence, 1960). "By common interest and cooperative efforts there are [in Kansas City] those individuals and organizations which reach across horizontally to form a 'goodwill' or 'better–human relations' community. Included are the local N.A.A.C.P. chapter, the Urban League, the Commission on Human Relations, the Jewish Community Relations Bureau, Fellowship House, National Conference of Christians and Jews, the Panel for Americans, Y.W.C.A. and Y.M.C.A. committees, certain labor unions, ministers, church lay groups and others" (pp. 55–56).

10. Interview No. 6, October 6, 1964.

11. See Neighbor (1962) for an analysis of the 1959 election.

12. This man had himself introduced a public accommodations ordinance in 1956. The City Council defeated it.

13. See Interview No. 12, October 24, 1964. The mayor under whom the legislation was enacted said: "The 1959 ordinance was passed for political expediency."

14. See Silberman (1964:194–223) for an excellent discussion of the need by Negroes for power as the only effective solution to the problem of Negro identity in American society.

15. See Ehle (1965) for a discussion of the effect upon the court of racial opinions and relative power during the Chapel Hill, North Carolina, civil rights activities.

16. *Kansas City Times,* August 6, 1963.

17. Ibid.

18. *Kansas City Star,* September 5, 1963.

19. Ibid.

20. Interview No. 9, October 19, 1964. Almost all those who qualified to vote between the time the referendum was called and the day of the vote were those recruited by the pro–public accommodations forces.

21. For an excellent summary of the response of the public accommodations movement, see a privately distributed letter by the director of the Jewish Community Relations Bureau entitled, "Observations on the Public Accommodations Ordinance."

22. Some estimates run as high as 25,000. See "Footnotes from a Referendum, Newsletter of Presbyterian Neighborhood Center" (Kansas City, Mo., April 15, 1964).

23. Interview No. 6, October 6, 1964.

24. See Silberman (1964:217) for further elaboration of the difference of goals for Negroes and whites in the civil rights movement.

11

The Civil Rights Movement and Social Change

MAURICE JACKSON

In studying the relationship of social movements to social change, one is immediately struck by the relative inattention given to the impact of social movements (Killian, 1964:426). This chapter is a presentation of the effect that one social movement, the civil rights movement, has had on social change. The thesis is that the civil rights movement seems to have had sufficient effect on change within and possibly change of the American society to warrant more attention to social movements. By social movement we refer to the more or less continuous interaction of conscious human beings in an emergent collectivity striving toward a goal (Killian, 1964:427). Most generally, by social change we mean both the development of new phenomena within a society and the overall transformation of a society. Examination of the effect of the civil rights movement on social change appears justified in light of such statements as that made by a sociologist that the movement has been "one of the most widespread and successful social movements in American history" (Laue, 1966:111–12); or that of another sociologist that "the development in American race relations from 1942 to 1964 [is] among the most rapid and dramatic of social changes to have ever been achieved without violent revolution" (Rose, 1967a:126); or that by a historian who mused, "I wonder if there has

"The Civil Rights Movement and Social Change," by Maurice Jackson is reprinted from *American Behavorial Scientiat* Vol. 12, No. 4 (March/April 1969) pp. 8–17 by permission of the author and the Publisher, Sage Publications, Inc.

been anything quite like it [the movement] since the Middle Ages, there was certainly nothing like it in the First Reconstruction" (Woodward, 1967:31).

Since no attempt can hope to be either definitive or comprehensive at this point in time, this study can be considered a preliminary step toward more detailed research of the civil rights movement and subsequent consequences. Rather than conduct a study of the effects of the movement upon social change, which would involve more time and personnel than was available for this report, we have mainly investigated evaluations that intellectuals have made of the movement. We have also added our own observations. The intellectuals include social scientists, journalists, civil rights participants, and other interested persons who have expressed some assessment of the movement. To the extent that intellectuals have a favorable vantage point from which to view cultural events, it is useful to begin with their assessments which can furnish a starting point for further systematic research.

An interesting paradox appears in the study of social movements and social change in that social change theorists have tended to deemphasize or ignore social movements while collective behavior theorists have accorded social movements a high priority in the area of change. To begin with, classical theorists were not of one opinion regarding the relationship. Some, such as Spencer, Spengler, and Toennies left little room if any for human participation in the process of change (Etzioni and Etzioni, 1964:3–9). Somewhat differently, Marx proposed that collective behavior accompanied the development of class consciousness, but he basically felt that human fate was predestined (Etzioni and Etzioni, 1964:6). Other theorists stressed human participation in change. Comte believed that human thought plays an important part in producing change. Toynbee saw change resulting from the response of creative minorities. Weber and Durkheim came closer than these theorists to viewing collective behavior as influential in change. Weber emphasized the change-producing character of ethics and charismatic leaders with accompanying communities (Etzioni and Etzioni, 1964:3–9). Durkheim (1951:124–33) stressed the creation of new social facts through the fusion of individual minds in interaction.

Current social change theorists who focus on the role of human agents do not show a commensurate interest in the role of social movements. They tend either to deemphasize social movements or to emphasize other types of social characteristics. Moore (1963:45–69) views the changes in relationship among individuals and groups as "small-scale" changes which are not thought to have any immediate and major consequences for the general structure of society. More recently (1966), he accords greater weight to human agents by stressing the importance of future views (utopias) in the development of social change. Bennis, Benne, and Chin (1961:11) ignore social movements as a consequence of their orientation to planned rather than spontaneous emergent actions. La Pierre (1965) argues that social movements result in transitory social change of little importance. For him, innovators (products of failures in socialization who have unconventional minds, a desire to innovate, and exceptional confidence) are the source of significant changes in society. Martindale (1962:54) also sees innovators and intellectuals as persons responsible for social and cultural change. Hagen (1962:30) feels that elite groups whose members had lost the secure place they once had in the social order are the leaders in societies in transition to economic growth. Etzioni (1966: vii) declares that power elites initiate and guide social change. As a final example, McClelland (1964) proposes that the main forces that propel societies rest in individuals with high achievement motivation.

Why do social change theorists grant so little importance to social movements? Killian (1964:426–27) suggests several reasons for the lack of attention given to the role of social movements in social change: concern with evolution, an implicit premise of determinism, a greater interest in culture than in groups, orientation to material rather than ideal factors, the dominance of the quantitative approach, and a preference for functional-equilibrium explanations.

Whatever the underlying assumptions of social change theorists might be, collective behavior theorists differ sharply from them in their evaluation of social movements in social change. Among the founders of collective behavior theory was Gustave Le Bon who believed that crowds play a part in destroying the old so it may be replaced by the new, even though "civilizations as yet have only been created and directed by a small intellectual aristocracy, never by crowds" (1960:17–18). A different role was assigned to crowds by Gabriel Tarde who felt that crowds, through imitation, spread the innovations of individuals (see Turner and Killian, 1957:4–5).

Contemporary collective behavior theorists are more in agreement about the influence of social movements on social change. Consider the following definitions of social movements which center around social change, although some definitions are more cautious than others. Social movements are characterized as efforts: "to bring about fundamental changes in the social order" (Heberle, 1951:6); "to inaugurate changes in thought, behavior, and social relationships" (King, 1956:27); "to alter or supplant some portion of the existing culture or social order" (Cameron, 1966:7); "to change the social order" (Brown,

1965:724); "to promote a change or resist a change in the society of which [they are] a part" (Turner and Killian, 1957:308); "collective enterprises to establish a new order of life" (Blumer, 1951:169); "collective action in pursuit of an objective that affects and shapes the social order in some fundamental aspect" (Lang and Lang, 1961:490); or as the processes through which "societies are disintegrated" and "brought together again into new relations to form new organizations and new societies" (Park and Burgess, 1942:924–25).

To avoid giving the impression that collective behavior theorists are solely interested in social change, it needs to be pointed out that many of them have focused on the emergence, development, and changing structure of social movements.

The civil rights movement is an excellent test case for assessing the extent to which social change or collective behavior theorists are justified in their differing evaluations of the role of social movements in social change. The ability to make the assessment rests upon certain considerations. First, in discussing change as the end result of a social movement, such as the civil rights movement, it is not necessary to maintain that the degree of change brought about must be congruent with that advocated. Conceivably the civil rights movement may have failed to achieve its goal of change but, in its process of development, may have fostered other important changes in society. On the other hand, any observed change may be the result of factors other than the civil rights movement.

Another problem in evaluating change is the absence of stable criteria for assessing the degree to which changes are short-run or long-run. The risks involved in carrying out such a determination are outweighed by the advantages of studying a movement in its course or shortly after it has run its course.

One additional problem is the determination of the unit of social change to examine. Since the civil rights movement has possible implications for the entire society, it seemed reasonable on the one hand to employ large subdivisions of society such as the political, economic, educational, and religious institutions as units of analysis. They tended to be a logical choice as many of the observers of the movement are specialists in a particular institutional sphere. On the other hand, it will be useful to point to extrainstitutional changes imputed to the movement.

THE CIVIL RIGHTS MOVEMENT

The movement can be understood as the activity of organized groups such as the National Association for the Advancement of Colored People (NAACP), Congress of Racial Equality (CORE), National

Urban League, Southern Christian Leadership Conference (SCLC), and Student Nonviolent Coordinating Committee (SNCC). Rather than restrict the civil rights movement to these groups, we will use the term to refer both to the activities of these organized groups, and to the activities of other organized groups and the "unorganized" mass who have been involved in the effort for civil rights.

The beginning of the civil rights movement has been defined in a number of ways by stressing either general or specific origins. At the earliest, Simpson and Yinger (1965:535) say that several events could serve as the general start of the current movement: the Jewish prophets of the eighth century b.c, the Sermon on the Mount, the eighteenth-century Enlightenment, the American and French revolutions, or the Emancipation Proclamation.

The later general beginnings of the movement were preceded by certain changes in the American society and in the world at large: industrialization; urbanization; labor and social welfare legislation; legal developments (extension of Bill of Rights to states through the Fourteenth Amendment); mass migration of Negroes from the rural South to northern cities; emergence of a Negro "middle class"; breakdown of the colonial system; emergence of formerly colonial societies into independence; and great enhancement of American position of power.

A number of specific recent events or times have been selected by various writers as the beginning of the civil rights movement. Among them are: the early sit-ins; the Supreme Court decision on desegregation May 17, 1954; the Montgomery bus strike in December 1955; or the lunch counter sit-ins February 1, 1960, at Greensboro, North Carolina. But, activities increased in frequency, intensity, and continuity from the time of the later sit-ins in ways that had not been true before.

Therefore, with the understanding that the movement has deep and extensive historical roots, by the civil rights movement we refer to such events as the following: the 1954 Supreme Court decision on education represented the culmination of the efforts of organized groups, primarily the NAACP, in litigation. This act has been typically viewed as promoting desegregation, not integration. Many of the subsequent acts were geared toward integration and involved direct action: the bus boycott in Montgomery, Alabama, 1955; sit-ins beginning in Greensboro, North Carolina, in 1960, followed by wade-ins at segregated beaches, read-ins at segregated libraries, kneel-ins at segregated churches, walk-ins at segregated theaters and amusement parks; freedom rides in 1961; marches in 1962 and many others concerned with voting, highlighted by the March on Washington in 1963;

freedom schools, rent strikes, job blockades, school boycotts, and Birmingham marches in 1963; school boycotts, bridge sit-downs, and the traffic-stall at the World Fair in 1964; the Selma-Montgomery march of 1965, and Chicago marches of 1966.

These and similar events have been conceptualized in at least two general ways. One set of writers thinks the single, continuing movement has undergone several changes, another set feels the movement has terminated with the cessation of nonviolent direct action activities. Some of the first group of writers conceive of the movement in terms of stages, but do not agree on the stages. Writing in the early period of the movement, Lomax (1963:131–34) feels that the 1960 sit-ins heralded a change from an emphasis on legalism alone to that of direct action. Rustin (1966*b*:411–12) terms the 1954–64 decade one of a protest movement attempting to remove the barriers to full opportunity and the decade beginning in 1964 one of a social movement involved in the politics of achieving the fact of equality. Moynihan (1966:134) sees virtually the same division: an earlier phase centered upon the idea of liberty and a later one of equality. Birmingham, 1963, was the turning point of the movement, according to Silberman (1964:140–44), since for the first time the poor became involved and their interest has more to do with jobs, identity, and so forth than with civil rights. Rustin (1966*b*:408) basically agrees with this conclusion. In 1966, Brink and Harris (1966:20–23) indicated that the goal of the movement had changed from equality under the law to equality in fact. Marx (1967:209–13) thinks the interest in the movement has shifted from integration to equality. One final view is held by Killian (1968:7), who feels that the Negro protest movement has become a revolution since it challenges the authority of the ruling class and the legitimacy of traditional values, and attempts to create fear in the public.

Changes in the movement may be dichotomized in other ways from: specific concerns to diffuse concerns, value interests to power interests, opposition to segregation to opposition to discrimination, and pursuit of the value of individualism to that of equality.

If the stage analysis is tenable, it is possible to characterize the current civil rights movement in a broader set of overlapping stages—all representing various ways to improve the situation of black people in this country, to improve their participation in the society, and to give them a sense of their humanity. Stage 1 emphasized legal means to reach these goals. Nonviolent direct confrontations with problems and issues to expose them for solutions represented Stage 2. Stage 3, the violent stage, involved symbolic identification with black victims of violence in the South, a concern with perceived misery combined with hopes of improvement, and subsequent striking back. Black power, the emphasis in Stage 4, represents a time of reassessment in which various ideas are being explored: from separatism through the acceptance of segregation and the use of power to achieve integration to an open society with choices. In brief, the sense of power is as variously understood in the civil rights movement as it is in the larger society.

One other way in which the civil rights movement is seen as continuing is presented by Wehr (1968:65), who sees the basic process as one of progressive structural differentiation rather than one of linear transformation. Hence, he regards the movement as a cluster of submovements using different basic tactics which gain ascendancy in certain periods.

A number of reports have indicated that the civil rights movement is over. The explanations tend to be particular to the American society and do not involve the world at large as was true of explanations of the rise of the movement. If the same historical factors have not changed but the civil rights movement is over, then a real question can be raised about the contributing effects of these factors to the movement. For instance, among the factors said to be responsible for a decline in the organized aspects of the movement are a decline in contributions to civil rights groups and the extension of limited resources to more areas of the country. A collapse in the less organized part of the movement has been attributed to a shift in volunteers to the antipoverty campaign and to groups protesting against the war in Vietnam.

It might also be said that some of the major goals of the movement in the South, voting rights and public accommodations, have been won. Looking backward, these goals may appear insignificant, but looking forward from 1960 they were of greatest importance for southern black people. The net effect of these victories might be the moving of the southern black people to a level on par with the northern black people. Their problems may be becoming similar. That is, southern black people may be expected to show increasing concern with traditional northern problems of better housing, schools, services, and the like. These problems, like other traditional concerns of northern black people, have been seen as more subtle and difficult to solve than those of the South in that northern racism has not been as blatant as southern racism. In Kenneth Clark's (1966a:607) words, "the difficult truth civil rights agencies must eventually face is that no technique has been developed which seems relevant to the problem [the peculiar cancerous growth of racism in American ghettos]."

Although these words were spoken a few years ago, as many facts indicate, no lasting solution for race relations in America has yet been established. The lack of a solution to the problem may have stultified the civil rights movement and sponsored other approaches. Certain conceptions such as the "vicious circle" interfere with the defining of the problem and its solution. The vicious circle hypothesis, for instance, proposes a symmetry in racial relations where asymmetry might be more adequate. In brief, if racial prejudice is developed and maintained without contact with members of other races, then nothing members of the groups can do will have any effect upon prejudice unless extensive and intensive contact is maintained.

Finally, it may be noted that the perceived collapse of the civil rights movement may not be total. C. Vann Woodward (1967:37) points to certain remaining assets which could result in a revival if warranted:

Foremost among these [assets] surely is a corps of Negro leaders that has not been surpassed in dedication, astuteness, and moral force by the leadership of any other great social movement of this century. . . . While there may be further defections among the whites, a younger generation of blacks and whites that shares a powerful sense of identity with this movement and has made it peculiarly its own is coming on strong. It will be heard from further.

Without attempting to resolve these differences, it can be said that all interpretations assume that the civil rights movement is a backdrop to certain subsequential activities. For instance, black power would not have been so eye-catching, effective, and influential without the sensitivity of Americans (both black and white) to black people, generated by the civil rights movement.

In brief, if the civil rights movement is over, it is an ideal time to evaluate the movement. If not, this study can serve as one of the base lines for future studies. Already, the movement has been said to have had certain consequences for social change. The question that we are addressing is this: in the opinions of intellectuals did the civil rights movement bring change? If so, in what areas of society?

EXTRAINSTITUTIONAL CONSEQUENCES

The civil rights movement has possibly affected the general society and subgroups within the society. For the society at large Turner and Young (1966:608) say:

There is no denying that without the picketing, the sit-ins, the marches, the nation would have progressed less rapidly, if at all, to its present position. . . . They [the protests] have drawn the young and not-so-young intellectuals, Negro and white, who have participated in an effort to rediscover the full meaning of democracy in today's age of scientific discovery.

They feel that the movement has revolutionary consequences for the society because it seeks and must find within the larger framework of social change a solution potentially involving modifications of traditional relations, between man and work and between man and his sociopolitical environment. [1966:684]

Rustin also argues that the movement is revolutionary in that it involves the qualitative transformation of fundamental institutions to bring about equality. To the extent that segregation and discrimination are overcome, to that extent, the movement would be revolutionary.

With regard to the black group, Talcott Parsons (1966a:722) feels that the civil rights movement was both an expression and implementation of the Negroes' demand for inclusion. The existence of the movement symbolically expressed and dramatized the demand. The activities, themselves, were both ways to implement the demands for inclusion and to "stir things up" further.

According to Yinger (1965:115–17), the movement also increased the self-respect and self-confidence of Negroes. For example, a poll conducted by *Newsweek* in the summer of 1966 (see *Newsweek,* August 22, 1966, pp. 20–58) showed that two out of three Negroes felt things were better for themselves and their families than previously. It may also be the case that the increased confidence drawn from the civil rights experience made black militancy possible.

An additional consequence of the movement, according to Yinger, was the creation of a context in which nondiscrimination could be facilitated nonviolently. For instance, within months after the sit-ins in 1960 at least 126 Southern cities had desegregated some eating facilities. By 1964 thousands of facilities (including lunch counters, laundromats, theaters, and hotels) had been desegregated in approximately 200 Southern cities.

Finally, Yinger felt the movement brought the situation of Negroes to public attention. As a matter of fact, according to Turner and Bright (1965:ix), it is only the second time in history (the other being the Civil War period) that the Negro has penetrated the consciousness of other Americans. The movement also played a part in communicating the dissatisfaction black people feel and an answer to the pervasive question—what do Negroes want? For instance, over time, the specific goals of black people were similarly perceived by black and white Americans. Equal job opportunities and the right to vote were seen as the most important goals and, added later, self-respect, dignity, and identity, as well as other specific goals.

Rustin (1966b:413–14) added another general effect of the movement on groups. He says, "this struggle may have done more to democratize life for whites than for Negroes." What he had in mind was the subsequent interest in politics, quality education for all, war on all poverty, and so forth, which may be more profitable for whites than for blacks.

James Q. Wilson, as well as Talcott Parsons, noted that many features of the movement had been taken over by whites. In Wilson's (1966:444) words:

> The nonpolitical strategies developed by the Negro for gaining bargaining power—the sit-ins, the protest march, and passive resistance—have already been adopted by whites concerned with everything from American foreign policy to university administration. Physically obstructing the operation of an organization—often illegally—has, in the 1960's, become a commonplace method for attempting to change the behavior of that organization. This "spill-over" of civil rights tactics into other areas of social conflict has probably been one of the most important consequences of increased Negro militancy.

We might add that the movement played a part in the activities of another group, the American youth, by involving many of them directly in the movement and by generally increasing youth's awareness of tactics of protest. Some civil rights activists went into youth-oriented protest, politics, and education—others became "hippies." In brief, some young people responded to the crises uncovered by the civil rights movement and to resistance to the movement in two broadly contrasting ways: becoming more active or dropping out.

Finally, the movement activated other minority groups, especially the Mexican-Americans.

INSTITUTIONAL CONSEQUENCES

Within the political, economic, educational, and religious institutions important changes were also attributed to the civil rights movement.

Political

Especially since the work of Emile Durkheim the study of laws has been of great importance for sociologists (Simpson, 1933). To the extent that laws are, as he said, important indicators of social solidarity, the legal institution should reflect the impact of a widespread social movement. These rules of the game are, in fact, the definition of what Durkheim called the "morality of principle," a morality that is often deviated from as members of society grant greater importance to the "morality of duty" (Wilson and Schnurer, 1961). Nevertheless, laws are not without measurable influence. Specifically, the movement should have consequences for the three phases of law-making, law-interpreting, and law-enforcing. Indeed, Kenneth Clark (1966b:xiii) is of the view that:

Today, the civil rights movement has clearly been successful in terms of attaining the limited goal of enlisting all branches of the federal government in the commitment to use the power of the federal government in the struggle for the ideals of racial equality.

It might also be observed that before the 1960s entertainers attracted the most attention in the society, but as the civil rights movement brought the federal government into more activities, politicians and politics became the center of attention.

In the area of law-making we find such views as that of Joanne Grant (1968:367):

There can be no doubt that the movement is responsible for the passage of the Civil Rights Acts of 1960 and 1963, and the Voting Rights Act of 1965, and the Interstate Commerce Commission order of 1961 to desegregate.

With regard to specific acts, Arthur Waskow (1967:231) claims that through the Civil Rights Act of 1964

the original goal of the sit-in movement was accomplished even where voluntary desegregation under direct pressure of sit-ins had been refused—by legislative action that had been born out of the pressure generated by the sit-in movement.

Harold Fleming (1966a:397) supported this general view by saying:

The Civil Rights Act of 1964 was more than a simple Congressional response to a national emergency and moral crisis. It was also a recognition that the civil rights forces had assembled a coalition which any practical politician could respect.

A similar relationship was proposed between the movement, especially the religious element, and the civil rights law of 1965. Joseph Fichter (1966:397) felt that the effect of the movement upon subsequent legislation was more apparent in this instance:

A clearer sequence [than in 1964] is seen in the active religious leadership of the march on Montgomery in 1965, which was followed immediately by President Johnson's proposal for a voting rights law.

In the judicial sphere, Paul Freund (1966:362) pointed to changes he felt proceeded from the civil rights movement. In general terms he states, "the movement has had a remarkable effect on the doctrine, structure, attitudes, and presuppositions in this country toward the law and the court."

The most frequent and common theme in the presidential election of 1968 was "law and order." Although many individuals interpret the phrase as being racial in intent, increased concern with "law and order" may have the effect of increasing respect for civil rights laws as well. Concern with "law and order" may be largely a response to urban riots, but it is indirectly related to the civil rights movement, particularly the civil disobedience feature.

Not only did Freund discern general effects, but he felt the movement specifically fostered "reexamination and change in the whole relationship of state and Federal courts in that Federal courts are not showing the same deference to state courts that they formerly did" (1966:361). Furthermore, the civil rights movement stimulated development of the law of freedom of speech and press and the law of demonstration and public assembly (Freund, 1966:360). An example of a specific change which he considered to be a "path-breaking decision" in constitutional law was "the approval of legal representation as advisory counseling not merely as court counseling" (1966:360–61). Another example Freund (1966:360) mentioned was the Supreme Court judgment that gives protection to the press in their discussions of the actions of public officials.

It is important to note at this point that many of the decisions stemming from civil rights cases affect all people. The last mentioned judgment was extended to invasion of privacy involving private citizens. The Supreme Court also ruled for the first time that the Constitution requires states to give a criminal suspect a "speedy trial." This decision on a civil rights case applies with full force to state court proceedings. Other examples can be found in the cases dealing with voting rights, selection of juries, and eviction of tenants. The point is that federal decisions in civil rights do not remain restricted to civil rights nor to the national level. They have implications for all citizens and for all levels of courts.

As with the national legislative and judicial branches of government, there was reason to expect that the civil rights movement had an effect upon the executive branch. Harold Fleming (1966a:362) concluded after his investigation of the relationship between the federal executive and civil rights that "the story of increasingly vigorous and far reaching federal action is in large part response to crisis and the rising militance of the civil rights movement." And further,

the quality of federal civil rights performance, then, depends directly on the ability of Negro Americans to dramatize their cause in such a way that it enlists the support of other influential segments of the society. . . . [While] New federal laws and programs . . . rely for the most part on complaints to trigger the enforcement mechanism. [Fleming, 1966b:397]

Talcott Parsons (1966b:xxvi) reached a similar conclusion:

We have emphasized the participation of many categories of whites in the movement itself, and in various kinds of support of the "cause." Indeed, the prominent role of the federal government would not be understandable without this, for the American system requires strong political "pressure" from various sectors of the public to generate this magnitude of governmental action.

The civil rights movement has also made police activity more visible, especially in the South, and has led to increased interest in and knowledge of the police. The violent phase or violent by-product of the movement has continued to generate further concern with police, their role and function in society, methods of improving their activities, and their relationship with members of communities.

Economic

Changes in the economic sphere of life have been traditional goals of Negroes. It follows that the civil rights movement would be oriented toward economic changes in large part. The movement did play a part in improving the employment situation of black professional and white-collar workers but not that of the bulk of black blue-collar and service workers or of the black poor. The War on Poverty, second perhaps only to the New Deal as a comprehensive approach to the problems of the poor, initiated by the Johnson administration has been viewed as a response to the movement.

In Earl Raab's (1966:46) words:

this aim (a more perfect equality of opportunity for the individual) has been the traditional aim of the civil rights movement as well. . . . The administration's anti-poverty program was, among other things, an accommodation to these demands [civil rights]. . . . This billion dollar program did not spring full-born out of a conscience. . . . It was part and parcel of the Negro revolution, of the direct action demonstrations and anarchic ghetto restlessness.

James Wilson (1966:434) views the War on Poverty as a strategic reaction to the movement: "some of the programs—particularly anti-poverty programs—were in part intended by supporters to dampen the civil rights revolution by improving the material conditions of Negroes."

There is some felt indication that the War on Poverty is having this dampening effect. Indeed, Raab (1966:52) observes that the individuals who participated most in the War on Poverty programs were from the civil rights movement:

But the people who drew the concept of "participation" to its ultimate definition of political power were the local militants. And they were not generalized spokesmen for the poor: they were the Negro and Spanish-speaking activists left over from the civil rights movement. As a matter of fact, they tended to be the newer, younger, more militant, more chauvinistic wing of the old civil rights movement.

If the conclusion is correct, one might suppose that reduction in poverty programs might result in a revival of more intense continuance of the civil rights movement. This need not occur if the War on Poverty programs are providing experience, training, and positions which become independent of the programs. For our purpose, however, it is sufficient to note that there is some feeling that the movement has affected the large-scale federal attack on poverty.

Finally, it may be the case that the great interest in black-owned business and black involvement in business generally reflects a confidence built up in the civil rights movement.

Educational

Education, like employment, has been one of the foremost goals of Negroes. Whether or not the civil rights movement has had a differential impact in the two institutions, their relative permeability should be noted. It is interesting to note that the federal government may find it easier to initiate change in the economic institution than in the educational one. The relatively less resistance to poverty programs may be associated with the intended self-help character of some of the programs.

On the other hand, desegregation of educational facilities has encountered rather stiff opposition, ranging from massive resistance in the South to school boycotts in the North. To some extent the resistance is based on the value placed on neighborhood schools. In part, however, the newness of poverty programs may result in their being viewed as less threatening than changes in old patterns of education.

A number of writers have indicated that some educational gains that have occurred followed directly or indirectly from the civil rights movement. In Oscar Handlin's (1964:14) words:

Pressure from these sources (organized political agitation and litigation and new techniques of sit-in and nonviolent protest) has already produced striking improvement. . . . There has been a marked rise in the quality of education available to colored children.

Parsons, among others, has stated: "The movement has certainly been a direct agent for bringing about certain specified changes, such as the desegregation of schools, lunch counters, and bus stations" (1966b:xxv).

In brief, the civil rights movement functioned in this area to bring out legally directed change to desegregate schools. The current lack of desegregation may reflect other factors such as residential and employment patterns. Oscar Handlin (1966:662) noted that schools in the North have moved to solve problems which arise from residential distribution, not from segregation by law. The point here is that current school shifts, redrawing of district lines, and compensatory education may be clearer instances of reaction to the civil rights movement than to legal decisions or other considerations.

Rustin (1966b:414) suggested another effect of the movement:

Clearly, it was the sit-in movement of young Southern Negroes which . . . galvanized white students. . . . It was not until Negroes assaulted de facto school segregation in the urban centers that the issue of quality education for all children stirred into motion.

Project Head Start, an important and successful educational innovation, has roots in the civil rights movement. Black student unions in high schools as well as in colleges and universities are another offspring of the movement which prepared the way for more intensive demands of black students for increased enrollment of minority students, increased recruitment of minority faculty, and increased knowledge of minority groups. These demands represent a way of including black people in the educational process on an equal, representative basis and of demonstrating the extent to which black people have existed as subjects as well as objects, even though they have had different experience in the society.

Finally, local control of schools has been generated as a consequence of resistance to busing or other efforts to desegregate.

Religious

One of the most apparent effects of the civil rights movement was the participation of religious leaders in marches, mass demonstrations, and so forth. Many of the Negro leaders were ministers who were joined by white ministers in many of the activities of the movement. Here, in Fichter's words (1966:417), was an example of "deliberate, moral impact of religious leaders on extra-church institutions of the American culture."

The other side of the coin was the effect of the movement upon the religious institution itself. There have been many discussions concerning the proper role of the ministry with regard to social problems. The discussions are continuing, implying that the impact of the civil rights movement was of great moment. Fichter further suggested (1966:415) that the movement attracted and stimulated a certain feature of religion: "What has come to the fore in the civil rights movement is the prophetic, creative, and positive role of religion."

Finally, it is possible that the movement had some effect upon the organization and doctrinal orientation of American religion. That is, it is likely that congregational membership has been reconstituted to a degree. At the same time, American religion has been stimulated by the movement to engage in self-analysis with regard to clarification of the moral dilemma of race.

To summarize, this study is not to be seen as a test of the proposition that social movements produce social change. Hence, it cannot be considered an answer to the correctness of either the social change or collective behavior points of view. But, there is sufficient reason to suggest that a closer, more intensive investigation is warranted. In the opinion of many intellectuals, in accordance with collective behavior theorists, the civil rights movement resulted in a large measure of change, all of which cannot adequately be accounted for at the present time. To establish the veracity of the suggested hypotheses, it will be necessary to set up a more systematic design to attempt a solution of at least some of the following problems.

How much change is required before one can safely say that large-scale change has occurred? Does the change have to be even throughout the society or its institutions? The civil rights movement, for instance, may have initiated a high degree of change in the legal institution and virtually none in the housing area. In addition, how does one identify transitory or enduring change? Finally, the importance of the civil rights movement, relative to other activities, as a factor in change has to be determined systematically.

The Movement: Discovering Where It's At and
How to Get It

JAMES H. LAUE

The Movement, first and foremost, the Movement. Insurrections. As-
sassinations. Viet Nam. Death. George Wallace. ABM. Death. Senator
Russell's "first people." Growing disparities between rich and poor,
black and white. Out and In. Black Power. Brown Power. Red Power.
Woman Power. The moon. The ghetto. The barrio. More death. Billy
Graham. The White House. The National ego. The Movement.

These words represent some aspects of social reality in the United
States in the 1960s—the "raw data" out of which sociologists say sense
(or at least order) can be made. As a sociologist concerned with conflict and social change, I have chosen to view the emergence, growth,
impact, and transformation of what has come to be called the Movement as an ordering principle for the data of the 1960s. It is, from this
perspective, a dominant social process of the decade that will have a
lasting and growing impact on American life in the 1970s and
beyond.

WHAT HAPPENED TO THE CIVIL RIGHTS MOVEMENT?

During the 1960s, for the first time in American history, there
emerged a national social movement for civil rights. It had its roots in

Reprinted by permission of the author and publisher from the *Urban & Social
Change Review* 3, No. 2 (Spring 1970).

190

a long and continuous history of individual and group protests against slavery and discrimination, and most immediately in direct action protests in cities like Montgomery, Orangeburg, Tallahassee, and Kansas City in the late 1950s.

Beginning with the Negro student sit-ins at lunch counters across the South in February 1960, a national movement quickly emerged, creating new national organizations (SNCC and SDS) [1] and strengthening others (CORE and SCLC).[2] By mid-decade, there was the feeling that nationally the movement was dead. But in reality it was returning to the local level, gathering ever broader issues such as war, poverty, economic exploitation, and political centralization.

What crystallized in 1960 as a movement for minor social change goals (desegregation of public accommodations and facilities) has emerged today as a movement challenging the centers of economic and political control in every metropolitan area and in national economic and governmental institutions.

Participation has broadened in proportion to expanding goals. Hundreds of new indigenous community organizations have developed in the last three years. They are in virtually every city, and they have strikingly similar goals from city to city: self-determination, community control, turf control, and economic development rather than assimilation at any cost. Constituent groups include not only blacks, but browns, Indians, women, welfare recipients, students (junior high through postgraduate), and, most recently, military personnel, rural poor whites, and urban white ethnics.

A COMPARISON: 1960 AND 1970

So what has changed since 1960? For middle class blacks and browns, some important things:

virtual nationwide desegregation of public accommodations and facilities

registration of tens of thousands of black Deep South voters, and commensurate emergence of political power is some local situations

OEO, Model Cities, and other programs with some funds for minority communities

black studies

Black Power, black unity, black consciousness

significantly more jobs, many of them high-paying, in government at all levels and in white-controlled businesses

hundreds of local projects for economic development, community development, community control, self-determination

radical movements and caucuses: black, brown, women's

new establishment institutions following the trend: Urban America, the Urban Coalition, the Urban Institute, and hundreds of urban study centers at universities

consulting fees for rapping black.

Most important of all the changes is the emergence of protest as a legitimate activity for large groups of Americans who have heretofore been apolitical and a sense that things can be changed, and the experience that organizing for confrontation and change is highly reinforcing. That peculiar combination of American fatalism ("They run things") and individualism ("But what can one person do?") is being eroded as the Movement educates white ethnics and Westchester housewives as well as Indians who want to fish in Washington state.

Much less has changed for grass-roots ghetto, barrio, and reservation residents. Disparities between white and nonwhite indices are, for the most part, staying the same or widening—in unemployment rates, life expectancy, infant and mother mortality, nonwhite median income as a percentage of white median income, and so forth.[3] Dominant institutions, in short, are strong, unified in their resistance to major changes (i.e., in control of decisions), adept at coopting, and rigid. Despite the growth of the Movement and the sampling of changes listed above, consider what else has either remained the same or changed in a nondemocratizing direction since 1960:

continued poverty, especially among blacks, browns and Indians (40 percent of all black families are poor)

the military-industrial-academic complex is stronger than ever

public opinion polls show increasing hostility toward protest in general and toward youth protest in particular

continued centralization of urban decision-making functions among the technocrats

House and Senate committee structures controlled by rural and small town legislators (in a nation now more than 70 percent urban), and chaired by men whose median age is sixty-seven (in a society where median age is twenty-eight)

growing repression of significant efforts at social change, ranging from the Green Amendment [4] (and now another Administration's further steps to depower community action efforts), to more sophisticated police-community relations programs, to the police attacks on Black Panther activities, headquarters, and leaders as the Panthers turn their program from racial to class and social welfare goals.

But the Movement remains. It is still a driving, hopeful phenomenon. Its constituent groups—from the New University Conference
and the Women's Liberation Movement to La Raza, the Black Panthers, and the radical caucus in the American Sociological Association—are united in their perception of the common issue: power.
This issue is no longer a limited radical one—integration versus segregation—as it was at the beginning of the decade. It is power (and
therefore some choice about one's destiny) versus no power (and no
choice). This is the legacy of the 1960s: a politicized society in which
the decision-making process at all levels is fair game for exposing and
influencing.

1970S: AGEISM, SEXISM, AND CAUCUSES

The root structural source of the Movement that has developed in
the United States today is a status system in which, throughout American history, the important decisions at every institutional level have
been made by adult white males—incumbents of a status constellation
of the three basic ascribed characteristics of age, race, and sex. The
civil rights movement of the 1960s challenged and began to break the
hold of one of these statuses on power prerogatives. We will see in the
1970s, I believe, the logical extension of the Movement beyond racism
to ageism and sexism—institutional inequalities generated by the centrality of the other two ascribed statuses. The student movement is, of
course, established and growing, and (if Martin Oppenheimer's
[1969] estimates are correct) is pouring upward of 80,000 activist,
politicized students a year out of college and into graduate schools
and the job market. The Women's Liberation Movement (encom-
passing thousands of women in hundreds of organizations like
WITCH and NOW) is spawning female caucuses everywhere. Will
there soon be a Presidential Commission on Sexism?

Add to the young, the black, and the beautiful, the white ethnics,
who are backlashing and organizing. Browns and reds are angry and
organizing. Antimilitary caucuses are building an insurgent network
throughout the armed services. The 1970s will be a decade of escalated and prolonged intergroup conflict as all of these groups and
others extend the major learning of the blacks in the 1960s: that significant group gains in a pluralistic society come not from the benevolence of the rulers, but from organization, negotiable power, self-ad-
vocacy, and confrontation.

What forms the conflict will take, how severe and how prolonged it
will be, depend to a great extent on the flexibility of the institutional

structures being challenged. Much also depends on the level and types of changes being sought by the Movement. The civil rights movement of the 1960s was largely reformist, with such "getting-in" goals as eating at lunch counters, voting, having decent housing, holding a job, and owning income-producing property. As military and foreign policy issues have become more frequent targets of protest in the last five years, a good deal of revolutionary ideology has emerged, but with little strategic planning and support for actual institutional overthrow and replacement. Slow progress in race relations also has promoted impatience with institutional reform per se and a call for more radical approaches.

The goals of movements among racial and ethnic minorities, students, and antiwar groups are indeed more radical at the end of the 1960s than they were at the beginning, as serious questioning of the value-assumptions underlying America's foreign and domestic policies intensifies. The nation's response may largely determine whether revolutionary sentiment gains support. Current repressive tendencies make me believe it will.[5]

But most persons and organizations in the Movement are still committed to radical institutional reform, I believe—and not to institutional overthrow except, perhaps, in rhetoric. Unless large numbers of persons are willing to employ guerrilla tactics, the macro-institutional structure of the United States will continue to stand—corporations, the Pentagon, the media, the major political parties, the committee structure of Congress, and so forth.

The way many persons now find themselves participating in the Movement, then, is through a radical reform caucus within existing institutions and organizations. This may be the most important new direction of the Movement structurally in the 1970s.

The caucus movement provides a readily accessible form of participation for the thousands of younger members of faculties, government agencies, and other establishment organizations who did their training in the civil rights movement of the early 1960s, and are now approaching or passing thirty and being called to account for support of themselves, spouses, and children. As professionals, they have considerable leverage on boards and higher administrators because of the seller's market (until very recently) in virtually every field. And in many cases they maintain their ties with action organizations on the outside whose pressure gives insiders the leverage to elicit change.

Caucuses now exist in virtually every organization, agency, university, professional association, and religious body in the United States that is at all alive to the issues of the day and that has not willingly shared its power prerogatives with the non-old, the non-white and the non-male, however noble its intentions.

Many federal, state and municipal agencies have black (or brown) and women's caucuses attempting to break the cycle of previous occupational discrimination, lower entry status, and restricted promotional opportunities.

The National Committee of Black Churchmen (now three years old) and the National Conference of Black Lawyers (formed in January 1970) represent well-organized caucuses within religion and law.

In higher education, it is the New University Caucus—a national coalition of students and faculty members who represent hundreds of locally effective caucuses.

Professional associations have been a particularly fertile ground, ranging from the predictable radical caucuses in the American Sociological Association and the National Association of Social Welfare to those within the Asian Studies Association (which held a counterconvention a year ago to get such topics as Vietnam and Taiwan on the agenda) and the Modern Language Association (in which a small group pulled a coup in December 1968 and gained control because not many members attend convention business meetings).

In politics, the "citizens caucus" may be emerging as a major innovation for preprimary party endorsement, as successfully illustrated in Massachusetts where a District Citizens Caucus endorsed a peace candidate as opposition to a man whom some consider a longtime incumbent hawk.[6]

In short, more organizations can expect to be confronted with situations similar to that facing the board of missions of a major Protestant denomination at its last annual meeting: challenges to everything from the very concept of foreign missions to the ownership of stock in a napalm producer, coming from a black staff task force, a youth board task force, a caucus of young black ministers, and a loose coalition of women board members.

This situation is suggestive of the way the Movement will grow in the 1970s and put American institutional structures to even more severe tests than they faced in the 1960s. Challenges from without increasingly will be aided from within, as masses of people try to deal with the massive unresponsiveness of community and national institutions to human needs.

The institutional intransigence is what the now very In "urban crisis" is all about—and was about long before overt racial conflict helped the media and the rest of us discover what was always there. The corporations did not move on jobs or economic development for minorities until they literally saw Detroit burning. University presidents (to say nothing of Richard Nixon, John Mitchell, and Billy Graham) insist on turning the discussion to the tactics of protestors instead of the life-or-death issues they raise. Congressmen complain about the "coercive" tactics of protestors with legitimate grievances, while they gladly submit to coercion by lobbyists who wear suits and ties instead of overalls and beads. All this happens against the backdrop of a steadily worsening fiscal situation for the cities as demands for service expand and revenue sources wither.

And now, after the 1960s, the Movement is geared up to meet each new resistance to power-sharing with further challenges at every level—organizational, institutional, community, and national. This interplay between challenge and resistance will be the scenario of the 1970s, rerun many times. Where we will stand at the beginning of the 1980s, then, depends on how the Movement applies its considerable but disparate resources, and whether establishment institutions decide on a strategy of minor cooptational concessions, repression, or real sharing of power with Outs who now know where it's at and are determined to get it.

NOTES

1. The Student Nonviolent Coordinating Committee, which came together early in 1960 to provide a channel of information and coordination between student sit-inners across the South; and Students for a Democratic Society, an outgrowth of the League for Industrial Democracy. These two organizations helped produce leaders of national prominence in the Movement today, among them Julian Bond, Stokeley Carmichael, James Forman and H. Rap Brown (SNCC), and Tom Hayden (the founder of SDS). SNCC recently changed its name to the Student National Coordinating Committee.
2. The Congress of Racial Equality was established in 1942 by James Farmer and others as the first nonviolent direct action organization in the United States working specifically for racial integration; and the Southern Christian Leadership Conference was organized in 1957 around Dr. Martin Luther King, Jr., after the successful Montgomery bus boycott.
3. Howard Ehrlich's paper for the Missouri Symposium on Urban Confrontations, "Social Conflict in America: the 1960's" (University of Missouri, Department of Sociology, June 27, 1969), documents this more recently and more impressively than any other source I have seen.
4. Which gave municipal governments the option of taking control of OEO community action programs away from indigenous groups.
5. For example, the responses to the Pentagon demonstration in October 1967, the Chicago convention demonstrations in 1968, and the People's Park protest in Berkeley in May 1969 (including the first air raid on an American community in history—on citizens by the government). Panthers may gain support from respectable moderates in the face of continued police killings of their leaders. And it should be remembered that establishment responses to the urban racial disorders of the late 1960s resulted in upward of 85 percent of the dead and 60 percent of the injured coming from the minority communities.
6. John Saloma, "Citizens Caucus—Political Innovation," *Boston Globe,* February 28, 1970, p. 7.

part 4

The Consequences of Effecting Change

Introduction

Normally, if not inevitably, there are unanticipated effects of a movement upon the larger society. In addition, any measure of success gained by the movement has unanticipated consequences for the movement itself. The selections in this final part illustrate the way in which movements themselves have been affected by their own successes.

This raises the question, of course, of the meaning of success. As Turner and Killian pointed out, "success" in reference to a social movement can have a number of different meanings, and can be gauged in various ways (Turner and Killian, 1957:320). For one, a movement may be judged to be successful if the number of members continues to increase. Second, a movement may be defined as successful if the organizational structure is maintained. And third, success may involve the extent to which the values of the movement are realized.

In other words, some observers—both adherents and non-members—will define a movement as successful even though it may not achieve any of its original goals, while others will maintain that success must involve at least a partial realization of movement ideals. For purposes of this section, I am defining success in terms of the achievement of some—however small—explicit goal. I am then asking the question, what happens if a movement is successful? One fact seems certain: success of any kind inevitably changes the movement.

As I noted in the Introduction, O'Neill has shown through his analysis of the American feminist movement that in some cases success

199

may be disaster in disguise. The victories of the feminists were hollow because they were "avoiding fundamental questions for the sake of immediate advantages" (O'Neill, 1968:289). The two selections in this part give further examples of the ways in which movements may be altered by achieving some kind of success.

In the first selection, Von Eschen, Kirk, and Pinard ask why the black movement in the United States shifted from a nonviolent ideology and strategy to a violent one when the former "had brought significant gains." That is, a number of successes had been wrought through nonviolence such as the opening of public facilities and the gaining of voting rights. But these very successes contributed to the shift toward violence for a number of reasons. For one, success attracted new members, including many working-class individuals. Both the larger number of adherents and the changed class composition of the movement facilitated the shift toward violence. Also, the successes were gained for more socially legitimate goals. The movement then had to strive for goals less legitimate and less realizable through nonviolent means. In addition, opponents of the movement learned from the successes that their harsh responses were counterproductive. In future encounters, antimovement responses were modified to minimize unfavorable public reaction and thereby minimize the force of nonviolent means.

Other factors were involved, of course. But the point is clear: certain circumstances facilitated the success of nonviolence, and that very success altered the circumstances and facilitated the shift toward violence. We see, then, a dialectical development of movement ideology and strategy on the one hand, and the social reality in which the movement functioned on the other hand.

Ideological alteration as a result of movement success also appears in the final selection. But in contrast to the militant shift evidenced in the black movement, Tucker shows us the process of deradicalization. The "successes" involved in Marxist movements include membership growth, the creation of a large organizational structure, and the attainment of legitimacy in the social order. The consequence is deradicalization, which Tucker defines as the loss of revolutionary other-worldliness and alienation, and "accommodation to the world as it stands."

These two selections both clearly delineate changes in movements which follow upon success, though the changes are in opposite directions. How can we account for this? Although more detailed analyses are necessary, at least one point seems clear: both movements changed in the direction that would maximize the possibility of further successes, where success is here defined as gaining access to social rewards. The black movement, in order to secure more of the rewards available in American society, could neither become less militant nor even remain wholly nonviolent according to our three authors. And when a radical movement becomes strong, says Tucker, with the potential for even further growth, it "acquires a definite stake in the stability of the order in which this success has been won." In other words, in both cases the changes which resulted from success were related to the acquisition of additional social rewards. It is not simply the internal dynamics of the movement, then, but interaction with the larger social order that is decisive for the course of development of any social movement.

13

The Disintegration of the Negro Non-Violent Movement

DONALD VON ESCHEN, JEROME KIRK, AND
MAURICE PINARD

A major problem in the theory of nonviolence is to determine its empirical limits both in terms of when an oppressed group will be willing to use it and when it will be effective. In this chapter we probe these limits by asking why blacks in the United States, after adopting nonviolent tactics in 1960, abandoned them only six years later, in spite of the fact that such tactics had brought significant gains. That such gains had occurred is undeniable. The nonviolent boycotts, picketing, sit-ins, wadeins, marches, and the like opened public facilities that had long been closed to blacks, often through the passage of public accommodations laws, and compelled the federal government to enforce voting rights in the Deep South.[1] That nonviolence was abandoned, however, is equally clear. In spite of its successes, by 1966 the nonviolent movement began to dissolve. CORE leaders began to speak of the right of self-defense; SNCC leaders glorified as rebellions the riots that had started in 1964. Within a few years the remaining nonviolent leaders found themselves largely without followers.[2] What accounts for this? Why should a movement, once so successful, so quickly have

Reprinted from the *Journal of Peace Research,* No. 3 (1969), by permission of the authors and the publisher, Universitetsforlaget, Oslo, Norway.

dissolved? By answering this question, we should gain considerable insight into the limits of nonviolent action.

Our approach shall be as follows. We shall argue that once one understands the circumstances under which the nonviolent movement succeeded, one can then understand at least part of the reason for its subsequent dissolution. By circumstances, we mean here such things as the movement's size, its social composition, the problems and dynamics of recruitment, its methods, and the responses of friends and opponents. Thus, in this chapter, we shall develop a theory, based on data, about how (i.e., the circumstances under which) the movement succeeded; then we shall use this theory to explain, at least in part,[3] why the movement dissolved.

Our theory about how it succeeded will be based primarily on three empirical studies: 1) a study we carried out of the Maryland movement from 1961–64, based on interviews and questionnaires from demonstrators, participant observation within the movement, and documents;[4] 2) a study of the movement in Nashville, Tennessee, during these same dates, carried out by Lyle Yorks in which he reconstructed the history of that movement by interviewing all available participants, including those against whom the movement was aimed;[5] and 3) an interview study by Killian and Grigg (1964) of biracial committees in Florida. In addition, we shall use whatever other information can be gleaned from journalistic reports, unsystematically gathered accounts by participants and leaders, documents, and the like.

A common image of the movement is that it overcame its opponents largely through the sheer weight of its numbers. This image is suggested by: 1) newspaper reports and publications of civil rights organizations which describe massive demonstrations—for instance, CORE, in its July 1963 CORE-LATOR, reported that "from 2 to 4,000 students marched daily into . . . [Greensboro, N.C.] joined by hundreds of adults";[6] and 2) counts of the number of people who have participated in the movement made by survey organizations—in polls, for instance, up to 8 percent of the eligible Negro population claimed that they had participated in the sit-ins (Brink and Harris, 1964:67), a figure rising to 15 percent for Negro students in southern schools (Matthews and Prothro, 1966:413)—and by such organizations as the Southern Regional Conference, which reported that about seventy thousand Negroes and whites had demonstrated in over one hundred communities in the first year and a half of the movement (Matthews and Prothro, 1966:408).

Nevertheless, evidence indicates that this image is false, that data of this sort are highly misleading. In both the Maryland and Nashville studies, where data consisted, instead, of interviews, questionnaires, and/or participant observation, the finding was one of low participation. From a vantage point inside the movement, the most frequent experience was one of great difficulty in assembling enough people to carry out a demonstration of any significant size. Almost always the number of demonstrators fell far short of the numbers hoped for. This was true in spite of the fact that newspaper accounts or survey data, and so forth, would have given a contrary impression.

The reports of large demonstrations carried in the newspapers and elsewhere were misleading for three reasons. 1) Such demonstrations were atypical. It is true that, on occasion, the movement was able to get hundreds of people out on the streets. So, for example, some eight hundred Negro college students in Maryland demonstrated in a massive assault against a segregated movie theater near their campus, and in Nashville hundreds demonstrated in similar actions against theaters there. But although such demonstrations established an image of widespread participation, they were not representative. Most demonstrations were small. Usually, a few days after a large demonstration it was impossible to put together one of any noticeable size whatsoever. 2) Demonstrations were large often only because they involved considerable numbers of outsiders. Thus, in one of the biggest demonstrations, the Route 40 Freedom Ride, a majority of participants were from out of state. This concentration in one place of demonstrators from a wide geographic area made the movement seem larger than it in fact was. Its actually smaller size was revealed by the fact that only rarely could it stage newsworthy demonstrations in more than one or two localities simultaneously. Thus, in Maryland, a CORE official explained to reporters that demonstrations had been unusually small that weekend because a demonstration was going on in New York at the same time. 3) As we shall explain in more detail later, many nonmembers (i.e., bystanders, friendly or hostile) were mistakenly enumerated by the press and television as participants, thus exaggerating the movement's actual size.

Similarly, survey data would have greatly exaggerated participation. It is probable, for instance, that over a third of the student body of the Negro college in Maryland mentioned above participated in the theater demonstrations. A survey would thus have revealed high participation. Yet these figures would have been misleading. What counts in a sustained drive for social change is not the number of people who have participated at one time or another, but the number who can be assembled for particular demonstrations. These were not the same. Firstly, participation tended to be sporadic; and secondly, the turnover in participation was high, each demonstration seeing both many new participants and the dropping out of many old ones. As a result, in no more than a few demonstrations were there more than a dozen or two students from that Negro college.

In short, in spite of widespread impression to the contrary, participation in Maryland and Nashville was low.

Can we generalize these findings of low participation to the movement elsewhere? This seems likely for several reasons: 1) In terms of importance, as measured by media coverage and the like, the Maryland and Nashville movements were among the major ones in the United States during this period. Participation in them, then, should have been as great as in most other instances.[7] 2) The data used to support the idea of massive participation elsewhere we now know to be suspect. With respect to reports of large demonstrations, such demonstrations may have been atypical; outsiders were clearly involved in some of the most important of them (in Selma, for instance); and bystanders were clearly mistaken at times for participants, as we shall indicate shortly. Similarly, with respect to counts, if participation was as sporadic as it was in Maryland and if turnover was as high, the impact of the numbers reported would be severely diluted.[8] 3) Random accounts of participants also suggest low participation. Organizers in the South have, at times, complained about the difficulty of mobilizing Negroes. Furthermore, SNCC organizers have claimed that the large demonstrations led by Martin Luther King in the South were sporadic, lasting only the length of his stay.[9] 4) The recruitment processes which led in Maryland to low participation almost certainly were at work elsewhere.

Participation was low because it required socially contradictory characteristics. This was shown by questionnaire data collected from Maryland demonstrators.[10] These indicated that active participation required, first of all, sufficient deprivation so that the person would have a strong reason to be active in the movement. At the same time, it required characteristics particularly rare among highly deprived people: a sense of political efficacy so that participation might appear worthwhile, or organizational involvement so one might be dragged through one's social connections into activity. In short, it required characteristics that, in the real world, are rarely found in the same persons. This limited participation in two ways. 1) It limited the numbers available to the movement. Because the most deprived are the least likely to possess a sense of efficacy or high organizational involvement, the movement was by and large denied access to them. 2) It meant that participation was sporadic. Because the movement was forced to recruit from among the less deprived, those with less reason to participate, participation was inconstant.

Evidence and argument for these propositions has been presented in detail elsewhere.[11] The essence of the data, however, is this:

1) Deprivation is necessary for high participation. This is shown in Table 1, where it can be seen that, among the demonstrators, activity in the movement (measured by how often a person went out on demonstrations) was highest among those of lower social status and of downward social mobility. The same was true for those dissatisfied with their jobs, those whose job aspirations greatly exceeded their expectations, and so forth. On the other hand, the less deprived showed a lower rate of participation.

1. The most deprived were the most active participants (percent more active *)

	Negroes		White		Both	
	%	N	%	N	%	N
Socioeconomic status † (all respondents)						
High	32	28	49	76	44	104
Medium	44	63	59	108	54	171
Low	67	27	83	18	73	45
Social mobility ‡ (non-students only)						
Upward	42	12	61	23	54	35
Stable	46	11	67	12	56	23
Downward	100	2	80	15	82	17

* Percent who reported to have been out on demonstrations three times or more, in answer to the question: "How many times have you been out on demonstrations before today?"

† Socioeconomic status: determined by North and Hatt scores for occupations given in response to the question: "What job are you training for in school?" (students), or "What is your job?" (non-students). A high status corresponds to a score of 85 or above; a low status, to a score of 71 or below. (Notice that many low-status participants had at most a lower-middle-class occupational level, i.e., below, approximately, the status of an undertaker, a grade school teacher, or a reporter.)

‡ Social mobility: comparison, for non-students, of their socioeconomic scores with that of their fathers ("What is your father's main occupation?"). The scores were broken into four classes (less than 72; 72–74; 75–84; 85 or more), and differential positions in these four classes were taken to measure social mobility.

2) Participation requires characteristics rare among the highly deprived. Although the most deprived were the most active, the movement was made up predominantly of the less deprived. Thus, virtually all the students involved were training for high-status professional and managerial occupations; while of the older, non-student demonstrators, 81 percent of the whites and 60 percent of the Negroes already occupied such positions. Similarly, Table 2 shows

2. Participants over twenty-five years old had a much higher educational level than did the population of Maryland as a whole

	White (percent)		Negro (percent)	
Education	Freedom Riders	Maryland Population	Freedom Riders	Maryland Population
College graduates	74	10	47	4
Some college	22	9	34	4
High school graduates	4	24	6	12
Some high school	0	19	9	20
Grade school or less	0	38	4	61
	100	100	100	101
	(N = 55)		(N = 47)	

Maryland figures from 1960 census.

that the demonstrators came from the higher reaches of the class system.

How may we explain this paradox? Analytically, the answer lies in Tables 3 and 4 which show that, although the most deprived were the most active once they were in the movement, they were among the last to join. Thus, although deprivation was necessary for intense activity, it inhibited joining.

But why were the most highly deprived late joiners? We suggest it is because other attributes are necessary for participation besides deprivations. Two major ones are these: 1) A belief in the efficacy of political action. People are not likely to join a movement if they do not believe it will be effective.[12] This is indicated in Tables 5 and 6. Table

3. The most deprived, in terms of socioeconomic status, were among the latest recruits (percent early joiners *)

	High		Medium		Low	
Socioeconomic status †:	%	N	%	N	%	N
Total sample	27	97	36	161	27	45
Negro non-students	43	7	44	18	18	17
Negro students	35	20	40	42	30	10
White non-students	40	5	42	40	33	18
White students	22	65	26	61	—	0

* Percent who first participated prior to 1961.

† Socioeconomic status: as in Table 1.

4. The most deprived, in terms of social mobility, were among the latest recruits (percent early joiners *)

	Negroes		White		Both	
	%	N	%	N	%	N
Social mobility † (non-students only)						
Upward	25	12	41	22	35	34
Stable	50	10	33	12	41	22
Downward	0	2	29	14	25	16

* As in Table 3.

† Social mobility: as in Table 1.

5 indicates that those highly pessimistic about the chances of desegregating restaurants in Baltimore, a major goal of the movement at that time, were late joiners. Table 6 indicates that, among Negroes, a general lack of faith in political activity, i.e., political alienation, led to late joining (the relation was different for whites, for reasons too complicated to go into here).[13] On the other hand, if demonstrators did have faith in the possibilities of political action, they were able to join early. One such group were ideologues whose beliefs embodied a deep conviction that history was on their side. They were among the earliest joiners, as is indicated in Table 7. 2) Organizational involvement. Previous studies have indicated that organizations function to drag people into political activity.[14] That the sit-ins were no exception is indicated in Table 8. Not only were those involved in civil rights organizations more likely to join early, but so also were those involved in other organizations.

5. Deep pessimism inhibits early joining

	Deeply Pessimistic *		Somewhat Pessimistic		Not Pessimistic	
	%	N	%	N	%	N
Percent active †	55	(22)	42	(84)	43	(210)
Percent early joiners ‡	10	(21)	31	(81)	33	(202)

* Deeply pessimistic are those who strongly disagreed with the statement: "Baltimore restaurants will be desegregated by the middle of 1962." Somewhat pessimistic are those who disagreed, but not strongly. Not pessimistic are those who agreed with the statement.

† As in Table 1.

‡ As in Table 3.

6. Politically alienated Negroes were late joiners

	Politically Alienated * (blacks only)		Not Politically Alienated (blacks only)	
	%	N	%	N
Percent active †	55	(31)	40	(80)
Percent early joiners ‡	17	(29)	38	(76)

* Those who agreed that "there is really little difference between the Republican and Democratic parties," and did not feel strongly that "letters are a good way for a citizen to make his voice count in public policy." The same relations hold for the statement: "All politicians are corrupt," when a control is made for ideology.

† As in Table 1.

‡ As in Table 3.

Thus, a sense of efficacy and organizational involvement are two additional factors necessary for active participation. But we know from numerous studies, that such characteristics are particularly rare among the highly deprived.[15] Here, then, is an explanation for their late joining. Additional evidence is given in Table 9. This shows that where lower status persons do possess a belief in the possibilities of action—for instance, when they possess an ideology whose belief system guarantees success—they are early, rather than late, joiners. Unfortunately, due to a lack of sufficient case bases, we cannot make similar controls for either political alienation or organizational involvement. However, in a later study of recruitment to another social movement, sufficient cases did exist. When feelings of hopelessness and non-involvement in organizations were controlled in this study, class differences in joining disappeared.[16]

3) The consequence of these processes was low participation. Active participation required socially contradictory characteristics: deprivation on the one hand; and a sense of efficacy on the other. Thus:

7. Ideologues were early joiners

	Socialists		Non-socialists	
	%	N	%	N
Percent active *	76	(59)	47	(245)
Percent early joiners †	41	(58)	29	(237)

* As in Table 1.

† As in Table 3.

8. Those involved in alienating organizations were early joiners even when the organizations were not civil rights organizations

Civil Rights Organizations Only

Number of alienating organizations into which respondent reported himself integrated *

	≥2 alienating		1 alienating		no organizations	
	%	N	%	N	%	N
Percent early joiners †	75	(4)	36	(28)	32	(165)
Percent more active ‡	100	(4)	68	(28)	49	(181)

Non-civil Rights Organizations Only

Number of alienating organizations into which respondent reported himself integrated

	≥2 alienating		1 alienating		no organizations	
	%	N	%	N	%	N
Percent early joiners	71	(7)	40	(20)	32	(165)
Percent more active	86	(7)	65	(20)	49	(181)

* Alienating organizations are those with goals in opposition to the larger society, but with little power. For further explication, see Von Eschen, Kirk, and Pinard, "Organizations and Disorderly Politics," cited in note 4.

† As in Table 1.

‡ As in Table 3.

1) The numbers available to the movement for recruitment were limited. It had to draw on that relatively narrow stratum possessing both characteristics to some degree. This accounts for the curvilinear relations in Tables 3 and 4. The highly deprived did not possess the sense of efficacy or organizational involvement necessary to join; while the least deprived while possessing these, did not possess sufficient deprivation. The movement was, thus, denied access both to the bulk of the Negro population—working class Negroes (see Tables 2 through 4 again)—and to the Negro upper class. Its numbers were, thus, restricted. 2) Because it, therefore, had to recruit from those only moderately deprived, participation was sporadic; for the moderately deprived were less motivated to participate intensely (see Table 1 again).

Were these processes operating outside Maryland? This seems almost certain. Matthews and Prothro (1966:419, 426) found in their study of Negro students in the South that joining was disproportion-

9. Ideology permitted a lower status person to join early (percent early joiners *)

Party	Left of Mother † (Ideologues)		Not Left of Mother (Non-ideologues)	
Preferences	%	N	%	N
Socioeconomic status ‡				
High	29	28	29	49
Medium	38	61	34	71
Low	43	14	18	22

* As in Table 3.

† Based on a comparison of respondent's and his mother's party preference. The reason the socialist-non-socialist distinction is not used in this table is that the case base among those of low status was too small. Instead, we are using a wider measure of ideology. The purpose of the comparison of respondent's with mother's preference is to separate those who have consciously adopted their political positions from those only weakly committed to them. We did this because we found no relation between ideology and participation for those who inherited their politics. We used left of mother rather than father because of the absence of data on father's political preference for many participants and because in those cases where parents were split politically, most participants agreed with their mothers. As about half of those classified as "left of mother" were socialists and most of the rest independents who were left of the Democratic and Republican parties, this group is not only "left of mother," but left politically as well.

‡ As in table 1.

ately low among those attending the poorer schools and coming from the least advantaged social backgrounds. The same was found by Searles and Williams (1962:219) in their study of Negro students in Greensboro and Raleigh, North Carolina. In addition, both teams of investigators found that joining was inversely related to pessimism about the probable resistence of whites. Finally, Searles and Williams found that those who joined the sit-ins were more likely to have participated in previously established organizations, i.e., had a higher level of organizational involvement. Also an examination of data on the composition of all movements for which such data could be gathered showed that, without exception, the most deprived were underrepresented even though, for many of these movements, they would have had the most reason to participate.[17] Thus, such processes seem to be universal.

We, therefore, have further reason to think participation was low everywhere. But, if this is true, how then did the movement succeed?

Although the movement was itself nonviolent, disorder frequently followed in its wake. The intense racist sentiments of the whites led them violently to attack demonstrators; and, in response, Negro nonmembers of the movement often retaliated by rioting.

That such disorder was essential to the movement's success is clear. Except when accompanied by a boycott, demonstrations had an impact only when they generated, or at least threatened, disorder. This was clear in all three studies.

Maryland. In 1960 and 1961, numerous peaceful demonstrations were carried out in Baltimore with virtually no impact. A close examination of the newspapers during this period shows practically no coverage given to these demonstrations; and, as far as can be discerned from the few accounts that do appear, the targets of the demonstrations gave them equally scant attention. What was missing was disorder. It was finally provided by the violent reaction of racists, not in Baltimore, but in Birmingham and Anniston, toward the Freedom Riders. After these events, when CORE announced a demonstration on Route 40 in Maryland, the mood communicated by the newspapers was one of hysteria. The inevitably selective attention of the media was focused on images of burning buses, uncontrollable mobs, and the like. The elites now began to respond. Restaurateurs said they would desegregate. Political elites began to pay attention to the movement. In short, only when the demonstrations appeared to threaten disorder did they get attention.

A similarly striking example occurred later on Maryland's Eastern Shore, where sentiments similar to those in the Deep South are prevalent. For some time demonstrations had been held in this area, yet with little effect. Subsequently, however, peaceful demonstrations led to violent racist attacks until finally some of the less sophisticated (and, therefore, difficult to organize) elements of the Negro population began to lash back violently at their opponents in Cambridge, a small Eastern Shore community. The impact was startling. Towns around Cambridge began desegregating at a rapid rate as soon as civil rights groups announced proposed demonstrations in these towns. Again, only with disorder was attention, and sometimes capitulation, given to the movement.

Nashville. The Nashville movement occurred in two major waves. In the first, demonstrations combined with a nearly complete boycott desegregated lunch counters in the downtown department stores. In the second, a drive was made to desegregate all restaurants. Here, a boycott could not be effective, as these restaurants did not depend on Negro clientele. For almost two years, a series of peaceful demonstrations failed to bring any progress whatsoever. The turning point finally came when the movement leaders hit on the idea of recruiting high school students. When these students entered the picket lines, the whole character of the demonstrations changed. These students and their friends who came to watch were unwilling to practice non-violence in the face of the attacks of white racists. Rioting ensued. The movement, nevertheless, continued to hold demonstrations, each generating more disorder than the last. Within the week, the leaders of the community had called a general meeting and persuaded restaurateurs to make a settlement.

Florida. The importance of disorder was also indicated in Killian and Grigg's investigation. In their study of a biracial committee, they wrote that, "in the absence of issues raised through the application of power [in this case, the failure of Negroes to hold a wade-in at the nearby beach, an action that would have brought mob violence,] the committee not only failed to act, but ceased to meet" (Killian and Grigg, 1964:75).

Why disorder was so important is not hard to determine: disorder mobilized friends and sanctioned opponents.

Although many whites in powerful positions were favorable to Negro equality, in general they did not act strongly on these beliefs. They had other goals that consumed their time and energies. Often the realization of these goals was dependent on those unsympathetic to Negro rights, and so forth. Thus, for example, northern liberal senators often compromised their commitment to civil rights to gain the support of southern senators for other pieces of liberal legislation. One function of disorder was to force these liberals, by creating a crisis, to set Negro rights over their other goals.

Secondly, disorder brought economic and political sanctions. For example, in Cambridge, Maryland, tourist trade was severely injured after the riots there. In Nashville, one reason financial leaders gave for their attempts to persuade restaurateurs to settle after the disorders was their fear that industry would not locate in a town torn by riots. In a Florida city studied by Killian and Grigg (1964:137) Negro demonstrators

demonstrated their ability to invoke the sanctions of notoriety upon the community, as national newspapers, radio and television broadcast descriptions of mob violence on the city's main streets. A group of economically powerful white leaders became convinced that this sort of notoriety could be extremely harmful to the city's industrial growth, as the experience of Little Rock had demonstrated.

Finally, the Southern Regional Conference put out a general report documenting the adverse economic consequences of demonstrations throughout the South.

Disorder brought political sanctions as well. Both the public and elected officials regard the maintenance of order as a primary function of government. Thus, officials not only feel responsible for maintaining order, but they know that if they do not succeed, the public may hold them accountable. In addition, politically, disorder is a symptom of politicization in the population. Such a process, if not discouraged, may increase mass interest in politics, bringing new forces into the political arena and threatening the position of established politicians. Thus, in Cambridge, Maryland, the moderate leaders were replaced with extreme conservatives after the racist masses had been activated by the disturbances. The same phenomenon occurred elsewhere in the South.

Disorder could be created by small numbers. Given the intense reaction of white racists and the resentment of the Negro community, even a handful of demonstrators could spark disorder. For instance, only a few dozen demonstrators were sufficient to generate violence in Cambridge after the situation there had become intense.

This fact was of utmost importance to the movement. It meant that it could have an impact despite its small numbers. In a sense, the necessary numbers were supplied by its opponents and by Negro bystanders who were caught up in the ensuing melee. For example, in Baltimore the media gave great attention to a mob that surrounded only a handful of demonstrators in Little Italy. In speaking of the Birmingham demonstrations that figured so importantly in the national movement, an aid of King told Robert Penn Warren (1965:226)

[The white press corps] can't distinguish between Negro spectators. All they know is Negroes, and most of the spectacular pictures printed in *Life* and in television clips had the commentary "Negro demonstrators" when they were not that at all. . . .

On the first Sunday of the demonstration, we had twenty-three demonstrators in the march. But people began to stand around, and it swelled to about fifteen hundred . . . and when UPI took pictures they said: fifteen hundred demonstrators, twenty-two arrested. Well, that was all we had.

So we devised the technique, we'd set the demonstration up for a certain hour and then delay it two hours and let the crowd collect.

Not only were few numbers necessary to create disorder, but once disorder had been created, it was no longer necessary to use even these few. As any demonstration came to have, for whites, a violent potential, in time it was necessary only to announce a demonstration to get effects. Thus, in Maryland, certain areas on the Eastern Shore were partially desegregated through threats of demonstrations, rather than by actually carrying them out. This tactic was consciously used by a leader of one of the major civil rights organizations in the state. The importance of not having to demonstrate cannot be underestimated in a situation where the movement organizations involved had trouble mobilizing people for action.

Thus, disorder was essential to the movement's success. But, of course, it was not sufficient. Confronted with disorder, elites had at least two alternatives open to them—capitulation to demands or suppression of the demonstrators. Why was suppression not used? The answer specifies the other conditions for the movement's success.

American values stress equalitarianism, while the subordinate position of the Negro in the United States society conflicts grossly with these norms. In short, there is, in Gunnar Myrdal's terms, a dilemma (Myrdal, 1944). Thus, as Hyman and Sheatsley have shown through the use of public opinion polls, from 1944 to 1963 the public became increasingly sympathetic with the plight of the Negro (Hyman and Sheatsley, 1964). By the time national legislators were confronted in 1963 with demands for open accommodations and protection of voting rights, a majority of whites were at least somewhat sympathetic.[18] Thus, the dilemma meant that elements among the white population were willing to work for legislation supporting the movement's goals and to agitate against suppression. The importance of this cannot be underestimated. Had there not been this sympathy, suppression would surely have been the alternative chosen. This can be seen by examining what happened in the Deep South where the white population was nearly uniformly against Negro demands. Here, at the local level, attempts at repression was the response. Even the mass demonstrations of SCLC in Birmingham, Albany, and the like, seem to have brought little change locally. That the civil rights movement was not totally destroyed in these areas was due to the fact that northern sentiment inhibited total repression and that the issue was finally settled outside the Deep South by federal legislation sponsored by national elites with constituencies either in favor of or, at worst, indifferent to Negro demands.

The impact of the dilemma was heightened by its concentration among the elite. Public opinion pools have universally shown that the higher the education of a person, the more likely he is to favor civil rights for Negroes.[19] That is, sensitivity to the dilemma is greatest among the more powerful. This meant that the impact of the dilemma could be greater than its average acceptance in the population might suggest—particularly important in those border state areas where the majority of whites were opposed to Negro rights. Thus, in Maryland, referendums and a George Wallace primary held late in the conflict revealed that whites, in general, opposed public accommodations. Elite sentiment minimized the impact of this fact. During the struggle for a public accommodations law, ministers, Young Democrats, junior members of the bar, editors of one of the major newspapers, and the like, all spoke out in its favor. The result was to create a climate of opinion in which it was illegitimate among established leaders, whatever their private opinions, publicly to oppose equal public accommodations. In short, no established leader dared to agitate the segregationist masses. Thus, even those who voted against the public accommodations law in the Baltimore City Council and in the State Assembly, refused, in general, to make speeches defending their beliefs. This meant that the masses were left without leadership throughout most of the conflict and, therefore, remained disorganized and ineffective.

Still, we have not yet arrived at the whole answer. Public or elite sympathy for the movement's goals does not entirely account for capitulation rather than suppression. Since the means used by the movement were illegitimately nonroutine, opponents could have used this issue as a way of publicly opposing the movement without having to appear segregationist. And, in fact, it was common to hear opponents say that they did not oppose integration, but that it should not be brought about by picketing and the like. That this was not a successful or widely used tactic was due to two additional factors.

The movement depended for success on using means less illegitimate than those of its opponents. The movement chose the least illegitimate of all nonroutine means—nonviolence. This minimized not only its illegitimacy, but also the danger that the disorder so necessary for the movement's progress would be attributed directly to the movement and its organizations. Had the violence arising from demonstrations been advocated by the movement, or even informally encouraged by it, there would have been far less hesitation in suppressing its activity. This choice of nonviolence, it should be added, was closely related to the small size of the movement. Few people have the sophistication and self-control both to see the necessity of nonviolence and to live by that principle. The very smallness of the movement made it possible to behave in a disciplined and even self-sacrificing manner.

Almost always the behavior of the opposition was more illegitimate than that of the movement. Throughout the Maryland demonstrations, the movement never departed from nonviolent means. The opponents on the other hand engaged in numerous illegitimate acts, from beating the grandson of a distinguished public servant (in front of a television camera, it might be added) to kicking a pregnant woman in the stomach. The same was true for the movement in other areas. When the movement picketed, its enemies screamed and jeered; when the movement sang freedom songs, it was squirted with mustard, spat on, and beaten. The result of this behavior on the part of the segregationists was to make the movement appear extremely virtuous; indeed, it made the system of segregation appear far more brutal than it had prior to the demonstrations. It meant that the illegitimacy of the movement's methods was greatly outweighed by that of the opposition's. It meant that it was very difficult for established leaders outside the Deep South to ally themselves in any way with the lawless opposition. The movement owed no little of its success to the Jim Clarks and "Bull" Connerses.

The movement depended for success on concentration. Because of the movement's small size, it was forced to concentrate its effort geographically. In Maryland, for instance, either the demonstrations were being held in Baltimore, or in the country, or on the Eastern Shore, but rarely in all places at the same time. The effect of this was striking. First, areas that had not yet been attacked tended to criticize the resistance of areas under siege. Apparently they were willing to refer the issue to their abstract values of equality. Second, after an area had been attacked and had capitulated, it tended to support the movement in other areas. There seem to have been a number of reasons for this. First, an ideological one: once an area had done what was right, even if forced to do it, it felt virtuous. Second, there were material reasons: businessmen feared that if only their area were desegregated, customers might go elsewhere. Concentration had similar effects on the national movement. Again, partly because of limited resources, the movement tended to concentrate on the South. This permitted the North to refer the issue to its abstract values, to feel superior, to offer support. The potency of concentration can perhaps be seen in the deep resentment expressed by northern whites in those few instances where civil rights leaders publicly stated that conditions in the North were just as bad as in the South.

In sum, the movement did not depend on large numbers for success. It could not, for active participation required the participant to be highly deprived, but such persons were held out of the movement by feelings of low political efficacy. Instead, the movement relied on the creation of disorder—disorder which could mobilize friends and sanction opponents, and which could be created by small numbers. That this method did not lead to suppression was due to several factors: that there existed in the society a dilemma, a dilemma to which the most powerful were the most sensitive, that the movement chose the least illegitimate of all nonroutine means while its opponents responded without restraint; and that, because of its small numbers, the movement was forced to concentrate its efforts geographically, permitting most people to refer the issue to their abstract values rather than their self-interest.

This understanding of the circumstances under which the nonviolent movement succeeded permits us to arrive at a partial explanation of why, despite these successes, it shortly thereafter dissolved. In brief, these circumstances were such that a) the will of blacks to use nonviolence inevitably weakened,[20] and b) the conditions for effective nonviolent action inevitably became attenuated, so that, even had the will persisted, a viable movement would no longer have been possible.

First, because the movement used disorder as a major sanction, it was inevitable that many of the later participants would draw the conclusion that violence works, failing to perceive the more subtle conditions under which such violence can be effective (e.g., the use of means less illegitimate than those of one's opponents, the necessity of a dilemma, and so forth). Second, the need for and the dynamics of recruitment inevitably pushed the movement away from nonviolence.

As we have seen, the movement during its nonviolent phase was not large: its core, in fact, was small. This smallness was one of the major features permitting the use of nonviolence. Only those committed to nonviolence were likely to participate intensely, leaders could reach each member for training in nonviolence, and small groups were easy to discipline. But the movement, inevitably, could not remain small. For reasons given below, larger numbers were necessary and, being necessary, the movement actively sought them. Also, the movement, by demonstrating success, was bound to break down a major inhibition to participation—pessimism about its potentialities—and increased recruitment was bound to follow. But as the movement, for these two reasons, became larger, selectivity, discipline, and training inevitably weakened. This was evident in the Chicago housing demonstrations of 1966 where a segment of the movement refused to obey King's order to cease demonstrating in order to prevent violence.

Also, as we have seen, the movement was heavily middle class. This probably aided nonviolence in that such an ethic, requiring a sophisticated theory of its effects and strong self-discipline, is more congenial to middle class personality and cognitive development.[21] But the movement could not remain solely middle class, for two reasons. The shift to welfare goals, mentioned below, meant that the movement would have less appeal to middle class individuals and that, therefore, if it were to maintain even the numbers it had before, it would have to extend its roots into the working class. Second, the success of the movement would remove a major barrier to working class participation, belief that action is not effective. That the movement did, in time, begin to attract more working class individuals was indicated in the Maryland study, where, in some of the later demonstrations, considerable numbers of working class individuals did begin to participate. This is also evident in the questionnaire data above where lower status individuals reported themselves as having recently joined the movement.

The dependence of the movement on its small, middle-class character for nonviolence is indicated in this quote from Robert Penn Warren (1965:214):

Stokeley Carmichael, of Snick, tells me that in some of the demonstrations in Cambridge, Maryland, only a few Negroes were willing to enter a non-violent demonstration, but that when Snick demonstrators, committed to nonviolence, moved into the street they were followed by a crowd of the local people who had refused to demonstrate. Then when the Snick demonstrators confronted the police, the local people behind the screen, threw bricks and bottles at the police.

In short, the mass of the population, most of whom were working class, were not committed to nonviolence. One consequence of this in Cambridge was that when they did become fully involved in the struggle, a riot ensued in which a number of people sustained serious injuries.

Even had the will to use nonviolence persisted, the conditions for its effectiveness were bound to disappear. First, the dilemma inevitably had to weaken. The movement initially sought goals with the most legitimacy in the eyes of the public—open public accommodations, and voting rights. This was not because these were the highest goals of the leaders: on the contrary, in Nashville, for instance, the leaders were primarily interested in jobs and welfare. This was, instead, due to recruitment requirements. A movement needs victories. Movements, thus, seek easily obtainable goals first, to demonstrate to those inhibited from joining by feelings of political futility that action is, in fact, not futile—and thereby ease the difficult process of recruitment. But this meant that once the initial goals were obtained, the movement had to move on to less legitimate ones—ones where the dilemma would be less strong.

This did in fact happen. The movement shifted to two new sets of goals: 1) Welfare goals. In summer 1966, Martin Luther King led a drive to end housing discrimination in Chicago. But public opinion polls showed that integrated housing did not have the legitimacy that open public accommodations had, surely one of the reasons why resistance to King's drive was so great and the results so meager.[22] The movement also began to press for compensatory hiring and education; and again, goals stressing special benefits rather than equalization had less legitimacy. 2) Acceptance of the legitimacy of black culture. Assimilation of ethnic groups in the United States has always consisted more of legitimizing than of erasing the culture of the group assimilated, and one of the mechanisms of collective social mobility has been pride in the knowledge that the group culture is shared from childhood. By 1966, some Negro leaders began to ask whether Negroes should be required to give up their culture. But this idea is not highly legitimate to most whites. As most Negroes are not far from the culture of the Delta and the slum, United States Negro culture represents poverty, symbolizing total failure to most Americans, as well as expressive behavior and immediate gratification. This runs counter to the whole moral burden of child socialization in the United States, and Negroes arguing that there may be elements of dignity in this culture are latently suggesting that the devil of America's secular ethic be permitted to walk the street.

Second, concentration of the dilemma among the elite inevitably had to become less important. Although sensitivity to the dilemma by elite elements may make it initially difficult for the masses, being thus deprived of leadership, to make their views heard politically, this is clearly a temporary situation. If established elites will not represent a popular view, new leadership which does will in time be developed. This happened in Maryland toward the end of the public accommodations struggle, when previously unknown individuals began to organize a counter movement, and later in 1966 when George Mahoney, once regarded as a near amateur in political circles, ran on a platform of opposition to open housing.

In addition, the masses may act through referendums. Although masses must act normally through elites if their voice is to be heard, where referendums exist, they may in time bypass elite unresponsiveness. Ultimately, therefore, concentration of the dilemma matters little. Thus, in Maryland, by the third year of the movement and after a public accommodations bill had been passed by the state legislature, a referendum was held in which the majority of whites voted against open accommodations. In California, whites, through a referendum, voted down a law integrating housing. The importance of referendums in permitting masses to bypass elites is seen by the following statement: "Despite the support of most clergymen, prominent citizens, of most leaders of both parties, the new housing law was overwhelmingly repealed by the voters" (Bell, 1968:177).

Third, the comparative legitimacy of the movement's means to those used by its opponents was bound to change. The response of the movement's opponents was bound to become less extreme. For one thing, a movement is a school in which both the movement and its opponents learn by trial and error the most appropriate moves. Thus, much of the success of the movement had depended on the untutored, emotional responses of the southern police. In time, however, authorities learned that such responses were counterproductive. In some areas, authorities learned responses sufficiently appropriate to deny the movement its instrument of disorder and to disorganize totally its leadership. In Maryland, for instance, Mayor McKeldin responded to CORE's announcement that Baltimore was to become CORE's target city with a warm welcome and an offer of aid, and the temporary chief of police, Gelston, used highly sophisticated tactics to defuse CORE's strategies.[23] In addition, the shift to goals where discrimination was far more subtle than in the case of public accommodations and voting meant a shift to geographical areas where the population was less likely to respond in a violently racist manner. Thus, when the movement tried in New York to press for desegregation of de facto segregated schooling, whites responded not by violence, as they had in the South, but by peaceful picketing, a tactic both legal and less disruptive than staying away from school, the means used by the Negroes.

Simultaneously, the perceived means of the movement were bound to become less legitimate. We do not refer here to the fact that many in the movement, for reasons given above, were bound to become less committed to nonviolence, as in Chicago where demonstrators asserted the right of self-defense and responded to white attacks by throwing bottles back at their tormentors. Even had this not occurred, even if the movement had remained entirely nonviolent, its means would have come to appear less legitimate. For one thing, under the religious leadership of Martin Luther King, the nonviolent means used by the movement between 1960 and 1965 generally employed a rhetoric of moral persuasion, an emphasis overtly on morally converting one's opponents. This meant that the movement had the tone of nonviolently asking whites to give greater status and power to blacks. Of all types of nonviolent action, this is likely to appear the most legitimate. But such moral nonviolence was inevitably unstable. As the movement was forced to shift to new and harder goals, as leadership developed among the white masses, as whites learned to respond without creating disorder, it became necessary for the movement to recruit greater numbers. Only larger numbers were likely to bring gains in the face of this greater, but more subtle resistance. As we have shown, however, recruitment is difficult, inhibited by feelings of low political efficacy. One way to overcome this barrier is, as Table 9 indicated, to propagate an ideology stressing the possibilities of action. It was inevitable, therefore, that black power or some similar ideology should have been developed by the movement.[24] Among other things, black power attempts to break down feelings of low efficacy by emphasizing to the Negro his potential political power. But such an ideology, while functional for recruitment, no longer creates in the minds of whites an image of a movement that is asking them to give it concessions. Black power tells whites that blacks are going to take what is due. This may be done, of course, nonviolently, through such actions as bloc voting, massive economic sanctions (boycotts), and so forth. But such nonviolence, emphasizing in rhetoric not moral persuasion but coercion, appears less legitimate. In addition, the previous successes of the movement through disorder inevitably led working-class members of the Negro community to engage in riot-ing.[25] As such rioting by people not in the movement became ever more frequent, as it occurred more and more on the heels of non-violent demonstrations carried out by the movement, and as move-ment members themselves increasingly made black power statements, it became harder and harder for the public to distinguish the riots from the actions of the movement itself. This meant that the non-violent means of the movement, by becoming merged in the public mind with the riots, came to appear less and less legitimate.

Fourth, the advantages of concentration inevitably had to be lost. This was true for at least two reasons. 1) Insofar as the previous suc-cesses of the movement aided recruitment, the movement gained the ability to carry on demonstrations in many areas at once. 2) Even had the movement tried to concentrate its efforts, as was done when King made Chicago and CORE made Baltimore their target cities, the movement had no control over rioting which broke out everywhere.

In sum, the will to nonviolence declined as blacks concluded cor-rectly that disorder works, and as the inevitable expansion and chang-ing composition of the movement brought in people whose life styles were inconsistent with nonviolent action. Simultaneously, the condi-tions for effective nonviolent action attenuated as the movement was forced to shift to new goals where the dilemma was less strong; as the segregationist masses developed their own leadership or gained polit-ical access through referendums; as both they and the authorities began to respond in less disorder-creating ways; as the perceived means of the movement became less legitimate; and as the movement lost the advantages of concentration. All these changes were largely inevitable. The result was the disintegration of the movement. The loss of potential effectiveness made the creation of a viable movement exceedingly difficult. When combined with the loss of will, the move-ment dissolved.

What, then, is the future of nonviolence in the Negro movement? It is clear that nonviolence as we have known it in the past is dead; few leaders now espouse a nonviolent ideology. Yet, it can be argued that, in some sense, the actions of certain of these leaders is still nonviolent. Some are presently engaged in the attempt to create parallel institutions, i.e., to develop black-controlled businesses, black-controlled schools, and even, in the case of one leader, fully black communities. This action is clearly nonviolent, although quite different from the previous nonviolent action, for it does not attempt to throw off oppression by confrontation with whites. Instead it attempts to withdraw from such confrontation and establish peacefully the same bases of power-capital, educational systems, and community institutions now predominantly in the hands of whites. If these efforts succeed, a new and perhaps more powerful nonviolent method will have been found.

NOTES

1. For background information on the history of the nonviolent movement, see Matthews and Prothro (1966:407 ff.), or Lomax (1963).
2. For documentation of this abandonment of nonviolence, see Bell (1968). CORE stands for the Congress on Racial Equality and SNCC for the Student Nonviolent Coordinating Committee, two of the major groups leading the nonviolent movement of that period. The third was SCLS, the Southern Christian Leadership Conference, the group led by Martin Luther King. This organization has not abandoned nonviolence.
3. It must be emphasized that we are not in this chapter trying to give a complete explanation of why nonviolence was abandoned. Rather, we are delineating only those reasons implied by our understanding of the circumstances under which the movement succeeded in attaining its initial goals. Other reasons, supplementing ours, are given in Bell (1968).
4. See Pinard, Kirk, and Von Eschen (1969); Von Eschen, Kirk, and Pinard (1969); D. Von Eschen, J. Kirk, and M. Pinard, "Organizations and Disorderly Politics" (Paper delivered at the Sixtieth Annual Meeting of the American Sociological Association, Montreal, 1964); J. Kirk, M. Pinard, and D. Von Eschen, "The Revolutionary Movement as a Political Organization" (Paper delivered at the Sixtieth Annual Meeting of the American Sociological Association, Montreal, 1964).
5. Lyle Yorks and Donald Von Eschen, "The Micro-Dynamics of the Civil Rights Movement, 1960–1964: The Case of Nashville" (Paper delivered at the Thirty-first Annual Meeting of the Southern Sociological Association, 1968).
6. *Core-Lator,* No. 101, July 1963.
7. This is not to say that no local movements experienced higher participation, only that most probably did not.
8. The impact of some of this data is diluted even before interpreting it in terms of our Maryland and Nashville findings. For instance, the claim by the Southern Regional Conference that seventy thousand persons participated in over eight hundred sit-ins in over one hundred cities during the first year and a half of the movement indicates that, on the average, only seven hundred persons participated per city carrying out only an average of eight or so sit-ins

per city or an average of one every two months throughout the period. When our Maryland and Nashville findings are applied to this data, it becomes even less impressive. Assume, as is plausible in light of these findings, that, say, out of every eight demonstrations, one was large and seven small, and that, on the average, most people (excluding the hard core of activists) participated in one large and two small demonstrations. This would mean that each city, on the average, experienced one demonstration of seven hundred people and seven of two hundred (instead of eight of seven hundred people). Of course, there were probably many small demonstrations which the Southern Regional Conference failed to report. But this is precisely our point. Most demonstrations were, in fact, small.

9. See Warren (1965:367–68) for reports of complaints by student activists in the South about the complacency and apathy of their fellow students. Data about the attitudes of SNCC workers toward King's demonstrations were gathered by Louis Goldberg in summer 1965 (personal communication).

10. The data were collected from participants in one of the major demonstrations in Maryland, the "Route 40 Freedom Ride." African diplomats, in their travels between the United Nations in New York and their embassies in Washington, D.C., had been denied service in restaurants along the major route between these two centers, Route 40. In December 1961, some five to six hundred members of CORE and other civil rights organizations drove along the Maryland section of the route requesting service at restaurants previously known to be segregated, variously sitting-in, picketing, or submitting to arrest if service was refused. By passing out questionnaires at the Baltimore terminal of the ride, we obtained data from 386 of the participants (i.e., 60 to 80 percent). The reason why some participants did not fill out the questionnaire is that they either did not arrive at the Baltimore terminal or, more often, were organized into groups leaving for a demonstration before they could complete it. While the sample is, thus, not random, so that confidence or significance measures cannot be applied, we have been unable to discern any source of systematic nonresponse bias and we feel satisfied that these data present an undistorted picture of the group.

11. See the references cited in note 4.

12. The importance of a sense of efficacy for participation in routine politics has been shown in many studies. See, for instance, Campbell et al. (1960:104–5).

13. See, however, Von Eschen, Kirk, and Pinard (1969).

14. See, for example, Lipset, Trow and Coleman (1956), especially pp. 69–105; or Erbe (1964:198–215).

15. For data showing that feelings of political efficacy are much lower among those toward the bottom of the stratification system, see, for instance, Campbell et al. (1956:172–73). Note that such feelings are particularly absent among Negroes as compared with whites. For data that higher organizational involvement is much less frequent among those at the bottom of the stratification system, see, for instance, Erbe (1964:207). Also see Rose (1967b:22), where Rose surveys the literature on social class and organizational involvement.

16. Pinard (1971). Chapter 8, "The Response of the Poor," contains the tables controlling for feelings of hopelessness. Chapter 11, "Mass Society and Social Credit," contains the tables controlling for organizational involvement. Pinard (1967) is a condensed version of chapter 8, in Pinard (1971).

17. See Pinard (1971), section in chapter 8 entitled, "The Poor in Other Movements." Among these movements were the socialist C. C. F. party in Saskatchewan, Canada, the Social Credit Party in Quebec, Canada, the Poujadist movement in France, and the popular rebellions of the eighteenth century in France.

18. A Louis Harris poll published in *Newsweek* on October 21, 1963, showed that a majority of whites favored equal accommodations.

19. See, for instance, the Louis Harris poll reported in the *Washington Post* of August 13, 1966, in which 57 percent of "affluent" whites, but only 24 percent of "low-privileged" whites "backed" Negro protest.

20. For additional reasons why blacks lost the will to use nonviolence, see Bell (1968).

21. Bell (1968:15, 80) also makes this point.

22. In the 1966 Louis Harris poll, cited in note 19 above, only 16 percent of whites objected to sitting next to a Negro in a restaurant, while most objected to living next door to a Negro.

23. An excellent account of the successful strategies used by McKeldin and Gelston to "tame" CORE in Baltimore is given by Louis Goldberg, "Cops and CORE: The Case of Baltimore" (Manuscript, Department of Sociology, McGill University, 1968).

24. The ideology of black power is well laid out in Carmichael and Hamilton (1967).

25. The way in which riots were generated by the nonviolent movement is more complicated than indicated in this sentence. Essentially, the nonviolent movement 1) raised the expectations of blacks, 2) showed them that disorder works, and 3) that sanctions were not as likely to be meted out as might have been anticipated, protest having become legitimate. As a result, when it became clear that hopes (expectations) were not going to be quickly realized, blacks engaged in acts (disorder in the form of riots) which sanctioned whites without being prohibitively costly to blacks.

14

The Deradicalization of Marxist Movements

ROBERT C. TUCKER

INTERPRETATIONS OF POST-STALIN IDEOLOGICAL CHANGE

Marxism-Leninism, as the Soviet Marxist ideology is called, has never been wholly static; it has evolved over the years by a process of accretion, elimination, and redefinition of dogma. But in the first post-Stalin decade, there were changes of unusual scope and significance in this sphere, accompanying and in some ways mirroring the general processes of systemic change which Stalin's death precipitated in Soviet society. This essay seeks to interpret the post-Stalin Soviet ideological changes, especially as they bear upon the politics of world revolution. In doing so, it attacks the broader theoretical problem of what goes on in radical political movements and their ideologies as these movements settle down and accommodate themselves to the existing world. For some such tendency appears to be involved in the Soviet case.

The year 1956 was the watershed of post-Stalin ideological change in the U.S.S.R. In the Central Committee's report to the Twentieth Party Congress—the first congress held after Stalin's death—Nikita Khrushchev announced a series of doctrinal innovations affecting particularly the line of Communist Marxism on international relations and the further development of the world Communist revolu-

Reprinted from the *American Political Science Review* 61 (June 1967), by permission of the author and the publisher, the American Political Science Association.

tion. One was the revision of the Leninist thesis on the inevitability of periodic wars under imperialism. On the ground that the worldwide forces for peace were now unprecedentedly strong, it was proclaimed that wars, while still possible, were no longer fatally inevitable even though "imperialism" continued to exist in large areas. Not only could the antagonistic socioeconomic systems peacefully coexist; they could and should actively cooperate in the maintenance of peaceful relations. At the same time, coexistence was a competitive process, economics being the principal arena of competition. In the long-range nonmilitary contest for influence, the Communist countries would strive to show the superiority of their socialist mode of production over the capitalist mode and would thereby make the Communist socioeconomic model compellingly attractive, particularly to the developing countries. Communism would spread, then, not by force but by force of example. And even as a strictly internal process in the countries concerned, the Communist revolution no longer need necessarily be accomplished through large-scale armed violence. New nonviolent forms of "transition to socialism" (i.e., to communism) might be found, especially in countries where capitalism was not yet very strong. Notwithstanding the Leninist tenet that ruling classes do not voluntarily surrender their power, it might now be possible for socialism to come to power in various places by a parliamentary path. The revolutionary forces would strive to "win a firm majority in parliament and to turn the parliament from an agency of bourgeois democracy into an instrument of genuinely popular will." [1]

Such was a large part of what came to be known in the Communist world as the "Twentieth Congress line." There were other elements as well. One was the proposal for rapprochement and cooperation between Communist parties and their historic Marxist enemies, the Social Democratic parties. Another was the formal recognition of Yugoslavia as a member of the family of Communist states, and therewith the recognition of diversity in Communist methods and institutions as legitimate within certain limits. The Twentieth Congress line was, moreover, accentuated and further elaborated in a series of important Soviet pronouncements in the ensuing years. In elaborating the new thesis on the non-inevitability of wars in the present era, Soviet leaders argued that the rulers of the non-Communist powers, or the more moderate and sober elements among them, could perceive the unprecedented dangers implicit in the rise of nuclear weapons and were inclined to take account of these dangers by pursuing a foreign policy designed to avoid another major war. Accentuating the optimistic idea that competitive coexistence could remain peaceful, the Twenty-First Soviet Party Congress in 1959 declared in its resolution that "even before the complete triumph of socialism on earth, while capitalism still exists on a part of the globe, a genuine possibility will arise of excluding world war from the life of human society" (Gruliow, 1960:214). To be sure, "national-liberation wars" were proclaimed to be legitimate and deserving of assistance from Communist states. But, at the same time, Soviet leaders warned against the dangers of escalation inherent even in small local armed conflicts, and advocated that independence be granted to peoples still under alien rule so that armed struggle would not be needed to attain this goal. And the idea of the desirability of peace-keeping cooperation between competitors, particularly the Soviet Union and United States as the military superpowers of the two coalitions, was elaborated at length in Soviet writings.[2]

The Twentieth Congress line also gave strong endorsement to a new Soviet policy of rapprochement with non-Communist nationalist revolutionary regimes and movements in newly independent nations of Asia, Africa, and Latin America. Governments of countries outside the Communist bloc were invited to join an expanding worldwide "peace zone" by adopting the policy of non-alignment with existing military blocs. Neutralism, the very possibility of which had been denied in Moscow in Stalin's final years, was thus given Soviet support; and what has come to be called the "third world" was recognized as such in a new tripartite world view which contrasted sharply with the Stalinist bifurcation of the contemporary political universe into two warring camps. That the developing countries would eventually develop into Communist states was postulated, but it came to be recognized that nations choosing the "non-capitalist path" of development might inaugurate socialist economic practices in various different ways and not necessarily under Communist party auspices. Moreover, a political way station on the long journey to Communism was envisaged in the concept of a "national democracy," which was defined as a non-Communist regime committed to internal developmental goals, tolerant of its own Communist movement, and friendly to the Soviet Union and associated states. Soviet writings meanwhile continued to emphasize the possibility of a peaceful parliamentary path of transition to communism. And the association of communism with the idea of dictatorship and violence was further softened with the introduction in 1961 of the notion that the contemporary Soviet state had ceased to be a "dictatorship of the proletariat" and become a "state of the whole people" in continual process of democratization.

All these doctrinal modifications were formally incorporated into the new C.P.S.U. Program adopted by the Twenty-Second Party Congress in 1961. Taken in their interrelated entirety, they marked the passage of Soviet Marxist ideology into a new stage of its history. In the decade since the Nineteenth Party Congress of 1952, which met in Stalin's presence and under his aegis, orthodox Leninism-Stalinism had been supplanted with a new Soviet ideological amalgam which might be called "neo-Communist Marxism." Needless to say, it showed continuity with the past, as in the reaffirmation of the ultimate goal of a world Communist society. On the other hand, there were definite breaks with the Communist ideological past. The doctrines of the non-inevitability of wars and the parliamentary path to communism were deviations from Leninist-Stalinist orthodoxy as derived from such fundamental works of Lenin as *Imperialism* and *The State and Revolution*. The idea of a nonclass all-people's state deviated not only from Leninism-Stalinism but from its classical Marxist premises, one of which held that the state qua state is a class agency of repression. And old ideological concepts had in some cases been infused with new content. The most notable example is the altered conception of coexistence, which had once been pictured as a condition of unremitting political warfare and was now seen as a long-range peaceful competition of socioeconomic systems for predominant world influence. True, the peacefully coexisting systems were envisaged as remaining adversaries between which no "ideological coexistence" would be possible.

The rise of neo-Communist Marxism in the Soviet Union has stimulated a worldwide debate over the meaning of the ideological changes. Three broad lines of interpretation have emerged. One is the official Soviet position, which holds that the ideological changes of the post-Stalin period are simply a new stage in a regular process of adaptation and development of Marxism-Leninism to keep it in tune with changing historical realities. Soviet ideology, according to this view, is a "creative Marxism-Leninism" that does not and cannot go unchanged in various particulars although it always remains true to its foundation principles. In particular, such profoundly important developments of the middle twentieth century as the spread of the Communist system and the rise of nuclear weapons necessarily affect the validity of such an ideological thesis as that concerning the inevitability of wars under imperialism. In Khrushchev's words, "one cannot mechanically repeat now what Vladimir Ilyich Lenin said many decades ago regarding imperialism, or continue asserting that imperialist wars are inevitable until socialism triumphs throughout the world." And he went on: "We live in a time when we have neither Marx nor Engels nor Lenin with us. If we act like children who study the alphabet by compiling words from letters, we shall not go very far." [3]

The dominant Western interpretation of the post-Stalin ideological changes is not wholly dissimilar to the Soviet view. Impressed by the vigor of Soviet reaffirmations of commitment to the ultimate goals of world communism, many Western students of Soviet affairs have tended to interpret the ideological innovations as essentially tactical. What has changed to some extent, according to this conception, is the Soviet doctrine on the ways and means of achieving the world Communist society that remains the cherished end of Soviet Communists. Moreover, the tactical changes represent to a very large extent a forced adjustment of doctrine (and practice) to the necessities of the nuclear age. Because of the enormity of the dangers posed by general war in the present era, the Soviet leadership has been compelled to reconsider its working assumptions concerning the feasible methods of spreading communism. The modified Communist credo, with its emphasis upon peaceful competition of systems and its discovery of a peaceful path to Communist revolution, has resulted.

A third interpretation, which has been advanced by the Maoist leadership of Communist China in the course of the Sino-Soviet controversy of recent years, finds a much deeper significance in the Soviet ideological changes after Stalin. It holds that they are symptoms of a degenerative process, a decline of revolutionary commitment on the part of the post-Stalin Soviet leadership or the dominant element of it that found in Khrushchev a natural leader and spokesman. Between the Twentieth and Twenty-Second Party congresses, it maintains, these Soviet leaders developed a complete and rounded system of revisionist views: "They put forward a revisionist line which contravenes the proletarian revolution and the dictatorship of the proletariat, a line which consists of 'peaceful coexistence,' 'peaceful competition,' 'peaceful transition,' 'a state of the whole people' and 'a party of the entire people.' " [4] Hence the Soviet Union's "creative Marxism-Leninism" is in fact a species of revisionism—"Khrushchev revisionism." It expresses, and at the same time endeavors to conceal, the surreptitious departure of the Soviet ruling group from the spirit and practice of revolutionary Marxism-Leninism as taught primarily by Marx, Engels, Lenin, Stalin, and Mao Tse-tung. And Chinese Communist writings have suggested that this phenomenon of Soviet deradicalization (to introduce a term of our own) goes along with, if indeed it does not grow out of, a process of *embourgeoisement* that is taking place in contemporary Soviet society, in which a new middle class has come into being with typical middle-class aspirations for material ease and stability.

"Revisionism" is a highly charged term, signifying in the Marxist context something similar to what various religions have meant by "heresy." For descriptive and analytical purposes, we may refer to the modified Soviet ideology simply as "neo-Communist Marxism." But with this reservation, and leaving aside for the moment the question of causation, I wish to suggest that the Maoist interpretation of the Soviet ideological changes may be close to the mark. The other two views unquestionably have some merit, for Soviet ideology has been creatively adapted to new historical circumstances and this adaptation does chiefly affect matters of strategy and tactics. Yet neither the Soviet official interpretation nor the dominant Western trend of thought does full justice to the phenomenon before us. The thesis of the present chapter, at any rate, is that the changes in question reflect a deradicalization of Soviet communism.

Here the methodological question arises of how such a judgment might be validated. How, in other words, would one know whether the Soviet Communist movement—or any other radical movement, Communist or non-Communist—was in the stage of deradicalization? To raise this question is to focus attention upon an apparent deficiency in our theoretical apparatus. We lack a general conception of deradicalization and, in particular, of the typical symptoms of the process, the characteristic behavior of radical sociopolitical movements, including those of the Marxist persuasion, in the phase when their radicalism has subsided or is subsiding. In general, our scholarship has shown a greater interest in the rise of radical movements than in their decline. Well known titles like *The Origins of Totalitarianism* and *The Origin of Totalitarian Democracy* reflect this bias. There is no disputing the legitimacy and fruitfulness of studying radical movements in their origins and vigorous youth. On the other hand, reflection shows that deradicalization must be the eventual fate of all radical movements, whether or not they achieve political power, and that this process, too, is well worth systematic analysis. Indeed, it may be that the study of such movements in the phase of deradicalization may be one avenue of deeper insight into the psychology and politics of radicalism as such.

The present essay is as much or more concerned with this theoretical problem as with the particular case at hand. It seeks to conceptualize the process of deradicalization in terms of its symptoms, and thereby to suggest certain possible guidelines for analysis of recent phenomena in the development of Soviet communism. These theoretical formulations will necessarily be quite tentative and provisional since they are derived from the study of a single historical instance of the phenomenon in question. The European Social Democracy around the turn of the century provides an example of a Marxist movement that was indubitably in the phase of deradicalization and therefore may be a profitable case to analyze from this point of view.

First, however, a few general remarks on the nature of radical movements, and on deradicalization as a stage in their development.

RADICALISM: A GENERAL VIEW

There are various ways of viewing radical politics and political movements. Some, for example, may think of radical politics as extremist politics and radical movements as those which rely upon extreme or violent methods of action. The difficulty with definitions turning on the mode of action is that extremist means are no monopoly of radical politics but are used on occasion by groups that no one would call radical.

A more promising way of arriving at a working conception of radicalism is to consider the attributes of the type of mind or outlook in which radical politics generally has its source and inspiration. Let us postulate that 1) radical social doctrines arise from time to time as expressions of the radical mind in individuals of outstanding creative power, and 2) under propitious circumstances such doctrines attract followers in significant numbers and become the ideologies of organized sociopolitical movements which may be described as radical by virtue of their being dedicated to the realization of a radical social doctrine. What, then, are the attributes of the radical mind as reflected in the type of doctrines it creates?

There is, to begin with, an intense element of negation in it. The radical is first of all someone who says "No!" to the surrounding society. He mentally and emotionally rebels against the existing order, repudiates the world as it stands, or as he perceives it to stand. For example, Marx—a quintessential example of the modern radical mind—started with a total uncompromising denial and rejection of existing reality. Already in notes to his doctoral dissertation of 1841 he propounded this fundamental theme in the notion that "philosophy," in the persons of Hegel's disciples, was in revolt against the world. What was needed, he wrote somewhat later to his friend Arnold Ruge, was *"a merciless criticism of everything existing,* merciless in two senses: this criticism must not take fright at its own conclusions and must not shrink from a collision with the powers that be." And, in his original formulation of Marxism in the *Economic and Philosophical Manuscripts of 1844,* he foretold the revolutionary transformation of this "alienated world" in which man was everywhere estranged from his own nature and being. Subsequently, his terminology changed somewhat, but his Weltanschauung did not. World-denial is a theme running through the writings of his mature and later years as well as the early works. In a speech of 1856, for example, he pronounced sentence of capital punishment upon the bourgeois social order in the name of what he called the *Vehmgericht* or court of history, appointing the proletarian as "executioner." And for all its tortuous elaboration of abstract concepts, *Capital*, his supreme achievement, was in its way a nine-hundred-page cry of pain and outrage against bourgeois civilization as Marx perceived it.

But the radical is not adequately described as one who rejects existing reality. To understand the radical mind as found in modern Western history, we must penetrate the inner springs of its rebellion. The radical is not simply a rebel but a visionary. What inspires his rebellion against the world as it stands is his vision of an alternative universe, a perfect social order. His negation of what exists proceeds from an underlying affirmation, an idealized image of the world as it ought to be. Indeed, it is the very perfection of his alternative universe that explains the depth and totality, i.e., the radicalness, of his act of world-repudiation. And here again, though somewhat less obviously, Marx provides an illustration. He initially rebelled against the world in the name of the "realization of philosophy," meaning the Hegelian philosophy of man's apotheosis in history. A vision of mankind in a state of perfection was thus his starting point. As his thought developed further, realization of philosophy was redefined to mean transcendence of human self-alienation or "humanism." And humanism in this special Marxian sense was conceived as the essence of future communism, which Marx thought would come about through the socialization of private property in a worldwide proletarian revolution.

This visionary aspect of Marx's radicalism was more clearly apparent in his early writings than later on. It was superficially obscured by the attack that he and Engels made on their socialist predecessors as "utopians." In the *Communist Manifesto* and elsewhere, they derided attempts to design ideal socialist communities (such as Fourier's phalansteries) and set socialist theoreticians the task of demonstrating the necessity of capitalist society's revolutionary self-destruction. But notwithstanding their own preoccupation with this task, the founders of Marxism never lost sight of their communist utopia. The vision of a perfect communist order of the future remained integral to the Marxist social doctrine. The present bourgeois epoch represented the closing chapter of man's "prehistory," declared Marx in millenarian tones in 1859. Beyond it lay the true life of the species, when man would become fully man—a freely productive being developing his talents in all directions—in communist society. That would be humanity's great leap from the realm of necessity to the realm of freedom, wrote Engels in *Anti-Dühring*. Society, they foresaw, would become classless and conflictless with the abolition of the division of labor in all its manifold enslaving forms, and the state would disappear for lack of repressive function. Man would finally realize his own nature in a society based upon distribution according to need. Such, in broad outline, was classical Marxism's image of the ideal communist order.

One other general attribute of the radical mind remains to be mentioned: its activism. The radical not only rejects existing reality; he wants and seeks to transform it. He not only has a vision of an ideal order but a belief in the possibility of realizing it, of moving from the world as it is to the world as it ought to be. "The philosophers have only *interpreted* the world in various ways," as Marx put it in the last of his eleven theses on Feuerbach. *"The point is, to change it."* And the radical mind, at its most creative, has a prescription for action toward this goal, a conception of revolutionary politics. In classical Marxism the prescription for action was class struggle leading to a dictatorship of the proletariat. Marx had only scorn for a socialism that would renounce the "revolutionizing of the old world" and seek, like the early Christian communities, to "achieve its salvation behind society's back" (Marx, n.d., *b*:21). He informed the proletarians that they had "a world to win," and unfurled the banner of a "revolutionary socialism" that stood for "the class dictatorship of the revolution, the class dictatorship of the proletariat as the inevitable transit point to the abolition of class differences generally, to the abolition of all the productive relations that correspond to these relations, to the revolutionizing of all the ideas that result from these social connections" (Marx, n.d., *a*:126).

A full statement of the conditions under which radical movements arise in society is more than can be attempted here. But paraphrasing Lenin in *What Is To Be Done?*, we can say without much exaggeration that there can be no radical movement without a radical social doctrine to serve as its inspiration and ideology. The movement develops as an institutionalization of the radical doctrine, as the organized activity of a group (party, association, and so forth) dedicated to the realization of the vision of a new society. By the nature of the self-selective process of initial recruitment, the movement's leadership, which may originally include the author or authors of the radical creed, will consist in large part of persons attracted to the doctrine by their own radical tendency of mind. On the other hand, some may be persons chiefly gifted in practical organizing ability. If conditions are propitious, as in a time of widespread misery and discontent, the movement may attract followers in large enough numbers to turn into a genuine mass movement. But many in the mass following may join the movement for motives other than zeal for the radical cause. Cases in point would be radical socialist movements with a mass membership arising out of their association with trade unions.

It appears to be the fate of radical movements that survive and flourish for long without remaking the world that they undergo eventually a process of deradicalization. A loss of élan is not necessarily involved, for this process can go on in a movement at a time of significant growth and advance. Deradicalization signifies a subtle change in the movement's relation to the social milieu. Essentially, it settles down and adjusts itself to existence within the very order that it officially desires to overthrow and transform. This is not to say that the movement turns into a conservative social force opposed to social change. Rather, it becomes "reformist" in the sense that it accepts the established system and its institutionalized procedures as the framework for further efforts in the direction of social change. A resolution adopted by the Congress of Parties of the Second International at Amsterdam in August 1904 conveys a vivid sense of this process in a passage warning against it:

The Congress condemns in the most decisive fashion revisionist efforts to change the victorious tactics we have hitherto followed based on the class struggle, in such a way that instead of conquering political power by defeating our opponents, a policy of coming to terms with the existing order is followed. The result of such revisionist tactics would be that instead of being a party which works for the most rapid transformation possible of existing bourgeois society into the socialist social order, i.e., revolutionary in the best sense of the word, the party would become one which is content with reforming bourgeois society.

The phrase "coming to terms with the existing order" best indicates what deradicalization means. In the stage of deradicalization, the movement loses its revolutionary otherworldliness, the alienation from existing conditions arising out of its commitment to a future perfect order, and makes an accommodation to the world as it stands.

Among the numerous and complex causal factors in deradicalization, two are particularly noteworthy: leadership change and worldly success. So far as the first is concerned, it is clear that mere continued official adherence to a radical social doctrine cannot preserve radicalism in a movement if the leadership, through aging or change of leaders, ceases to be radical in its outlook. The radical tendency of mind, as suggested above, is likely to be dominant among the original generation of the movement's leaders. In the normal course of events, however, this situation will eventually change. Not only may some among the original generation of leaders mellow as they grow older. Younger persons who rise through the movement into leadership positions are less likely than the original leaders to be radical types. Ambition, organizing ability, and concern for the interests of the organization and its social constituency are likely to be their predominant characteristics. Successive generations of leaders will show less and less of the alienation from the existing order that characterized the radical founders of the movement and their associates.

Turning to the second factor, there seems to be an inverse relation between a radical movement's organizational strength and the preservation of its radicalism. Radical movements that remain small sectarian groups on the fringe of society are relatively impervious to deradicalization; the history of twentieth-century Trotskyism furnishes numerous illustrations. But when a radical movement grows large and strong, acquires a big organizational structure, a mass social constituency, and a recognized place in society, this very worldly success fosters deradicalization. The acquisition of a mass membership inevitably dilutes the movement's radicalism, and the influence of the relatively less radical rank-and-file will make itself felt in various ways at the leadership level. Moreover, when society begins to accord a measure of acceptance to a radical movement, this may tend to weaken, if not eventually dissipate, the sharp sense of alienation from this world and the commitment to a future order which characterized the movement in its earlier phases. Above all, a movement that grows strong and influential and has prospects of further growth acquires a definite stake in the stability of the order in which this success has been won—a stake that is no less real for the fact that it goes unacknowledged. Robert Michels stressed this point in his study of socialist parties. Observing that the revolutionary political party is at first a state within the state, pursuing the avowed aim of supplanting the present social order with a new one, Michels argued that the growth of the party as an organization weakens the commitment to the revolutionary aim. For revolutionary action can only endanger the position of a party that has achieved a mass membership, a bureaucracy, a full treasury, and a network of financial and moral interests extending all over the country. So it is that "from a means, organization becomes an end" and that "the party grows increasingly inert as the strength of its organization grows; it loses its revolutionary impetus, becomes sluggish . . ." (Michels, 1959:370, 371, 372–73).

DERADICALIZATION OF SOCIAL DEMOCRATIC PARTIES

Michels's thoughts on the deradicalization of revolutionary political parties were generalizations from the observed experience of European Marxist parties in the late nineteenth and early twentieth centuries, the German Social Democratic Party (SPD) in particular. The 1880s had witnessed the emergence in various West European countries of mass working-class parties professing revolutionary Marxism as their ideology. The largest and most influential was the SPD, which in 1875 had become a united body under the leadership of Wilhelm Liebknecht and August Bebel and with Marx and Engels as its mentors and advisers. Notwithstanding the harassment and repression endured under Bismarck's Anti-Socialist Law of 1878–90, the SPD waxed strong in late nineteenth-century Germany. In the elections of 1890, it received nearly a million and a half votes—about a fifth of those cast—and thirty-five seats in the Reichstag. Thirteen years later, a remarkable electoral victory gave the party over three million votes and eighty-one Reichstag seats. And by the elections of 1912, its membership totaled nearly a million and its electoral strength exceeded four million votes, making the SPD both the largest party in Germany and the largest socialist party in the world.

In the aftermath of persecution under the Anti-Socialist Law, the party firmly restated its radical goals and principles in the new program adopted at its Erfurt Congress in 1891. Yet by the turn of the century if not earlier, this formidable mass Marxist party and the movement over which it presided were far along in the process of deradicalization. Marx and Engels were now both dead, and a second generation of leaders, typified by Eduard Bernstein and the party theorist Karl Kautsky, had come to the fore. The party's radical orientation was tempered by its association with a decidedly unradical trade-union movement whose whole tendency was to work toward piecemeal economic reform. And deradicalization was fostered by the great growth of the movement—its wealth, organizational strength, widespread influence, and seeming prospects for further gradual increase of power under the prevailing social system.

It is beyond question that around the turn of the century the German and other European Social Democratic movements were settling down and coming to terms with the existing order. But what were the symptoms of this process? In what ways did the movements reflect and react to it? The principal manifestations of deradicalization were of four different kinds, having to do with the action-pattern of the movement, its relation to its ideological goals, the development of its strategy and tactics, and, finally, its inner conflicts. Taking the German Marxist movement as a classic case in point, let us now examine these points in order.

The accommodation with the existing system was shown first of all in the emergence of a reformist, as distinguished from a revolutionary, pattern of action. The movement's political action lost all meaningful orientation toward the coming great upheaval foretold in the Marxist ideology, and concentrated more and more on what was called the *Gegenwartrarbeit,* or everyday work of the party. The electoral activity of the party expanded with its electoral success. "Everywhere there is action for reform, action for social progress, action for the victory of democracy," wrote Eduard Bernstein in the famous articles in *Neue Zeit* that proved the manifesto of Marxist revisionism. "People study the details of the problems of the day and seek for levers and starting points to carry on the development of society in the direction of socialism." It would therefore be better, he argued, if the Social Democracy "could find the courage to emancipate itself from a phraseology which is actually outworn and if it would make up its mind to appear what it is in reality today: a democratic socialistic party of reform" (Bernstein, 1961:197, 199).

But that is precisely what the party, or rather its dominant, so-called orthodox faction, refused to do. It reasserted its ideological revolutionism at the very time when its practical reformism was becoming most pronounced. In the Erfurt Program, as mentioned above, the party had reaffirmed its radical mission as a revolutionary anticapitalist organization destined to unite and lead the working class in what was described as an ever more bitter class war between bourgeoisie and proletariat. And this in essence remained the party's line in the aftermath of appeals by von Vollmar, Bernstein, and others for abandonment of the Marxist theory of catastrophe and the gospel of revolution through class war. Not only did Kautsky at the turn of the century defend the radical goals and principles of the movement in response to Bernstein's critique. The party formally condemned the latter at its Hanover Congress in 1899 and again at the Dresden Congress of 1903. Furthermore, the Dresden Congress's resolution on this point was adopted by the Socialist International at its Amsterdam Congress the following year and thus was made binding upon all member parties. And right up to the eve of 1914, when the German party's support for war credits in the Reichstag demonstrated conclusively how far it had gone in deradicalization, it officially continued to regard itself as utterly alienated from bourgeois society. "Social Democracy differs from all other parties through its fundamental opposition to the social and governmental system of capitalism," declared the report of the Parliamentary Party to the SPD Congress in 1912.[5]

So it was that a deradicalized Social Democratic movement pledged its allegiance anew to ideological orthodoxy while adhering in practice to a reformist policy line. Instead of abandoning its radical principles and aims in accordance with the revisionist program, the party renewed and even intensified its formal commitment to these aims and principles. Why the dominant element of the leadership moved in this direction was hinted in a letter from an elder German Socialist, Ignaz

Auer, to Bernstein. "Do you think it is really possible that a party which has a literature going back fifty years, an organization going back forty years and a still older tradition, can change its direction like this in the twinkling of an eye," he inquired. "For the most influential members of the party to behave as you demand would simply mean splitting the party and throwing decades of work to the winds. My dear Ede, one doesn't formally decide to do what you ask, one doesn't say it, one *does* it." [6] This was to say that the party's interests militated against any tampering with its ideological *raison d'être*. To preserve the unity and stability of the movement, its leaders had to show great care and restraint in their capacity as custodians of its revolutionary ideology. Similar reasoning underlay the resistance of Austrian Social Democratic leaders like Victor Adler to demands raised in the movement in the 1890s for a theoretical reappraisal of some fundamental concepts of orthodox Marxism which were not being vindicated by contemporary economic development. Such demands, we are told, were "strenuously resisted by Adler, not so much on ideological grounds, for he was anything but a doctrinaire Marxist, but rather for fear of provoking dissensions which might once more endanger party unity" (Leser, 1966:118).

All this suggests that the process of deradicalization has a certain inner "dialectic." For deep-seated reasons, theory and practice diverge. The movement intensifies its theoretical adherence to revolutionary goals at the very time when in practice it moves down the path of reformism. The dominant leadership resists the counsel of the Bernsteins who want the radical theory to be revised to accord with the reformist practice and follows the contrary counsel of those who argue that "one doesn't say it, one *does* it." Far from succumbing to doctrinal revisionism, it resoundingly reaffirms its official revolutionism and pledges its allegiance anew to its original radical outlook. And it does so, at least in part, in an effort to preserve the movement's integrity, to prevent or lessen the demoralization and disunity that open avowal of reformism would tend to provoke. As we shall note presently, it may also be impelled in this direction by accusations from strongly radical elements within the movement that it is betraying the revolutionary cause.

The appearance of a serious discrepancy between revolutionism in theory and reformism in practice is thus one of the hallmarks of deradicalization. But for subjective reasons as well as vulnerability to accusations of hypocrisy from within the movement, the leadership is uncomfortable in the presence of this discrepancy and does what it can to lessen or blur it. While rejecting the formal revisionism that would disavow the radical principles or eschatological elements of the movement's ideology, the orthodox leaders modify the tactical part of the ideology by stressing immediate short-term objectives and non-radical means of attaining them. And in their exegeses of the authoritative writings and pronouncements of the founders, they highlight those statements that give (or seem to give) sanction to such a development of the tactical doctrine. This, at any rate, was the road taken by the Social Democratic leaders.

What had come to be called the "minimum program" of the movement, embracing lesser goals attainable without revolutionizing the existing order, was emphasized at the expense of the truly revolutionary "maximum program," but on the official assumption that every step in fulfillment of the movement's minimal program would likewise bring closer the realization of the maximal program. The democratic electoral road to power was increasingly treated as the highroad, and a doctrine of socialist "parliamentarianism" arose. Thus in his commentary on the Erfurt Program, Kautsky (1910:196, 197) reproved the early "proletarian utopians" like Wilhelm Weitling for having viewed as a betrayal of the movement "every form of the class struggle which was not aimed at the immediate overthrow of the existing order, that is, every serious, efficient sort of effort." Again, in lectures delivered before an Amsterdam socialist group in 1902, he extolled democracy as "light and air to the proletariat." Elections were "a means to count ourselves and the enemy," and further: "They prevent premature outbreaks and they guard against defeats. They also grant the possibility that the opponents will themselves recognize the untenability of many positions and freely surrender them when their maintenance is no life-and-death question for them." He foresaw that parliamentarianism, in decline under capitalism, would be "reawakened to new youth and strength when it, together with the total governmental power, is conquered by the rising proletariat and turned to serve its purposes." And how would the governmental power be conquered by the proletariat? Not by an armed uprising, Kautsky cautioned, save possibly in Russia. Unlike some past revolutions, the coming revolution would be a long-drawn-out political "civil war" without battles, barricades and blood, i.e., a figurative civil war. It would not, moreover, be a "battle of mobs," but rather: "It is a battle of organized, intelligent masses, full of stability and prudence, that do not follow every impulse or explode over every insult, or collapse under every misfortune (Kautsky, 1913:79–82, 88).[7]

In keeping with this concept of a well-behaved class struggle, orthodox Marxism gave an exegesis of the Marxist scriptures which laid particular emphasis upon everything that pointed in its own tactical direction. It is questionable whether Marx and Engels (particularly

Marx) ever wavered in their commitment to the radical Weltanschauung that they formulated as young men. But in their later
years, owing in part to involvement in the intricate politics of the revolutionary movement, they made various statements that seemed to
sanction gradualism, an electoral orientation, and a belief in a peaceful path of socialist revolution. Thus Marx's inaugural address to the
International Workingmen's Association in 1864 welcomed the ten-
hour day as a victory for the "political economy of labor," suggesting
that more such reforms within the capitalist order represented a real
path of progress to socialism. In a speech at The Hague in 1872, after
a congress of the International, he allowed that in countries like England and America, and possibly Holland as well, the worker might be
able to attain his goal by peaceful means. Engels too referred to the
possibility of a peaceful revolution in his critique of the Erfurt Program. More important still, in his 1895 preface to a new edition of
Marx's *Class Struggles in France,* Engels gave his blessing to the parliamentary mode of struggle by hailing the German Social Democracy's
two million voters as the decisive "shock force" of the international
proletarian army. "The irony of world history turns everything up-
side down," he went on. "We, the 'revolutionaries,' the 'rebels'—we
are thriving far better on legal methods than on illegal methods and
revolt. The parties of order, as they call themselves, are perishing
under the legal conditions created by themselves" (Marx, n.d.,
a:27–28).[8]

These and like texts proved of great importance to the leadership
of a movement in which all policy had to be legitimated by reference
to authoritative pronouncements of the founders of the ideology.
Having undertaken to paper over the discrepancy between its theoretical revolutionism and practical reformism by prescribing gradualist and peaceful *tactics* of revolutionary struggle, Social Democratic
Marxism naturally gave special attention and emphasis to such statements by Marx and Engels as those just cited. By the same token, it
tended to de-emphasize the many Marx-Engels texts which visualized
the socialist revolution as the forcible overthrow of all existing conditions by "illegal methods and revolt" and which visualized the regime
of the revolution as a violent dictatorship of the proletariat. Thus a
definite line in the exegesis of classical Marxism was part of the general process of deradicalization of the Social Democratic Marxist
movement. A sort of retrospective deradicalization of the radical god-
fathers of the movement, Marx and Engels, was one of its manifestations.

So, finally, was conflict in the movement between the orthodox
leadership and elements whose radical alienation from the existing

order and commitment to the revolutionary vision of a new world remained unimpaired by the movement's worldly success. Reflection shows that such conflict is virtually inescapable when a movement is in the stage of deradicalization, so much so that the absence of it may be treated as a sure sign that no fundamental deradicalization is taking place. What explains this fact is that the leadership (not to mention the rank-and-file) of a radical movement is never homogeneous in outlook. There are bound to be differences of temperament, of relationship to the ideology, of position in the movement. For reasons touched on above, some of the more adaptable leaders will preside over the movement's deradicalization. But other, more consistently radical-minded elements will rebel against this process, and here lie the seeds of inner conflict or even schism in the movement.

Seeing the discrepancy between the officially avowed revolutionary theory and the unrevolutionary day-to-day practice, the genuine radicals will be profoundly worried by the direction the movement is taking. What is happening, they will ask. Are we not giving up in practice our cherished goals, our effort to transform society totally? Is not the movement drifting into opportunism? Are we not, then, betraying the founders of the doctrine in whose name we continue to speak? Among the prominent figures in the Social Democratic movement who raised such troubled and troublesome questions were Rosa Luxemburg, Anton Pannekoek, and Wilhelm Liebknecht's son Karl, of whom it has been said that he inherited his father's political romanticism without his common sense (Joll, 1955:100).[9] Like revisionists of the Bernsteinian persuasion, the genuine radicals craved consistency. But the two groups moved in opposite directions in search of it. Whereas the revisionists wanted to revise the revolutionary theory to accord with reformist practice, the radicals wanted to abandon reformist practice out of fidelity to the revolutionary world-image. They took the movement's eschatology seriously.

The inner conflict attendant upon a movement's deradicalization may be all the more deep and disruptive if it is an international movement, as Marxist Social Democracy was in the early years of this century. For heterogeneity of outlook among the leaders is even more to be expected on an international scale than within a given national branch of the movement. One reason for this is that at any given time the movement may be in different stages of development in various countries. This may result in the ascendancy of a group of one outlook in one branch of the international movement, and of a group of opposed outlook in another. In that event, a schism may occur, as it did in the international Marxist movement in 1917 and after. German orthodox Marxism had a counterpart in the Menshevik wing of the younger Russian Social Democracy. But the Marxism that came to power in Russia in the October Revolution of 1917 was the radical Bolshevik Marxism of Lenin and his associates. The international Marxist movement was consequently split in two, and soon a deradicalized Social Democracy with its center of gravity in Western Europe found itself in hostile confrontation with a radical Marxist movement of Leninist persuasion centering in Soviet Russia and laying undivided claim to the Marxist heritage.

RADICALISM AND DERADICALIZATION UNDER LENIN AND STALIN

It is always risky to interpret a massive historical event in terms of a single cause or issue. But it seems undeniable that rebellious protest against the deradicalization of Social Democracy was a central motif in the great Marxist schism and in the rise of Communist Marxism as a new worldwide movement. The younger Lenin had venerated Kautsky as a Marxist teacher and adversary of revisionism. But during the world war, in which Kautsky and many other European Social Democratic leaders failed to oppose the warring governments in the name of the previously espoused principle of international working-class solidarity, Lenin turned against them. In a pamphlet published in Geneva in 1915, he accused Kautsky of paying mere "lip service" to Marxism. Speaking of the Kautskys of the international Social Democratic movement, he went on: "Those people castrate Marxism; they purge it, by means of obvious sophisms, of its revolutionary living soul; they recognize in Marxism *everything except* revolutionary means of struggle, except the advocacy of, and the preparation for, such struggle, and the education of the masses in this direction" (Lenin, 1947:359). In 1917, on the eve of taking power, Lenin insisted on changing the name of his party from "Social Democratic" to "Communist" in order to sharpen symbolically his break with Social Democratic Marxism. The subsequent creation of the Third International was a logical outgrowth of this step.

Leninist or Communist Marxism emerged as a kind of Marxist fundamentalism, a revival of the radical essence of Marx's thought. On the opening page of *The State and Revolution*—one of the great documents of Marxist radicalism—Lenin declared that the pressing need was to restore to Marxism its revolutionary soul and thus combat the efforts of vulgarizers like Kautsky to omit, obliterate, and distort the revolutionary side of the doctrine. Here and in other writings of this period, he hammered out the foundations of Communist Marxism in a savage polemic against Kautskyan Social Democracy and its interpretation of Marx and Engels. Kautsky, he contended, was guilty of "petty-bourgeois distortion of Marxism and base renunciation of it *in practice,* while hypocritically recognizing it *in words*" (Lenin, 1947:163). The essence of Kautskyism, as Lenin saw it, was, in our terms, the discrepancy between revolutionary theory and nonrevolutionary practice which shows up when a movement undergoes deradicalization.

Kautsky's exegesis of the Marx-Engels texts was a particular target of Lenin's polemic. "How Kautsky Transformed Marx into a Common or Garden Liberal" was the title of the opening section of *The Proletarian Revolution and the Renegade Kautsky.* And Lenin argued in this and other writings of the period for a fundamentalist reading of the views of Marx and Engels on revolution and dictatorship. To be a true Marxist, one had not only to accept the class struggle but also the proletarian dictatorship as its culmination and the necessary way station to the new world of communist society. A proletarian revolution meant the taking of power by an armed uprising; and Marx, were he alive now, would no longer allow for the possibility of a peaceful path to socialism in Britain and America, since the exceptional conditions that might have made peaceful revolution possible there in the nineteenth century no longer obtained. And the dictatorship of the proletariat—the theory of which constituted the very essence of Marxist teaching—was a revolutionary regime relying upon force and violence to suppress its class enemies.

Thus Communist Marxism took shape as the political doctrine of a new anti-Social Democratic Marxist radicalism. Now, nearly a half century after Lenin, the Soviet Communist movement still claims to be authentically "Marxist-Leninist." But if deradicalization, as suggested above, is the general fate of radical movements, the question arises whether this fate has been overtaking Soviet Communism in the recent past. One way of approaching it may be to inquire whether Soviet Communism has begun to show such symptoms of deradicalization as those displayed in its time by the Social Democratic movement. Such comparative treatment seems logically feasible despite the fact that in the one case we are dealing with a radical movement that came to power, while the other movement remained out of power.

It could be argued that Soviet Communism entered upon the phase of deradicalization long before Stalin's death. There were, for example, indications of deradicalization as early as the period of the New Economic Policy in the 1920s, most notably in the regime's action-pattern in both international and domestic affairs. True, the revival of revolutionary militance at the close of the 1920s, both internally and to some extent externally, points to the inconclusiveness of those earlier signs. Soviet foreign policy in the Popular Front period of the middle 1930s, however, could again be seen as symptomatic of deradicalization—and some in the West so saw it. Moreover, two of the factors in deradicalization that have been emphasized in these pages—change in the composition of the leadership and the worldly success that gives a one-time radical movement a stake in the existing order—were evident, or becoming so, as the Bolshevik old guard began to be replaced by a new generation of Soviet leaders. It might be mentioned, too, that the charge of deradicalization—couched in such terms as "bureaucratic degeneration" and "Thermidor"—bulked large in the Trotskyist polemic against Stalinist Soviet Communism. It was, in particular, Trotsky's fundamental thesis in *The Revolution Betrayed* (1937) that Soviet Communism, despite continued lip-service to revolutionary Marxism, had undergone a far-reaching deradicalization under the aegis of a basically conservative bureaucracy of which Stalin himself was the personification. The Great Purge of the middle 1930s and Stalin's supercautious foreign policy of that time appeared to Trotsky, along with much else, as evidence in support of this thesis. The Great Purge, in which most of the still-surviving old Bolshevik revolutionaries perished or were sent once more to Siberia, was seen as a counterrevolution of conservatism.

There is no denying that Stalinist Soviet Communism showed conservative features, particularly in its later years. But apart from the fact (or in connection with it) that Stalin himself was fundamentally misconstrued as a mere personification of the Soviet bureaucracy, there were deep flaws in the Trotskyist analysis. Although the Soviet Communist movement undoubtedly underwent very considerable deradicalization during the Stalin era, Stalin himself, a man of the original revolutionary generation, represented in his peculiar way a link with the radical Leninist past and a bar to full-scale development of the deradicalizing tendencies that had become strong in Soviet Communism. In internal policy, for example, he espoused in his *Economic Problems of Socialism in the U.S.S.R.* (1952) the idea that the Soviet agrarian economy should soon begin to be based not on monetary relationships but on direct "product-exchange"; and this radical prescription, along with his projection of a policy of economic austerity for the Soviet Union in its further advance towards "full communism," may help to explain why, in subsequent years of Soviet de-Stalinization, the Chinese Communist leader Mao Tse-tung has defended Stalin as a great Marxist-Leninist mentor for Communist movements.

In foreign policy, moreover, Stalin demonstrated his surviving —or reviving—commitment to Marxist revolutionism by presiding over a largely forcible expansion of the Communist system to other countries after the end of the Second World War. And whatever the mixture of motives actuating him, it is notable that an analysis of his action widely accepted in the West saw it as deriving from continued commitment to radical Marxist-Leninist goals.[10] It is true that Stalin's postwar revolutionism had its limits. Possibly fearing great-power competition from within the international Communist movement, he did not, for example, show initial enthusiasm for a Communist takeover of China. It is likewise true that Stalin acted with a certain circumspection and caution in the process of exporting communism to other countries. This is understandable when we consider that the age of atomic weapons had dawned and that Russia was not only without them but also weakened by the ordeal of war. But caution in the pursuit of radical ends is no derogation of radicalism itself. To this it should be added that so long as Stalin lived, there was no serious departure from the strategic and tactical fundamentals of the Marxist-Leninist doctrine of world revolution as codified in the 1920s and 1930s under Stalin's aegis. This fact is all the more significant in the light of available evidence, to which I shall refer presently, that Stalin in the last years of his life was strenuously resisting some doctrinal changes which were being advocated by other Soviet political leaders and which would have been indicative of Soviet deradicalization.

DERADICALIZATION SINCE STALIN

The real question, then, is not whether Soviet Communism began to deradicalize before Stalin died, although there are strong indications that it did. Rather, the question is whether the deradicalizing tendency already apparent in earlier years but always held in check may have come to much fuller fruition in the post-Stalin period, whether the passing of Stalin and the consequent emergence of a new generation of Soviet leaders has brought the Soviet Communist movement into a highly advanced or even final phase of deradicalization. In short, is Soviet Communism of the late 1950s and early 1960s to be seen as a basically deradicalized Marxist movement? If we can take the symptoms that were shown by the Social Democratic Marxist movement in its phase of deradicalization as criteria for judgment, an affirmative answer is indicated.

We see, to begin with, a coming to terms with the existing order, both internationally and internally, in the action-pattern of the Soviet Communist leadership. In Soviet foreign relations there have been, it is true, episodes in which force was egregiously employed or serious risks incurred; the Hungarian intervention of 1956 and the Cuban missiles venture of 1962 are, respectively, the obvious cases in point. Yet neither of these Soviet actions is necessarily to be interpreted as the action of a revolutionary power intent upon altering the international sociopolitical *status quo*.[11] And the general pattern of Soviet international behavior in the post-Stalin period has been distinctly unrevolutionary. The Soviet regime has sought a rapprochement with non-Communist nationalist regimes in the underdeveloped areas of the world. In certain critical junctures in international affairs, it has found it possible to support a non-Communist India engaged in conflict with Communist China. It has attempted to mediate a dispute between non-Communist India and non-Communist Pakistan. It has shown a desire to settle the war in Vietnam, even at the expense of full (or early) realization of Communist aims in South Vietnam. In addition to all this, it has intermittently sought to improve relations and institutionalize a measure of cooperation with the leading non-Communist power of the West. In internal policy, moreover, the Soviet regime has increasingly turned away from doctrinaire schemes toward a more pragmatic policy line in the economic and other spheres. The recent experimentation with market principles in the economy is only one of many expressions of this.

But the "dialectic" of deradicalization seems to have been operative too in the post-Stalin period. The tendency of the regime to adjust its conduct at home and abroad to existing situations and realities has been accompanied by no diminution of ideological rhetoric. On the contrary, verbal protestations of fidelity to Communist ideas have intensified, and there has been something of a Leninist revival in Soviet propaganda. Frequently and in the strongest terms the leadership has reaffirmed its dedication to the final goals of communism as laid down by Marx, Engels, and Lenin. It has insisted, as mentioned earlier, that peaceful coexistence can never embrace "ideological coexistence," i.e., that the ideological gulf between Communist and non-Communist societies remains unbridged and unbridgeable. It was, moreover, in this very period that a Soviet leader issued the warning that Soviet Communists would not renounce their Communist principles until "the shrimps whistle" and flung down the gauntlet to capitalist America in the famous phrase: "We will bury you!" The image of the future Communist social order reappeared in shining form in Khrushchev's address to the Twenty-First Party Congress in 1959 and again in the new Party Program in 1961; and never in Soviet history was so much official public attention bestowed upon the utopian vision of the Communist future. It is symptomatic that the new Party Program envisages, with the advent of a full Communist society in

Russia some time after 1980, the radical transformation of Soviet man himself into "a new man who will . . . combine spiritual wealth, moral purity and a perfect physique" (Mendel, 1961:468).[12]

The pledging of allegiance anew to communism's eschatology has, however, been accompanied by the third symptom of deradicalization—revision of the tactical doctrine, changes in the official conception of the means by which the ultimate goals may be achieved. As noted earlier, these changes center in the general idea that communism can spread in the world by peaceful means, without "export of revolution" (i.e., the use of armed force to impose Communist revolutions from without) or internal civil war. In elaborating the programmatic notion of a peaceful path to communism, Soviet sources have put forward a new doctrine of parliamentarianism which strikingly parallels the above-mentioned Kautskyan picture of a takeover of power through the winning of a parliamentary majority by the working class. In keeping with this same trend of thought, Soviet official writings have endorsed the essentially gradualist tactic (originally developed by the Italian Communist leader Palmiro Togliatti) of Communist advocacy of economic "structural reforms" within the frame of the existing order. And on the broader plane of general strategy, Soviet doctrine has broken with the Leninist thesis on the inevitability of wars and espoused, as we saw, the view that the Soviet Union can best contribute to the further spread of communism by winning the battle of economic development in peaceful competitive coexistence.

These doctrinal developments have been accompanied by appropriate adjustments in the official Soviet image of the movement's founders. To some extent, in fact, we see a retrospective "deradicalization" of the Marxist-Leninist classics. Thus the 1961 Party Program, in elaborating upon the theme of parliamentary transition to socialism, ascribes to Marx and Lenin the view that it may prove possible to buy out the bourgeoisie: "It may well be that . . . there will arise in certain countries a situation in which it will be preferable for the bourgeoisie, as Marx and Lenin foresaw it, to agree to the means of production being purchased from it and for the proletariat to 'pay off' the bourgeoisie" (Mendel, 1961:402). Lenin is said to have granted (and by implication to have preferred) the possibility that the Russian revolution would develop peacefully.[13] And great emphasis is placed upon an obscure Lenin statement to the effect that "we exert our chief influence upon the international revolution through our economic policy."[14] Thus, neo-Communist Marxism is projected back upon the radical founders of the movement, including Lenin.

The fourth mark of deradicalization—conflict in the movement between those who take the lead in this process and those who resist it—has also been present. The rise of neo-Communist Marxism in the Soviet Union was not a smooth and painless development reflecting a consensus of the Communist leadership. These doctrinal changes were the subject of an intense and bitter debate that began while Stalin was still alive. Irrefutable evidence on this point is contained in his final published work, *Economic Problems of Socialism in the U.S.S.R.*, which is a record of Stalin's interventions in a discussion carried on inside the Soviet regime in 1951–52 in preparation for the Nineteenth Party Congress. There he took issue with unnamed "comrades" who were contending that Lenin's thesis on the inevitability of wars under imperialism was obsolete and in need of revision, and that such wars had ceased to be inevitable. In other words, the new doctrine on non-inevitability which was first promulgated at the Twentieth Party Congress in 1956 had been advocated behind the scenes in Stalin's final years. But Stalin would have none of it.

"These comrades are mistaken," he declared. "To eliminate the inevitability of war, it is necessary to abolish imperialism" (Stalin, 1952:27–28, 30). Since, in other words, wars would remain inevitable so long as the world Communist revolution remained basically incomplete, the only road to peace was the roundabout road to forcible Communist revolution, with all that this implied for further growth of international tension. The call to moderate Communist tactics implicit in the thesis on the non-inevitability of wars in our time was thus rejected. This obdurate defense by Stalin of Marxist-Leninist ideological orthodoxy was indirectly a demand for indefinite prolongation of the cold war pending the spread of Communist revolution to other countries. It was of a piece, moreover, with his concluding speech at the Nineteenth Party Congress in October 1952. In what was to prove his valedictory, Stalin applauded the continuing progress of the world Communist revolution and set the course of the movement toward its further advance in the coming years. In the light of this and other evidence, it is impossible to accept the view of some Western scholars that Stalin in the final period of his life was preparing the realignment of Soviet foreign policy which took place after his death.[15] On the contrary, he was engaged in a determined struggle against change, against forces within his own regime that were pressing for an international detente and realignment of policy.

Stalin's death removed the most formidable opponent of the revision of the Leninist thesis on inevitability of wars and related doctrinal as well as policy changes. But "heirs of Stalin" remained strong within the Soviet leadership, and post-Stalin ideological change was contested. As late as October 1961, on the eve of the Twenty-Second Party Congress, Vyacheslav Molotov addressed a letter to the Party

Central Committee protesting against the doctrinal revisions in the draft Party Program scheduled for adoption by the Congress; and the storm of abuse he thereby brought down upon himself at the Congress suggests that his message struck a sensitive chord in many Soviet Communist minds. By this time, however, the conflict over the post-Stalin trend of development in Soviet Communism had been internationalized. Resistance to this trend from within the international Communist movement had found a powerful and vigorous champion in the Maoist leadership of the Chinese Communist Party.

Soviet sources have asserted that the great Sino-Soviet ideological dispute began in April 1960 when the Chinese Communist press published, on the occasion of the ninetieth anniversary of Lenin's birth, a series of implicitly polemical articles entitled "Long Live Leninism!" Chinese Communist sources have contested this, pointing out that "it takes more than a cold day for the river to freeze three feet deep." The real starting point, according to the Chinese view, was the Twentieth Party Congress: "Ever since the Twentieth Congress of the C.P.S.U., we have watched with concern as the C.P.S.U. leadership took the road of revisionism." To substantiate this claim, the Chinese have revealed that in April 1956, shortly after the adoption of an anti-Stalin line by the Twentieth Congress, Mao Tse-tung emphasized to Mikoyan and the Soviet ambassador in China that Stalin's "merits outweigh his faults." Repeatedly in subsequent months, the Chinese leaders, in private conversations with Soviet officials, opposed the anti-Stalin line. And in November 1957, when a conference of Communist leaders from all over the world took place in Moscow to formulate the international Communist line, conflict broke out over the issue of peaceful parliamentary transition to socialism. In an "Outline of Views on the Question of Peaceful Transition" which was submitted to the C.P.S.U. Central Committee, the Chinese maintained that it would be inadvisable to lay much stress on the possibility of peaceful transition, and especially on the possibility of seizing state power by winning a majority in parliament, for "it is liable to weaken the revolutionary will of the proletariat, the working people and the Communist Party and disarm them ideologically." The Chinese document went on to express doubt whether there was a single country where the possibility of peaceful transition was of any practical significance. And recalling Lenin's insistence that in a Communist revolution the old state apparatus must not simply be taken over but destroyed, the Chinese warned that peaceful transition should not be interpreted in such a way as solely to mean transition through a parliamentary majority. That, the document concluded, would be a Social Democratic view, and: "On the question of socialist revolution, our position is fundamentally different from that of the Social Democratic parties. This distinction must not be obscured." [16]

Soviet sources have furnished no evidence to refute this account of the early development of the conflict that in our time has shaken and threatened to disrupt and even split in two the international Communist movement. In the subsequent stages of the dispute, Chinese warnings against obscuring the distinction between the Social Democratic and Communist positions on socialist revolution have given way to the charge that the Soviet leadership has gone the deradicalizing way of the Social Democratic leadership in Lenin's time. Khrushchevism has been seen as a new version of the Kautskyism that took over European Marxism a generation ago, and Lenin's writings of that time have been studied anew in search of insight into contemporary Soviet development. "As Lenin pointed out, the 'orthodox' Marxists headed by Kautsky were virtually hidden opportunists," declared a Chinese Communist study of "Kautskyism" published in 1962. "Under their leadership the Second International adopted some revolutionary manifestos and declarations, but their aim was not to put them into effect but to win the trust of the masses by fraud and to continue to manipulate the workers' movement." [17] Four years later, all pretense of merely historical reference was thrown aside, and the Chinese Communist leadership was saying: "After Stalin's death, the leaders of the C.P.S.U. headed by Khrushchev gradually revealed their true features as betrayers of Lenin and Leninism and embarked on the old path of the German Social Democrats Bernstein and Kautsky, who betrayed Marx and Engels and Marxism." [18]

CHINA AND DERADICALIZATION

Detailed treatment of the Sino-Soviet conflict is beyond the scope of the present essay. The point I wish to make in conclusion is simply that in its inception, development, and basic content, this inner conflict in international communism shows a deeply significant similarity to (as well as significant differences from) the inner conflict that split the international Social Democratic Marxist movement a generation ago. Once again we see the leadership of some parts of the movement showing in their conduct and ideological pronouncements the symptoms of deradicalization. And once again we see rebellion against this trend on the part of radical elements of the movement in whom the need for integrity of theory and practice is still strong. Once again, moreover, the predominance of one element or the other is connected with the difference between the stages of development of the movement in one country and the other.

All this bears emphasizing in part because of a tendency of the Western mind to view the Sino-Soviet ideological controversy as a mere smoke screen for clashing national ambitions or great-power rivalry between Russia and China. To ignore the national, imperial, and personal factors in the conflict would be wrong. But it would be no less an error, and perhaps a greater one, to fail to perceive that ideological and political fundamentals of communism really are at stake in this dispute.

As recent events have clearly shown, moreover, the concern about Soviet deradicalization is accompanied in the mind of the Maoist leadership in China by a fear of deradicalizing tendencies in Chinese Communism itself, and the conflict now in progress in the Chinese Communist movement turns in large measure on this issue. To combat deradicalizing tendencies in the higher leadership as well as in the party and state apparatus throughout the country is an avowed main aim of the great Maoist "cultural revolution" that has convulsed the internal life of Communist China in 1966 and early 1967. This aim— and in general the radical mentality—is epitomized in the slogan that has been given the youthful Maoist Red Guards: "Let us destroy the old world, and build a new world!" Mao and his closest adherents appear to realize more clearly than radical leaders of the past that the changing of the generations is always a threat to the radical mentality. "Imperialism pins its hopes of 'peaceful evolution' on the third and fourth generations," runs their reasoning as expressed in the Maoist press. "China's young people must remember class hatred and carry the proletarian revolutionary cause through to the end." To inoculate Communist China's young in advance against the bacilla of "revisionism" appears to be the purpose of the frenzied campaign of indoctrination. But it is not by indoctrination that genuine radical minds are created. The history of radical movements, Marxist ones included, suggests that Mao's fear of the coming deradicalization of Chinese Communism is well founded.

Not often does a theoretical problem have such immediate relevance to the practical concerns of political leaders as in the present instance. Since statesmen in our time have had to deal with radical movements that have come to power and may have repeated occasion to do so in the future, an understanding of the dynamics of the behavior of such movements at various stages of their development is of great importance. Both the lack of such understanding and the need for it find illustration in the recent history of our thinking about Soviet Communism. The Western mind has tended to anticipate a mellowing of the Soviet Communist movement in terms of what has been called "ideological erosion." A decline or softening of official commitment to the final goals of the movement has, in other words, been taken as the prime criterion for judging whether Soviet Communism is undergoing genuine change away from its radical foundations. The analysis presented in this essay leads to a very different view. Not only would a Soviet Communist movement in process of deradicalization go on proclaiming its adherence to the final goals of the movement, it would, by virtue of the dialectic of the process, reaffirm the goals in very strong terms, as it has done. For intensified verbal allegiance to ultimate ideological goals belongs to the pattern of deradicalization.

What a sociologist has written of religious change seems to be applicable also to ideological movements of radical persuasion: "Religious change is usually a latent process, carried on beneath symbols of nonchange" (Yinger, 1963:70).[19] Not the end of ideology but rather the growth of a stable discrepancy between ideological symbols and political deeds is the true mark of deradicalizing change in once-radical movements.

NOTES

1. *Pravda,* February 15, 1956.
2. For details, see "Dialectics of Coexistence," in Tucker (1963).
3. *Speech to the Third Congress of the Rumanian Workers' Party, June 22, 1960* (New York: Crosscurrents Press, 1960), pp. 27, 28.
4. "The Leaders of the C.P.S.U. Are the Greatest Splitters of Our Times: Comment on the Open Letter of the Central Committee of the C.P.S.U. (VII)," *People's Daily,* February 4, 1964.
5. Quoted by Joll (1955:90).
6. Ibid., pp. 93–94.
7. All this bears out the comment of Alfred Meyer (1963:135) that "Kautsky still spoke about the proletarian revolution but demanded that it be a tame and civilized revolution." A detailed and useful discussion of trends in Social Democratic Marxism at the end of the nineteenth century is contained in chapters 5 and 6 of Meyer (1963).
8. Michels suggests that this influential endorsement by Engels of parliamentary methods for attaining socialism did not give expression to his true opinions. In this connection he quotes from a letter that Engels wrote to Kautsky saying, with reference to the preface: "My text had to suffer from the timid legalism of our friends in Berlin, who dreaded a second edition of the anti-socialist laws—a dread to which I was forced to pay attention at the existing political juncture." Michels concludes on this basis that "Engels would seem to have been the victim of an opportunist sacrifice of principles to the needs of organization, a sacrifice made for love of the party and in opposition to his known theoretical convictions" (Michels, 1959:370n).
9. On the radicals' rebellion against the tendency of deradicalization, see Meyer (1963:136–39). He writes of Rosa Luxumburg, in particular, that "her

entire political life was one momentous attempt to reunite the theory and practice of Marxian socialism in the radical spirit of its founders" (p. 137).

10. I refer to the analysis by George Kennan in his article, "The Sources of Soviet Conduct," *Foreign Affairs,* July 1947.

11. In the Hungarian intervention, the Soviet motivation was probably mainly defensive, since the preservation of the Soviet position in Eastern Europe was threatened by Hungarian departure from the Warsaw Pact. In the Cuban missiles episode, the Soviet aim may have been to redress an adverse balance of nuclear power inexpensively.

12. It may be noted that Khrushchev's phrase, "We will bury you!" was widely misunderstood abroad. In colloquial Russian, the words carry the meaning: "We will be present at your funeral," i.e., we will outlive you. The flamboyant statement was not, then, a threat to destroy but rather a boast that Soviet Communism would outlive the non-Communist system in the long-range competition of systems that Khrushchev called "peaceful coexistence."

13. See, for example, Khrushchev's public speech to the Twentieth Party Congress, *Pravda,* February 15, 1956.

14. Inozemtsev (1966:23).

15. See, for example, Shulman (1963). For a fuller presentation of the evidence against the view that Stalin was preparing a realignment of foreign policy, see Tucker (1963:20–35).

16. *The Origin and Development of the Differences Between the Leadership of the C.P.S.U. and Ourselves* (Peking: Foreign Languages Press, 1963), pp. 11, 12, 59, 61. Soviet sources have asserted that the possibility of a parliamentary path of transition was mentioned in the 1952 new program of the British Communist party on the suggestion of Stalin. It should be observed, however, that he did not at that time make a corresponding general revision in Soviet Marxist doctrine.

17. Li Fu, Li Ssu-Wen and Wang Fu-ju, "On Kautskyism," *Hung-ch'i,* Nos. 8/9, April 25, 1962. Quoted in Dallin (1963:277–78).

18. "Chinese Communist Party Cannot Send Delegation to C.P.S.U. Twenty-Third Congress," *Peking Review,* No. 13, March 25, 1966, p. 5.

19. See also Kautsky (1965:11–12). Of particular relevance to my argument is Kautsky's statement: "One may expect that the more the Soviet government changes its policies from those that were once associated with the goal of World Communism, the less can it afford to stop insisting that it continues to stand for this goal."

Afterword   Bibliography   Index

Afterword: Summary and Directives for the Future

ROBERT H. LAUER

We have arrived at a point of completion and a point of beginning. We have explored four kinds of interrelationships between social movements and social change, but that exploration has raised as many questions as it has answered. It will be worthwhile at this point, therefore, to review the ground we have covered and to specify at least some of the directives for future research to which this book has led us.

First, we sought to identify the impact of social change upon social movements. That impact is pervasive: social movements not only arise out of the matrix of change, but the development of the movement—its life cycle—is intimately bound up with changes occurring in its social milieu. The Chinese student movement arose out of the agony created by the intersection of a rigid social order and a rapidly changing environment. And the course of development of the movement has been intimately bound up with developments in the larger society. Similarly, the American student movement's fortunes rose and fell, and its focal concerns shifted, in accord with events of the larger society. The LSD movement led by Timothy Leary exhibited modifications in its ideology and program as the movement interacted with the larger society and tried to adapt to changes in that larger society. And, finally, both the ideology and the composition of the Woman's Christian Temperance Union altered significantly over time as the move-

259

ment struggled with the larger society and with the changing norms and behavior of that society.

With respect to the genesis of a movement, we discussed the importance of a sense of deprivation in the Introduction. I noted in my chapter on the LSD movement that the deprivation thesis was not helpful in explaining recruitment. That referred, however, to economic deprivation. The notion of relative deprivation must not be limited to an economic sense if it is to be useful in understanding recruitment to movements. Thus, the sense of outrage of the Chinese students, the political concerns of American students, the thirst for meaning of LSD advocates, and the moral concerns of the women of the WCTU can all be understood in relationship to varying kinds of deprivation.

We know, then, that change in the larger society can significantly alter various aspects of a movement as well as facilitate the genesis of a movement. Furthermore, we know that both events—such as occurred in the case of student movements and the LSD movement—and long-term shifts—such as occurred in the case of the WCTU—can affect the movement. But there is much to learn, and the following are some of the questions raised that offer directives for research.

What is the relative importance of unexpected events versus longer-term changes in the genesis and subsequent course of development of a social movement?

What kinds of events and what kind of changes in the larger society are particularly significant for understanding social movements?

What is the relationship between social change and the genesis of particular kinds of movements; that is, are certain kinds of changes more likely to generate particular types of movements (revolutionary, reformist, and so forth), and are certain kinds of changes and/or structural conditions related to specific kinds of deprivation?

How does social change bear upon the prosperity or decline of a movement?

What facets of social movements (ideology, program, recruitment, and so forth) are most likely to be altered by social change, and what kind of alteration is most likely to occur?

The second relationship we explored involved the strategies employed by movements to achieve their goals. We pointed out that strategies are important not only for goal attainment, but also for the recruitment and commitment of members. Radical strategies may guarantee failure to achieve goals. The question of strategy, therefore, confronts the movement with something of a dilemma.

A number of explicit or implicit assumptions underlie the choice of any particular strategy or strategies—assumptions about who it is that must implement the change, the amount of force required to effect the change, and the proximate target of the change effort. In some cases the strategy may focus almost wholly upon the membership of the movement; millenarian movements typically aim at an analgesic effect upon their own membership. In other cases, the strategy may focus upon the social structure itself. The civil rights movement evolved a power strategy as it interacted with a changing society—a society changing, in part, because of the previous activities of the movement. The aim of the strategy was nothing less than basic alterations in the social structure. But neither the millenarian nor the civil rights movements were unconcerned about changes at other levels; rather, each assumed that a particular proximate target was the most appropriate and each selected a strategy aimed at that proximate target.

As the chapter on the civil rights movement showed, the strategy of a movement, like virtually every other of its aspects, tends to alter over time. Even movements which acquire a revolutionary stance do not always start out that way. Consequently, our understanding of strategies and tactics will be partial at best until we probe into how and why strategies change over time as well as how and why particular strategies are selected.

What, then, are some of the important questions related to strategies that need to be pursued? Comparative studies are needed to test and refine the typology of strategies which I offered. In addition, the following questions suggest directions for research.

What is the relative effectiveness of multiple versus single strategies?

Are some strategies impotent in certain kinds of social contexts? What is the relationship between the strategy employed and the kind of changes effected? For example, do some strategies bring about more unanticipated consequences than others; are some strategies more likely to insure long-term consolidation of gains; and are some strategies inherently counterproductive in the long run?

Since the movement may be "remembered more for the methods of persuasion" which it employs than for its objectives (Wilson, 1973:226), do successful movements employ strategies which have as much public relations value as logical import for achieving stated goals?

The third relationship we have tried to illuminate involves the effects of the movement upon change. We noted that a movement might effect change at any number of levels—the individual, the organization, the institutional, the societal. Millenarian movements have consequences primarily for the individuals who comprise the movement. They tend to support, therefore, the existing social order. In fact, some religious movements may even recruit and socialize deviants back into an acceptance of the existing social order (Robbins, 1969). By contrast, other movements have effected various kinds of changes in the social order. The Chinese revolutionary movement has made significant alterations in the meaning of the female status-role. The civil rights movement has sought to effect institutional changes through changed laws. And that same movement has had numerous consequences throughout American society.

But we must distinguish between the changes aimed at by the movement and those it actually effects. Movements may have quite diverse effects, including those which are unintended and unanticipated. The unintended and unanticipated is not necessarily undesirable for the movement; to the extent that the civil rights movement has made protest a legitimate activity in America, it has achieved something for which it did not aim but which facilitates its own work.

One of the difficulties of researching the effects of movements upon change is rooted in the ambiguity of the concept of change. As Warshay (1964:322) has pointed out, we must come to terms with a number of issues: "what is changing; change versus variation; short-term/long-term change; the form of change; its rapidity." Furthermore, the shortcomings of structural-functionalism in adequately dealing with change has resulted in considerable criticism of "structure" as a static concept; this, in turn, "has frequently led to the reification of process, one consequence of this being the formulation of abstract laws of change regardless of what it is that is changing" (Warshay, 1964:323).

One task of the researcher, therefore, is to specify what he means by change. In this book, we have looked at change at different levels of social reality: the individual's beliefs and feelings; the societal definition of a particular status/role; the legal sphere; social institutions; and various extrainstitutional facets of the society. The chapter by Jackson attempted to describe the extensiveness of the changes which might result from a movement. But, as Jackson himself pointed out, his observations are not based upon any systematic empirical work. Much of value could be learned, consequently, by identifying a number of levels of change, specifying how we would define change (rather than mere variation) at each of those levels, and exploring how various social movements have affected change at each of those levels.

For example, millenarian movements obviously effect changes at the individual level. But have not those movements had an impact upon status/roles, or social institutions, or the pattern of social inequality? This problem is the basis for the first of the following questions all of which require much additional research.

What is the overall impact of a social movement; that is, to what extent does it effect change at various levels of social reality?

What is the impact of various kinds of social movements for change at each level of social reality?

What are the second- and third-order consequences of a social movement; that is, what are the subsequent effects of the changes which result from the social movement?

What is the relationship between changes specified by the goals of a movement and the changes actually effected by the movement?

What is the relationship between structural or ideological variations in social movements and the kinds of change effected?

How does the appearance of countermovements affect the movement's effort to effect change?

What is the relationship between the movement's own process of evolution and its efforts to effect change?

What is the bearing of a movement's leadership and the composition of its membership upon its efforts to effect change?

The final relationship we have explored involves the consequences for the movement of effecting or not effecting change. To some extent, the "successes" of the civil rights movement in the United States and of various Marxist movements in other societies led to changes in the movements themselves. The civil rights movement evolved a violent strategy to replace its previous nonviolent approach, and the Marxist movements typically followed a process of deradicalization.

In other words, what appears on the surface as some kind of success may have significant consequences for the movement itself, including a fundamental alteration of the initial character and goals of the movement. On the other hand, what appears at first as failure may have long-term consequences which are in accord with the initial aims of a movement. Killian (1964:452) notes that the failure and disappearance of a specific movement "may, within the framework of an enduring general movement, leave behind the seeds of another specific movement." He gives as an example the Garvey movement of the 1920s, which had apparently passed into oblivion; but the values of the movement have reemerged in more recent times in the Black Muslims.

Thus, our initial impressions of what success or failure may mean for the subsequent development of a movement may prove to be quite wrong. On the other hand, this is not to imply that successes and failures always have contrary consequences, with the former proving debilitating and the latter proving to be a hidden blessing for the movement. Rather, we can only say at this point that no simple conclusions can be drawn about the relationship between the success or failure of a movement's change efforts and the consequent impact upon the movement itself.

This line of thought leads to the first of some questions posed by our exploration of this area.

Is there any systematic relationship between success or failure of change efforts and the consequences of that success or failure for the subsequent development of the movement?

Are the consequences of a movement's success or failure related to the type of movement, to the social context of the movement, or to the combination of movement type and social context?

What facets of a movement are most susceptible to alteration as a result of success or failure?

What is the significance of the composition of the membership of a movement for the consequences of its successes or failures?

Finally, taken as a whole, the above summary and questions stress the importance of analyzing social movements as processes of interaction with the larger society. To sum up the interaction process in a sentence: social change leads to the emergence of social movements; these movements develop in the context of interaction with a changing society, effect or fail to effect certain changes, and experience various alterations as a consequence of the change effort's success or failure.

In essence, this means that the sociological analysis of any phenomenon, including social movements and social change, must not proceed upon the basis of the doctrine of "simple location." The latter was defined by Whitehead (1925:50–51) as the view that entities may be studied in and of themselves without reference to either their relationships with other entities or the passage of time. But even students of organizations have come to realize that interorganizational relationships and organization-environment interactions are crucial to our understanding. The goals of organizations, for example, shift over time as a result of interaction with the environment; we could hardly expect less to happen with respect to social movements. Thus, as social movements are conceived as processes and, further, as processes within the larger social process, we will gain important insights not only into the movement's development but also into those matters which have typically been the focus of sociological study—structure, leadership, motivation to join, and others.

Bibliography

Aberbach, J., and J. Walker
 1970 The meanings of black power: a comparison of white and black interpretations of a political slogan. American Political Science Review 64 (June):367–88.
Aberle, David F.
 1970 A note on relative deprivation theory as applied to millenarian and other cult movements. Pp. 209–14 in Sylvia L. Thrupp (ed.), Millennial Dreams in Action. New York: Schocken Books.
Ahneras, C.
 1960 La Revolte des Camisards. Grenoble, France: Editions Arthaud.
Altshuler, Alan A.
 1970 Community Control. New York: Pegasus.
Ash, Roberta
 1972 Social Movements in America. Chicago: Markham Publishing Company.
Bachrach, Peter, and Morton S. Baratz
 1970 Power and Poverty: Theory and Practice. New York: Oxford University Press.
Barclay, R.
 1876 The Inner Life of the Religious Societies of the Commonwealth. London: Hodder & Stoughton.
Barnes, Gilbert Hobbs
 1933 The Anti-Slavery Impulse. New York: D. Appleton-Century Co.
Becker, H. S.
 1953 On becoming a marijuana user. American Journal of Sociology 59 (November):235–42.

1960   Notes on the concept of commitment. American Journal of Sociology 66 (July):32–40.

Bell, Inge Powell
1968   CORE and the Strategy of Non-Violence. New York: Random House.

Bennis, Warren G., Kenneth D. Benne, and Robert Chin (eds.)
1961   The Planning of Change. New York: Holt, Rinehart and Winston.

Bensman, Joseph
1967   Dollars and Sense. New York: Macmillan.

Benson, J. Kenneth, and David L. Allen
1969   Organizational structure and rehabilitation of the disadvantaged. Pp. 172–201 in Joseph T. Kunce and Corinne S. Cope (eds.), Rehabilitation and the Culturally Disadvantaged. Columbia, Mo.: Regional Rehabilitation Research Institute.

Bernstein, Edward
1961   Evolutionary Socialism. New York: Schocken Books.

Bestor, Arthur, Jr.
1952   The ferment of reform. Pp. 251–82 in Richard Leopold and Arthur Link (eds.), Problems in American History. New York: Prentice-Hall.

Bieberman, L.
1967   The psychedelic experience. New Republic 157, August 5, pp. 17–19.

Blum, Richard, and associates (eds.)
1964   Utopiates: The Use and Users of LSD-25. New York: Atherton Press.

Blumer, Herbert
1939   Collective behavior. Pp. 167–222 in Robert Park (ed.), Principles of Sociology. New York: Barnes & Noble.
1951   Collective behavior. Pp. 199–212 in Alfred McClung Lee (ed.), Principles of Sociology. New York: Barnes & Noble.
1957   Collective behavior. Pp. 127–58 in Joseph B. Gittler (ed.), Review of Sociology: Analysis of a Decade. New York: John Wiley.
1966   Sociological implications of the thought of George Herbert Mead. American Journal of Sociology 71 (March):535–44.

Braden, William
1967   The Private Sea: LSD and the Search for God. Chicago: Quadrangle Books.

Brink, William, and Louis Harris
1964   The Negro Revolution in America. New York: Simon and Schuster.
1966   Black and White. New York: Simon and Schuster.

Brown, John
1928   John Bunyan, His Life, Times, and Work. London: Hulbert.

Brown, Roger
1965   Social Psychology. New York: Free Press.

Brunton, R.
1971   Cargo cults and systems of exchange in Melanesia. Mankind 8 (December):115–28.

Bunyan, John
  1925   The Pilgrim's Progress, Grace Abounding, and Relation of His Im-
         prisonment. Oxford: At the Clarendon Press.
Callis, Helmut G.
  1959   China: Confucian and Communist. New York: Henry Holt & Co.
Cameron, W. B. (ed.)
  1966   Modern Social Movements. New York: Random House.
Campbell, Angus et al.
  1956   Sense of political efficacy and political participation. Pp. 170–73 in
         Heinz Eulau et al. (eds.), Political Behavior. Glencoe, Ill.: Free Press.
  1960   The American Voter. New York: John Wiley.
Campbell, Donald T.
  1965   Variation and selective retention in socio-cultural evolution. Pp.
         19–49 in Herbert R. Barringer, George I. Blanksten, and Raymond
         W. Marck (eds.), Social Change in Developing Areas: A Reinterpre-
         tation of Evolutionary Theory. Cambridge, Mass.: Schenkman Pub-
         lishing Co.
Campbell, J.
  1938   Youth, religion, and peace. Socialist Review 6–7 (July–August):12.
Carmichael, Stokely, and Charles V. Hamilton
  1967   Black Power: The Politics of Liberation in America. New York:
         Knopf, Vintage.
Chasteen, Edgar
  1968   Who favors public accomodations: a demographic analysis. Socio-
         logical Quarterly 9 (Summer):309–17.
Chin, Robert, and Kenneth D. Benne
  1969   General strategies for effecting changes in human systems. Pp.
         32–59 in Warren G. Bennis, Kenneth D. Benne, and Robert Chin
         (eds.), The Planning of Change. 2nd edition. New York: Holt, Rine-
         hart and Winston.
Chow Tse-tung
  1960a The anti-Confucian movement in early Republican China. Pp.
         288–312 in Arthur F. Wright (ed.), The Confucian Persuasion.
         Stanford: Stanford University Press.
  1960b The May Fourth Movement. Cambridge: Harvard University Press.
Clark, Kenneth B.
  1966a The civil rights movement: momentum and organization. Pp.
         595–625 in Talcott Parsons and Kenneth B. Clark (eds.), The Negro
         American. Boston: Houghton Miffin.
  1966b Introduction: the dilemma of power. Pp. xi–xviii in Talcott Parsons
         and Kenneth B. Clark (eds.), The Negro American. Boston:
         Houghton Mifflin.
Clark, Kenneth, and Jeannette Hopkins
  1968   A Relevant War Against Poverty. New York: Harper and Row.
Clark, S. D.
  1949   Church and Sect in Canada. Toronto: University of Toronto Press.
Cobb, R.
  1965   Some aspects of the revolutionary mentality (April 1793–Ther-

midor, Year II). Pp. 305–37 in Jeffry Kaplow (ed.), New Perspective on the French Revolution: Readings in Historical Sociology. New York: John Wiley.

Cochrane, Glynn
  1970   Big Men and Cargo Cults. Oxford: At the Clarendon Press.
Cohn, Norman R. C.
  1957   The Pursuit of the Millennium. London: Secker & Warburg.
Coleman, J. S.
  1971   Conflicting theories of social change. American Behavioral Scientist 14 (May/June):633–50.
Compton, Boyd
  1952   Mao's China: Party Reform Documents, 1942–44. Seattle: University of Washington Press.
Conant, R., with S. Levy and R. Lewis
  1969   Mass polarization: Negro and white attitudes on the pace of integration. American Behavioral Scientist 13 (November–December):247–63.
Coser, Lewis
  1956   The Functions of Social Conflict. Glencoe: Free Press.
Croll, Elisabeth
  1974   The Women's Movement in China. Nottingham: Anglo-Chinese Education Institute, Modern China Series No. 6.
Cutten, George B.
  1927   Speaking with Tongues, Historically and Psychologically Considered. New Haven: Yale University Press.
Da Cunha, E.
  1902   Os Sertoes (S. Putnam translation of 1944 edition). Chicago: University of Chicago Press.
Dallin, Alexander (ed.)
  1963   Diversity in International Communism. New York: Columbia University Press.
d'Aureous, Skye
  1969   A guide to liberty—ACE I. Libertarian Connection, November 12, pp. 1–4.
Davies, J. C.
  1962   Toward a theory of revolution. American Sociological Review 27 (February):5–19.
Davis, J. L.
  1943   Mystical versus enthusiastic sensibility. Journal of the History of Ideas 4 (June):301–19.
Davis, Kingsley
  1949   Human Society. New York: Macmillan.
Dawson, Carl A., and Warner E. Gettys
  1929   An Introduction to Sociology. New York: Ronald Press.
Deardoff, M. H.
  1951   The religion of Handsome Lake: its origin and development. Pp. 77–107 in William Fenton (ed.), Symposium on Local Diversity in

Iroquois Culture Bureau of American Ethnology Bulletin 149. Washington, D.C.: U.S. Government Printing Office.

De Queroz, M. L. P.
  1958 L'influence du milieu social interne sur les mouvements messianiques bresiliens. Archives de Sociologies des Religions 3:3–30.

Dodds, Eric Robertson
  1965 Pagan and Christian in an Age of Anxiety. Cambridge: Cambridge University Press.

Donovan, John P.
  1967 The Politics of Poverty. New York: Pegasus.

Downing, Joseph J.
  1964 Zihuatanejo: an experiment in transpersonative living. Pp. 142–77 in Richard Blum and associates (eds.), Utopiates: The Use and Users of LSD-25. New York: Atherton Press.

Draper, Hal
  1967 The student movement of the thirties: a political history. Pp. 151–89 in R. J. Simon (ed.), As We Saw the Thirties. Urbana: University of Illinois Press.

Durkheim, Emile
  1951 Suicide. Translated by J. A. Spaulding and G. Simpson. New York: Free Press.

Earhart, Mary
  1944 Frances Willard: From Prayers to Politics. Chicago: University of Chicago Press.

Eddy, Samuel K.
  1961 The King is Dead: Studies in the Near Eastrn Resistance to Hellenism, 334–31 B.C. Lincoln: University of Nebraska Press.

Edwards, Harry
  1970 Black Students. New York: Free Press.

Ehle, John
  1965 The Free Men. New York: Harper and Row.

Engels, Frederick
  1968 Origin of the Family, Private Property and the State. Moscow: Progress Publishers.

Erbe, W.
  1964 Social involvement and political activity: a replication and elaboration. American Sociological Review 29 (April):198–215.

Essien-Udom, E. U.
  1962 Black Nationalism: A Search for Identity in America. Chicago: University of Chicago Press.

Etzioni, Amitai
  1966 Studies in Social Change. New York: Holt, Rinehart and Winston.

Etzioni, Amitai, and Eva Etzioni
  1964 Social Change. New York: Basic Books.

Festinger, Leon
  1957 A Theory of Cognitive Dissonance. Stanford: Stanford University Press.

Festinger, Leon, Henry W. Riecken, and Stanley Schachter
  1964   When Prophecy Fails. New York: Harper and Row.
Feuer, Lewis S.
  1969   The Conflict of Generations. New York: Basic Books.
Fichter, J. H.
  1966   American religion and the Negro. Pp. 401–22 in Talcott Parsons
         and Kenneth B. Clark (eds.), The Negro American. Boston:
         Houghton Mifflin.
Firth, C. H., and R. S. Rait (eds.)
  1911   Acts and Ordinances of the Interregnum, 1642–1660. London:
         HMSO.
Firth, Raymond
  1955   The theory of "Cargo" Cults: a note on Tikopia. Man 55: 130–32.
  1956   Elements of Social Organization. London: Watts.
Flacks, R.
  1967   The liberated generation: an exploration of the roots of student
         protest. Journal of Social Issues 23 (July):52–75.
Fleming, H. C.
  1966a Notes from the academy. Daedalus 95 (Winter):397.
  1966b The federal executive and civil rights: 1961–1965. Pp. 371–400 in
         Talcott Parsons and Kenneth B. Clark (eds.), The Negro American.
         Boston: Houghton Mifflin.
Form, W., and J. Rytina
  1969   Ideological beliefs on the distribution of power in the United States.
         American Sociological Review 34 (February):19–30.
Freud, W. H. C.
  1952   The Donatist Church: A Movement of Protest in Roman North
         Africa. Oxford: At the Clarendon Press.
Freund, P. A.
  1966   Notes from the academy. Daedalus 95 (Winter):360–62.
Friedman, D.
  1970   The economics of theft or what ruling class? Libertarian Connection
         (April):6–7.
Geschwender, J. A.
  1968   Explorations in the theory of social movements and revolutions.
         Social Forces 47 (December):127–35.
Gerlach, Luther P., and Virginia H. Hine
  1970   People, Power, Change: Movements of Social Transformation. Indi-
         anapolis and New York: Bobbs-Merrill Company.
Goffman, Erving
  1961   Asylums. Garden City, N.Y.: Doubleday.
Goode, William J.
  1963   World Revolution and Family Patterns. New York: Free Press.
Gosnell, Harold
  1942   Grass Roots Politics. Washington, D.C.: American Council on Public
         Affairs.
Grant, Joanne (ed.)
  1968   Black Protest. New York: Fawcett Publications.

Green, Gil
    1971   The New Radicalism: Anarchist or Marxist? New York: International Publishers.
Gruliow, Leo (ed.)
    1960   Current Soviet Policies III. New York: Columbia University Press.
Gusfield, Joseph R. (ed.)
    1970   Protest, Reform, and Revolt: A Reader in Social Movements. New York: John Wiley.
Hagen, Everett E.
    1962   On the Theory of Social Change. Homewood, Ill.: Dorsey Press.
Halbrook, S.
    1970   Towards a general theory of revolution. Libertarian Connection (April 26):35.
Handlin, Oscar
    1964   Fire-Bell in the Night. Boston: Beacon Press.
    1966   The goals of integration. Pp. 659–77 in Talcott Parsons and Kenneth B. Clark (eds.), The Negro American. Boston: Houghton Mifflin.
Hayden, Tom
    1966   A view of the poverty program: when it's dry you can't crack it with a pick. New York: New York University, Center for the Study of Unemployed Youth, Training Series.
    1969   Colonialism and liberation as American problems. Pp. 170–90 in Roland L. Warren (ed.), Politics and the Ghettos. New York: Atherton Press.
Heberle, Rudolf
    1951   Social Movements. New York: Appleton-Century-Crofts.
Hess, K.
    1969   Washington report. Libertarian Forum (August):3.
Hine, V. H.
    1969   Pentecostal glossolalia: toward a functional interpretation. Journal for Scientific Study of Religion 8 (Fall):211–26.
Hoffer, Eric
    1951   The True Believer. New York: Harper and Row.
Hook, Sidney
    1943   The Hero in History. Boston: Beacon Press.
Hornstein, Harvey A. et al.
    1971   Social Intervention: A Behavioral Science Approach. New York: Free Press.
Hospers, John
    1971   Libertarianism: A Political Philosophy for Tomorrow. Los Angeles: Nash Publishing.
Hsü Kai-yu
    1958   The life and poetry of Wen I-to. Harvard Journal of Asiatic Studies 21 (December):175–78.
Hyman, H., and B. Sheatsley
    1964   Attitudes toward desegregation. Scientific American 211 (July):16–23.

Inozemtsev, I.
   1966   Leninizm-nauchnaia osnova sovetskoi vneshnei politiki. Kom-
          munist, No. 7, p. 23.
Israel, John
   1966   Student Nationalism in China 1927–37. Stanford: Stanford Univer-
          sity Press.
   1967   The Red Guards in historical perspective. China Quarterly 30
          (April–June):26–30.
James, William
   1902   The Varieties of Religious Experience. New York: Modern Library.
Jarvie, I. C.
   1963   Theories of Cargo Cults: a critical analysis. Oceania 34 (September):
          1–31; (December):108–36.
Jellinek, E. M.
   1947   Recent trends in alcoholism and in alcohol consumption. Quarterly
          Journal of Studies on Alcohol 8 (June):1–43.
Johnson, B.
   1961   Do holiness sects socialize in dominant values? Social Forces 39
          (May):309–16.
Joll, James
   1955   The Second International 1889–1914. London: Weidenfeld and Ni-
          colson.
Kanter, R. M.
   1968   Commitment and social organization: a study of commitment mech-
          anism in utopian communities. American Sociological Review 33
          (August):499–517.
Kautsky, John H.
   1965   Myth, self-fulfilling prophecy, and symbolic reassurance in the east-
          west conflict. Journal of Conflict Resolution 9 (March):1–17.
Kautsky, Karl
   1910   The Class Struggle (Erfurt Program). Chicago: Charles H. Kerr.
   1913   The Social Revolution. Chicago: Charles H. Kerr
Keep, John
   1967   Lenin as tactician. Pp. 135–58 in Leonard Schapiro and Peter Red-
          daway (eds.), Lenin: The Man, the Theorist, the Leader. New York:
          Frederick A. Praeger.
Kelman, H. C.
   1958   Compliance, identification, and internalization: three processes of
          attitude change. Journal of Conflict Resolution 2 (March):51–60.
Killian, Lewis M.
   1964   Social movements. Pp. 426–55 in Robert E. L. Faris (ed.), Handbook
          of Modern Sociology. Chicago: Rand McNally & Company.
   1968   The Impossible Revolution. New York: Random House.
Killian, Lewis, and Charles Grigg
   1964   Racial Crisis in America. Englewood Cliffs, N.J.: Prentice-Hall.
King, Albion Roy
   1951   Drinking in colleges. Christian Century, July 18, pp. 842–43; ibid.,
          July 25, pp. 864–68.

King, C. Wendell
  1956 Social Movements in the United States. New York: Random House.
Knox, Ronald A.
  1950 Enthusiasm. A Chapter in the History of Religion with Special Reference to the Seventeenth and Eighteenth Centuries. Oxford: Oxford University Press.
Kramer, Ralph M.
  1969 Participation of the Poor. Englewood Cliffs, N.J.: Prentice-Hall.
Krimerman, Leonard I., and Lewis Perry (eds.)
  1966 Patterns of Anarchy. Garden City: Doubleday, Anchor Books.
Krout, John
  1928 The Origins of Prohibition. New York: Columbia University Press.
Kurland, Albert A., Charles Savage, John W. Shaffer, and Sanford Unger
  1967 The therapeutic potential of LSD in medicine. Pp. 20–35 in Richard C. Debold and Russell C. Leaf (eds.), LSD, Man and Society. Middletown, Conn.: Weslyan University Press.
Lang, Kurt, and Gladys Engel Lang
  1961 Collective Dynamics. New York: Thomas Y. Crowell Company.
Lang, Olga
  1946 Chinese Family and Society. New Haven: Yale University Press.
  1967 Pa Chin and His Writings: Chinese Youth Between the Two Revolutions. Cambridge: Harvard University Press.
La Pierre, Richard T.
  1965 Social Change. New York: McGraw-Hill.
Laue, J. H.
  1964 A contemporary revitalization movement in American race relations: the Black Muslims. Social Forces 42 (March):315–23.
  1966 An example: the civil rights movement. Pp. 111–20 in W. B. Cameron (ed.), Modern Social Movements. New York: Random House.
Lauer, Robert H.
  1971 The scientific legitimation of fallacy: neutralizing social change theory. American Sociological Review 36 (October):881–89.
  1972 Social movements: an interactionist analysis. Sociological Quarterly 13 (Summer):315–28.
  1973 Perspectives on Social Change. Boston: Allyn & Bacon.
Lawrence, Peter
  1964 Road Belong Congo: A Study of the Cargo Movement in the Southern Madang District, New Guinea. Manchester, England: Manchester University Press.
Leary, Timothy
  1962 How to change behavior. Pp. 50–68 in Gerhard S. Nielsen (ed.), Proceedings of the XIV International Congress of Applied Psychology, Vol. 4: Clinical Psychology. Copenhagen: Munksgaard.
Leary, T., and W. H. Clark
  1963 Religious implications of consciousness expanding drugs. Religious Education 58 (May–June):251–56.
Leary, Timothy, Richard Alpert, and Ralph Metzner
  1964 Rationale of the Mexican psychedelic training center. Pp. 178–86 in

Richard Blum and associates (eds.), Utopiates: The Use and Users of LSD-25. New York: Atherton Press.

Leary, T., G. H. Litwin, and R. Metzner
1963   Reactions to psilocybin administered in a supportive environment. Journal of Nervous and Mental Diseases 137 (December):561–73.

Le Bon, Gustave
1960   The Crowd. New York: Viking Press.

Lebra, T. S.
1967   An interpretation of religious conversion: a millennial movement among Japanese-Americans in Hawaii. Ph.D. dissertation, University of Pittsburgh.
1969–70   The logic of salvation. International Journal of Social Psychiatry 16 (Winter):45–53.
1970   Religious conversion as a breakthrough in transculturation: a Japanese sect in Hawaii. Journal for Scientific Study of Religion 9 (Fall):181–96.
1972   Reciprocity-based moral sanctions and messianic salvation. American Anthropologist 74 (June): 391–407.

Lee, A. M.
1944   Techniques of social reform: an analysis of the New Prohibition Drive. American Sociological Review 9 (February):65–77.

Le Fevre, R.
1965   Autarchy versus anarchy. Rampart Journal of Individualist Thought (Winter):1–20.

Lenin, Vladimir I.
1947–52   Selected Works. Moscow: Foreign Languages Publishing House.

Leser, N.
1966   Austro-Marxism: a reappraisal. Journal of Contemporary History 1, no. 2, pp. 117–33.

Lesser, A.
1933   Cultural significance of the Ghost Dance. American Anthropologist 35 (January/March):108–15.

Levin, Henry M. (ed.)
1970   Community Control of Schools. New York: Simon and Schuster.

Lewack, Harold
1953   Campus Rebels: A Brief History of the Student League for Industrial Democracy. New York: Student League for Industrial Democracy.

Lewis, Michael
1970   The Negro protest in urban America. Pp. 149–90 in Joseph R. Gusfield (ed.), Protest, Reform, and Revolt. New York: John Wiley.

Lifton, Robert J.
1961   Thought Reform and the Psychology of Totalism. New York: W. W. Norton & Company.
1967   Peking's "Thought Reform"—group psychotherapy to save your soul. Pp. 137–47 in Franz Schurmann and Orville Schell (eds.), Communist China. New York: Knopf, Vintage.

Lincoln, C. Eric
  1961 The Black Muslims in America. Boston: Beacon Press.
Linton, R.
  1943 Nativistic movements. American Anthropologist 45 (April/June):230–40.
Lipset, Seymour
  1950 Agrarian Socialism. Berkeley and Los Angeles: University of California Press.
Lipset, Seymour, Martin Trow, and James Coleman
  1956 Union Democracy. Glencoe, Ill.: Free Press.
Lipsky, M.
  1968 Protest as a political resource. American Political Science Review 62 (December):1144–58.
Lofland, John
  1966 Doomsday Cult. Englewood Cliffs, N.J.: Prentice-Hall.
Lomax, Louis
  1963 The Negro Revolt. New York: New American Library.
Lundberg, George A., Clarence C. Shrag, Otto N. Larsen, and William R. Catton, Jr.
  1963 Sociology. 4th edition. New York: Harper and Row.
McClelland, David C.
  1964 Business drive and national achievement. Pp. 165–78 in Amitai Etzioni and Eva Etzioni (eds.), Social Change. New York: Basic Books.
McCord, William, John Howard, Bernard Friedberg, and Edwin Harwood
  1969 Life Styles in the Black Ghetto. New York: W. W. Norton and Co.
Machan, T.
  1970 Just what the hell is Halbrook talking about. Libertarian Connection (April 26):29–30.
McKinney, John, and Charles P. Loomis
  1961 The typological tradition. Pp. 557–82 in Joseph Roucek (ed.), Readings in Contemporary American Sociology. Patterson, New Jersey: Littlefield, Adams & Co.
Mannheim, Karl
  1936 Ideology and Utopia. New York: Harcourt Brace.
Manuel, Frank
  1963 Isaac Newton, Historian. Cambridge: Harvard University Press.
Manzoni, Alessandro
  1954 I Promessi Sposi. Storia Milanese del Secolo XVII. Milan: Arnoldo Mondadori Editore.
Mao Tse-tung
  1954 Selected Works. Vol. 3. New York: China Books.
  1962 On the correct handling of contradictions among the people. Pp. 264–97 in Anne Fremantle (ed.), Mao Tse-tung: An Anthology of His Writings. New York: Mentor Books.
  1967 Selected Works of Mao Tse-tung. Vol. 1. Peking: Foreign Language Press.

Marris, Peter and Martin Rein
    1967   Dilemmas of Social Reform. New York: Atherton Press.
Martindale, Don
    1962   Social Life and Cultural Change. Princeton: D. Van Nostrand.
Marx, Gary T.
    1967   Protest and Prejudice: A Study of Belief in the Black Community.
            New York: Harper and Row.
    n.d., a   The Class Struggles in France (1848–1850). New York: Interna-
            tional Publishers.
    n.d., b   The Eighteenth Brumaire of Louis Bonaparte. New York: Inter-
            national Publishers.
Matthews, Donald R. and James W. Prothro
    1966   Negroes and the New Southern Politics. New York: Harcourt, Brace
            and World.
Mauss, Armand L., and Donald W. Petersen
    1973   The cross and the commune: an interpretation of the Jesus people.
            Pp. 150–70 in Robert R. Evans (ed.) Social Movements: A Reader
            and Source Book. Chicago: Rand McNally.
Meier, August, and Elliott Rudwick
    1969   Black violence in the 20th century: a study in rhetoric and retalia-
            tion. Pp. 380–92 in Hugh Davis Graham and Ted Robert Gurr
            (eds.), Violence in America. New York: New American Library.
Meier, August, Elliott Rudwick, and Francis L. Broderick (eds.)
    1971   Black Protest Thought in the Twentieth Century. 2nd edition. Indi-
            anapolis: Bobbs-Merrill Company.
Mendel Arthur (ed.)
    1961   Essential Works of Marxism. New York: Bantam Books.
Messinger, S. L.
    1955   Organizational transformation: a case study of a declining social
            movement. American Sociological Review 20 (January):3–10.
Meyer, Alfred
    1963   Marxism: The Unity of Theory and Practice. Ann Arbor: University
            of Michigan Press.
Michels, Robert
    1949   Political Parties. Translated by Eden and Cedar Paul. Glencoe, Ill.:
            Free Press.
    1959   Political Parties. New York: Dover Publications.
Middleton, R.
    1962   The civil rights issue and presidential voting among southern Ne-
            groes and whites. Social Forces 40 (March):219–22.
Miller, Perry
    1956   Errand into the Wilderness. Cambridge: Harvard University Press.
Miller, S., and M. Rein
    1969   Participation, poverty, and administration. Public Administration
            Review 29 (January–February):15–25.
Miller, S. M., and Pamela Roby
    1968   The war on poverty reconsidered. Pp. 68–82 in Jeremy Larner and

Irving Howe (eds.), Poverty: Views from the Left. New York: William Morrow.

Mills, C. Wright
1951   White Collar. New York: Oxford University Press.

Mooney, James
1951   The Ghost Dance Religion and Sioux Outbreak of 1890. Chicago: University of Chicago Press.

Moore, Wilbert E.
1963   Social Change. Englewood Cliffs, N.J.: Prentice-Hall.
1966   The utility of utopians. American Sociological Review 31 (December):765–72.

Morrison, D. E.
1971   Some notes toward theory on relative deprivation, social movements, and social change. American Behavioral Scientist 14 (May/June):675–90.

Moynihan, D. P.
1966   Employment, income, and the ordeal of the Negro family. Pp. 134–59 in Talcott Parsons and Kenneth B. Clark (eds.), The Negro American. Boston: Houghton Mifflin.
1969   Maximum Feasible Misunderstanding. New York: Free Press.

Muste, A. J.
1928   Factional fights in trade unions. Pp. 332–48 in J. B. S. Hardman (ed.), American Labor Dynamics. New York: Harcourt Brace.

Myrdal, Gunnar
1944   An American Dilemma. New York: Harper.

Myrdal, Jan, and Gun Kessle
1970   China: The Revolution Continued. Translated by Paul Britten Austin. New York: Knopf, Vintage.

Neighbor, Howard
1962   Reform Metamorphosis of Non-Partisan Politics in Kansas City, Missouri. Kansas City, Mo.: Community Studies, Inc.

Nickalls, John L.
1952   The Journal of George Fox. Cambridge: Cambridge University Press.

Niebuhr, H. Richard
1929   Social Sources of Denominationalism. New York: Henry Holt & Co.

Nimuendaju, C.
1914   Die sagen von der erschaffung und vernichtung der welt als grundlagen der religion der Apapocuva-Guarani. Zeitschrift für Ethnologie 46:284–403.

Nuttall, Geoffrey F.
1948   Studies in Christian Enthusiasm Illustrated from Early Quakerism. Wallingford, Pennsylvania: Pendle Hill.

Odegard, Peter
1928   Pressure Politics. New York: Columbia University Press.

O'Neill, William L.
1968   Feminism as a Radical Ideology. Pp. 274–300 in Alfred F. Young

(ed.), Explorations in the History of American Radicalism. DeKalb:
Northern Illinois University Press.

Oppenheimer, M.
  1969   The coming class struggle. Antioch Review 29 (Summer):181–83.

Orwell, George
  1946   Animal Farm. New York: Harcourt Brace.

Pa Chin
  1958   The Family. Peking: Foreign Languages Press.

Pagitt, E.
  1662   Heresiography. London. Cited on p. 138 in P. G. Rogers, The Fifth
         Monarchy Men. London: Oxford University Press, 1966.

Park, Robert, and Ernest W. Burgess
  1921   Introduction to the Science of Sociology. Chicago: University of
         Chicago Press.
  1942   Introduction to the Science of Sociology. 2nd edition. Chicago: Uni-
         versity of Chicago Press.

Parsons, Talcott
  1966a Full citizenship for the Negro American? A sociological problem.
         Pp. 709–54 in Talcott Parsons and Kenneth B. Clark (eds.), The
         Negro American. Boston: Houghton Mifflin.
  1966b Introduction: why "freedom now," not yesterday? Pp. xix–xxviii in
         Talcott Parsons and Kenneth B. Clark (eds.), The Negro American.
         Boston: Houghton Mifflin.

Paterculus, V.
  1924   Roman History. Loeb Classical Library. London: Heinemann; New
         York: Putnam.

Pinard, Maurice
  1967   Poverty and political movements. Social Problems 15 (Fall): 250–63.

  1971   The Rise of a Third Party: A Study in Crisis Politics. Englewood
         Cliffs, N.J.: Prentice-Hall.

Pinard, M., J. Kirk, and D. Von Eschen
  1969   Processes of recruitment in the sit-in movement. Public Opinion
         Quarterly 33 (Fall):355–69.

Pivan, Frances, and Richard Cloward
  1970   Disrupting city services to change national priorities. Pp. 471–80 in
         Steven E. Deutsch and John Howard (eds.), Where It's At. New
         York: Harper and Row.

Pope, Liston
  1942   Millhands and Preachers. New Haven: Yale University Press.

Purcell, Victor
  1963   The Boxer Uprising: A Background Study. Cambridge: Cambridge
         University Press.

Raab, E.
  1966   What war and which poverty? Public Interest (Spring):45–56.

Rand, Ayn
  1961   For the New Intellectual. New York: Signet Books.

Ranulf, Svend
  1938   Moral Indignation and Middle Class Psychology. Copenhagen: Levin & Munksgaard.
Ray, E.
  1969   Self-liberation ways: a compilation and evaluation. Innovator (Spring):1–4.
Reichert, W. O.
  1967   Toward a new understanding of anarchism. Western Political Quarterly 20 (December):856–65.
Ribeiro, D.
  1957   Uira vai ao encountro de Maira. Anais II Reuniao Bras. de Antropologia. Salvador.
Riecken, Henry W., and Stanley Schachter
  1964   When Prophecy Fails. New York: Harper and Row.
Riesman, David
  1950   The Lonely Crowd. New Haven: Yale University Press.
Robbins, T.
  1969   Eastern mysticism and the resocialization of drug users: the Meher Baba cult. Journal for the Scientific Study of Religion 8 (Fall):308–17.
Roberts, Ron E., and Robert Marsh Kloss
  1974   Social Movements: Between the Balcony and the Barricade. St. Louis: C. V. Mosby.
Rose, Arnold M.
  1967a The American Negro problem in the context of social change. Pp. 111–26 in Wilbert E. Moore and Robert M. Cook (eds.), Readings on Social Change. Englewood Cliffs, N.J.: Prentice-Hall.
  1967b The Power Structure. New York: Galaxay.
Rosen, G.
  1967   Emotion and sensibility in ages of anxiety: a comparative historical review. American Journal of Psychiatry 124, no. 6, pp. 771–84.
  1968   Enthusiasm: "a dark lanthorn of the spirit." Bulletin of History of Medicine 42:393–421.
Royce, Josiah
  1898   Studies of Good and Evil. New York: Appleton.
Rush, Gary B., and R. Serge Denisoff
  1971   Social and Political Movements. New York: Appleton-Century-Crofts.
Rustin, B.
  1966a Black power and coalition politics. Commentary 42 (September):35–40.
  1966b From protest to politics: the future of the civil rights movement. Pp. 407–19 in Raymond J. Murphy and Howard Elinson (eds.), Problems and Prospects of the Negro Movement. Belmont, Calif.: Wadsworth.
Sartre, Jean Paul
  1951   Le Diable et le Bon Dieu. Paris: Gallimard.

Scalapino, Robert A.
  1967 Prelude to Marxism: the Chinese student movement in Japan,
        1900–1910. Pp. 190–215 in Albert Feuerwerker, Rhoads Murphey,
        and Mary C. Wright (eds.), Approaches to Modern Chinese History.
        Berkeley: University of California Press.
Schechter, S.
  1908 Safed in the 16th century: a city of legists and nuptics. Pp. 203–
        306 in Studies in Judaism. Philadelphia: Jewish Publication So-
        ciety.
Schein, E. H.
  1956 The Chinese indoctrination program for prisoners of war: a study
        of attempted "brainwashing." Psychiatry 19:149–72.
Schlesinger, Arthur
  1950 The American as Reformer. Cambridge: Harvard University Press.
Schneider, L.
  1971 Dialectic   in   sociology.   American   Sociological   Review
        36 (August):667–78.
Schwartz, T.
  n.d.   The Cargo Cult: a Melanesian type response to change. Manuscript.
Scott, Walter
  1906 Old Mortality. London: Dent; New York: Dutton.
Searles, R., and J. A. Williams, Jr.
  1962 Negro college students' participation in sit-ins. Social Forces
        40 (March):215–19.
Selznick, Philip
  1952 The Organizational Weapon. New York: McGraw-Hill.
Shulman, Marshall D.
  1963 Stalin's Foreign Policy Reappraised. Cambridge: Harvard Univer-
        sity Press.
Siegfried, André
  1927 America Comes of Age. New York: Harcourt Brace.
Silberman, Charles
  1964 Crisis in Black and White. New York: Random House.
Silver, Abba Hillel
  1959 A History of Messianic Speculation in Israel from the First Through
        the Seventeenth Centuries. Boston: Beacon Press.
Simmel, Georg
  1950 The Sociology of Georg Simmel. Translated, edited, and with an in-
        troduction by Kurt H. Wolff. New York: Free Press.
Simpson, George (trans.)
  1933 Emile Durkheim on the Division of Labor in Society. New York:
        Macmillan.
Simpson, George and J. M. Yinger
  1965 Racial and Cultural Minorities. 3rd edition. New York: Harper and
        Row.
Smelser, Neil J.
  1962 Theory of Collective Behavior. New York: Free Press.

Smith, Roy L.
1953 Young Mothers Must Enlist. Evanston, Ill.: National WCTU Publishing House.
Snow, Helen Foster
1967 Women in Modern China. The Hague: Mouton & Co.
Soboul, Albert
1958 Les Sans-culottes Parisiens en l'an II. Paris: Librairie Clavreuil.
Sorokin, Pitirim A.
1942 The Crisis of Our Age. New York: E. P. Dutton & Co.
Spencer, Herbert
1874 The Study of Sociology. New York: Appleton & Company.
Spier, L.
1935 The prophet dance of the Northwest and its derivatives. General Series in Anthropology 1:1–74.
Stalin, Joseph
1952 Economic Problems of Socialism in the U.S.S.R. New York: International Publishers.
Stern, S.
1967 NSA-CIA. Ramparts 5 (March):29–39.
Stewart, Eliza
1888 Members of the Crusade. Columbus, Ohio: William G. Hubbard Co.
Suchman, E., R. K. Goldsen, and R. Williams, Jr.
1953 Attitudes toward the Korean War. Public Opinion Quarterly 17 (Summer):171–84.
Swain, J. W.
1940 The theory of the four monarchies: opposition history under the Roman Empire. Classical Philology 35:1–21.
Talmon, Y.
1962 Pursuit of the millennium: the relation between religious and social change. Archives européenes de sociologie 3, no. 1, pp. 123–48.
1966 Millenarian movements. Archives européenes de sociologie 7, no. 2, pp. 159–200.
Tannehill, Morris, and Linda Tannehill
1970 The Market for Liberty. Lansing: self-published.
Teng Ssu-yu and John K. Fairbank
1967 China's Response to the West. New York: Atheneum.
Thomas, K.
1967 Women and the civil war sects. Pp. 332–57 in Trevor Aston (ed.), Crisis in Europe 1560–1660. Garden City, N.Y.: Doubleday.
Toch, Hans
1965 The Social Psychology of Social Movements. Indianapolis and New York: Bobbs-Merrill Company.
Tocqueville, de, Alexis
1955 The Old Regime and the French Revolution. New York: Doubleday, Anchor Books.
Tomlinson, T. M.
1968 Riot ideology among urban Negroes. Pp. 417–28 in Louis H. Ma-

sotti and Don R. Bowen (eds.), Riots and Rebellion: Civil Violence in the Urban Community. Beverley Hills, Calif.: Sage Publications.

Townsend, James R.
1968   Political Participation in Communist China. Berkeley and Los Angeles: University of California Press.

Troeltsch, Ernst
1911   The Social Teachings of the Christian Churches. Translated by Olive Wyon. London: George Allen & Unwin.

Tuccille, Jerome
1970   Radical Libertarianism: A Right Wing Alternative. Indianapolis: Bobbs-Merrill Company.

Tucker, Robert C.
1963   The Soviet Political Mind. New York: Praeger.

Turner, Darwin T., and Joan M. Bright (eds.)
1965   Images of the Negro in America. Boston: Heath.

Turner, Ralph H.
1970   Determinants of social movement strategy. Pp. 145–64 in Tamotsu Shibutani (ed.), Human Nature and Collective Behavior. Englewood Cliffs, N.J.: Prentice-Hall.

Turner, Ralph H., and Lewis M. Killian
1957   Collective Behavior. Englewood Cliffs, N.J.: Prentice-Hall.

Turner, R. H. and W. M. Young, Jr.
1966   Who has the revolution or thoughts on the second reconstruction. Pp. 678–93 in Talcott Parsons and Kenneth B. Clark (eds.), The Negro American. Boston: Houghton Mifflin.

Turner, Victor W.
1969   The Ritual Process: Structure and Anti-Structure. Chicago: Aldine.

Tyler, Alice F.
1962   Freedom's Ferment: Phases of American Social History from the Colonial Period to the Outbreak of the Civil War. New York: Harper, Torchbooks.

United States Employment Service
1944   Dictionary of Occupational Titles. Washington, D.C.: Government Printing Office.

Useem, Michael
1972   Ideological and interpersonal change in the radical protest movement. Social Problems 19 (Spring:451–69.
1975   Protest Movements in America. Indianapolis: Bobbs-Merrill Company.

Vaughan, R.
1838   The Protectorate of Oliver Cromwell. London: H. Colburn.

Virchow, R.
1851   Die epidemien von 1848. Archiv für Pathologische Anatomie and Physiologie 3:1–12.

Voget, F.
1957   The American Indian in transition: reformation and status innovation. American Journal of Sociology 62 (January):369–78.

Von Eschen, D., J. Kirk, and M. Pinard
  1969   The conditions of direct action in a democratic society. Western Political Quarterly 22 (June):309–25.
Walker, D. P.
  1964   The Decline of Hell: Seventeenth Century Discussions of Eternal Torment. Chicago: University of Chicago Press.
Walker, Richard
  1963   Student, intellectuals, and "the Chinese revolution." Pp. 87–108 in Jeanne J. Kirkpatrick (ed.), The Strategy of Deception. New York: Farrar, Straus & Giroux.
Wallace, Anthony F. C.
  1956a Mazeway resynthesis: a biological theory of religious inspiration. Transactions of New York Academy of Science Series 2, 18:626–38.
  1956b Revitalization movements. American Anthropologist 58 (April): 264–81.
  1957   Mazeway disintegration: the individual's perception on sociocultural disorganization. Human Organization 16 (Summer):23–27.
  1961   The cultural composition of Handsome Lake religion. Bulletin of Bureau of American Ethnology 180:143–51.
  1970   The Death and Rebirth of the Seneca. New York: Knopf.
Waller, D. J.
  1970   The Government and Politics of Communist China. London: Hutchinson University Library.
Walton, R. E.
  1965   Two strategies of social change and their dilemmas. Journal of Applied Behavioral Science 1, no. 2, pp. 167–79.
Wang, Y. C.
  1966   Chinese Intellectuals and the West, 1872–1949. Chapel Hill: University of North Carolina Press.
Warner, Harry S.
  1946   The Liquor Cult and Its Culture. Columbus, Ohio: Intercollegiate Association.
Warren, Robert Penn
  1965   Who Speaks for the Negro. New York: Knopf, Vintage.
Warshay, Leon H.
  1964   Breadth of perspective and social change. Pp. 319–44 in George K. Zollschan and Walter Hirsch (eds.), Explorations in Social Change. Boston: Houghton Mifflin.
Washburne, Norman
  1954   Interpreting Social Change in America. New York: Random House.
Waskow, Arthur L.
  1967   From Race Riot to Sit-In. New York: Doubleday.
Weber, Max
  1947   The Theory of Social and Economic Organization. Translated by A. M. Henderson and Talcott Parsons. New York: Oxford University Press.

Wehr, P. E.
  1968   Nonviolence and differentiation in the equal rights movement. So-
          ciological Inquiry 38 (Winter):65–76.
Wesley, John
  1963   The Journal of John Wesley. New York: Capricorn.
Whalen, William J.
  1962   Armageddon Around the Corner: A Report on Jehovah's Wit-
          nesses. New York: John Day.
Wheeler, S.
  1966   The structure of formally organized socialization settings. Pp.
          51–116 in Orville G. Brim, Jr., and Stanton Wheeler (eds.), Social-
          ization after Childhood. New York: John Wiley.
White, Leslie A.
  1949   The Science of Culture. New York: Farrar, Straus & Giroux.
White, T.
  1967   A People for His Name. New York: Vantage.
Whitehead, Alfred North
  1925   Science and the Modern World. New York: Mentor Books.
Williams, George H.
  1962   The Radical Reformation. Philadelphia: Westminster.
Wilson, Everett K., and Herman Schnurer (trans.)
  1961   Emile Durkheim on Moral Education. New York: Free Press.
Wilson, John
  1973   Introduction to Social Movements. New York: Basic Books.
Wilson, J. Q.
  1966   The Negro in politics. Pp. 423–47 in Talcott Parsons and Kenneth B.
          Clark (eds.), The Negro American. Boston: Houghton Mifflin.
Wingo, W.
  1970   How students see you now. Nation's Business 58 (May):54–57.
Wittenmyer, Annie
  1878   History of the Woman's Temperance Crusade. Philadelphia: Anne
          Wittenmyer.
Wolf, Eric R.
  1971   Peasant rebellion and revolution. Pp. 48–67 in Norman Miller and
          Roderick Aya (eds.), National Liberation: Revolution in the Third
          World. New York: Free Press.
Wollstein, Jarret
  1969   Philosophy of social change (I). Rational Individualist (Octo-
          ber):7–10.
  1970   Society Without Coercion. Silver Spring, Md.: Society for Individual
          Liberty.
Woodward, C. V.
  1967   What happened to the civil rights movement? Harper's 234 (Jan-
          uary):29–37.
Worsley, Peter.
  1968   The Trumpet Shall Sound: A Study of "Cargo" Cults in Melanesia.
          New York: Schocken.

Yadin, Yigael (ed.)
 1962   The Scroll of the War of the Sons of Light Against the Sons of Dark-
        ness. Translated by B. Rabin and C. Rabin. Oxford: Oxford Univer-
        sity Press.
Yang, C. K.
 1959   The Chinese in the Communist Revolution. Cambridge, Mas-
        sachusetts: MIT Press.
Yinger, J. Milton
 1963   Sociology Looks at Religion. New York: Macmillan.
 1965   A Minority Group in American Society. New York: McGraw-Hill.
Zablocki, Benjamin
 1971   The Joyful Community. Baltimore, Md.: Penguin Books.
Zeller, E.
 1877   Vorträge and Abhandlungen. Leipzig: Fues.
Zimbardo, Philip, and Ebbe B. Ebbesen
 1970   Influencing Attitudes and Changing Behavior. Reading, Mass.: Ad-
        dison-Wesley Publishing Company.

Index

Aberbach, J., 111
Abolition movement: changed by Civil
   War, xviii–xix; membership of, 63
Agrarian movements, 63
All-China Federation of Democratic
   Women, 147–48
Alpert, Richard, 48, 49, 51, 52
Altshuler, Alan A., 120
American Libertarian movement:
   strategies used, xx, 88–92; anarchist
   tradition of, 86–87; philosophy of,
   86–88
American Student Union (ASU), 36–37
American Youth for Democracy (AYD),
   39
Analgesic strategy, 82
Antibureaucratic movements, xviii
Anti-imperialism: of Chinese Students, 9,
   11, 12, 24–25
Antipornographic movement, xviii
Anti-Saloon League, 65, 76n
Antiwar movement, 90
Ash, Roberta, xiii, xxvi, xxviiin

Bachrach, Peter, 113, 116–17
Baratz, Morton A., 113, 116–17
Bargaining strategies, 82, 93
Barnes, Gilbert H., 63, 76n
"Beatniks," 41
Becker, H. S., 59n
Bell, Inge P., 108, 224n, 226n
Benne, Kenneth D., 86, 176

Bennis, Warren G., 176
Benson, J. Kenneth, 83
Bernstein, Eduard, 239, 252
Bestor, Arthur, Jr., 76n
Bieberman, L., 55
Black movement: increasing militance of,
   xix; use of various strategies in, 85; four
   phases of, 95; shift from nonviolence,
   200–201
Black Muslim movement, 52, 108, 129–32,
   137, 139, 141, 142, 263
Black Panther movement: supported by
   Libertarians, 90
Black Panthers, 193, 196n
Black power movement: ideology of, 52,
   83, 108–11, 116–17, 120n; interrela-
   tionship with War on Poverty, 107–8,
   111–20; conflict with civil rights movement, 108; ideology supported by
   Negro masses, 110–11; relationship
   with other reform movements, 111;
   struggle for control of Community Action programs, 112–19; challenges
   ideology of civil rights movement, 119;
   as phase of civil rights movement, 180;
   mentioned, 190, 191
Blum, Richard, 51, 53, 54
Blumer, Herbert, 46, 76n, 85
Bright, Joan M., 182
Brink, William, 111, 179
Bruderhof: communitarian movement,
   94–95
Brunton, R., 138

287